D1083973

THE ARMED SERVICES AND ADULT EDUCATION

COMMISSION ON IMPLICATIONS OF
ARMED SERVICES EDUCATIONAL PROGRAMS

Appointed by the American Council on Education

THE ARMED SERVICES AND ADULT EDUCATION

BY *Cyril O. Houle, Elbert W. Burr, Thomas H. Hamilton* AND *John R. Yale* FOR THE COMMISSION ON IMPLICATIONS OF ARMED SERVICES EDUCATIONAL PROGRAMS

AMERICAN COUNCIL ON EDUCATION
Washington, D. C.

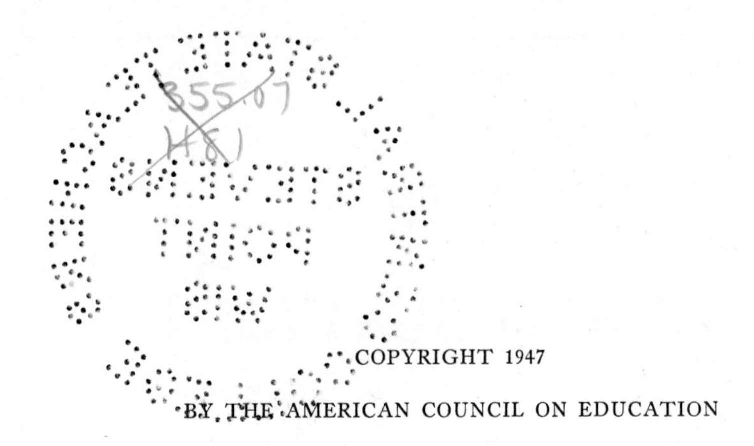

PRINTED IN THE UNITED STATES OF AMERICA

FOREWORD

ORDINARILY we think of wartime armed services training as consisting of duty-time activities embracing basic military and physical training, study and practice in the maintenance and uses of ships, aircraft, vehicles, and weapons, and the tactics of offense and defense. It will not do to overlook the off-duty voluntary educational activities designed to maintain high morale by affording a connecting link with the cultural facilities the fighting men had known at home, a stimulus to look ahead to eventual return to civilian life, and an encouragement to the development of a sound philosophy of the citizen-soldier.

These functions closely parallel some of the aims of the peacetime enterprise of adult education: Provide all adults with a stimulating means of using a part of their leisure time; make available to them the cultural facilities of their own communities; encourage them to plan their lives far ahead and to forge their philosophies as citizens of the nation and of the world. What does the experience of the armed services, in their several off-duty educational undertakings, suggest for the advancement of general adult education in America?

For this sector of its investigations, the Commission on Implications of Armed Services Educational Programs obtained the services of Dr. Cyril O. Houle, dean of University College, the University of Chicago. He was assisted by three collaborators: Elbert W. Burr of the department of education of Colgate University; Thomas H. Hamilton, assistant dean of University College, the University of Chicago; and John R. Yale, executive secretary, Science Research Associates, Chicago.

The Secretary of War and the Secretary of the Navy agreed to cooperate in the entire project of the Commission and facilitated its progress by designating as official liaison agencies respectively the Historical Division, War Department Special Staff, and the Standards and Curriculum Division, Training Activity, Bureau of Naval Personnel. These agencies provided full access to documentary materials and entree to armed services headquarters and training installations.

The same agencies also reviewed the studies in manuscript, gave valuable suggestions, and approved the drafts for factual accuracy and for safeguarding information vital to the national security. Opinions and assertions contained in the studies are private ones of the authors and are not to be construed as official or as reflecting the views of the War or Navy Departments or of the military or naval services at large.

Adult education, in the armed services as in civil life, proceeds through many agencies concurrently, and does not exhibit a stable and symmetrical organization. Among the principal agencies whose experiences are distilled in this report are the Army and Navy library services; the United States Armed Forces Institute; war orientation activities, subsequently included in Information and Education in the Army and in Educational Services in the Navy; the agencies of literacy training in the Army and the Navy; and the Army post-hostilities schools. Their varied problems and accomplishments, their merits and shortcomings, their advantages and handicaps, their successes and failures, hold many lessons bearing upon the future of adult learning in the United States.

ALONZO G. GRACE
Director

PREFACE

THE STUDY which is presented in the following pages has been influenced primarily by two important circumstances.

The first of these is that the scope of the study was limited to the location and expression of positive implications. Any negative evaluation which would appraise and point out weaknesses was therefore not appropriate. The authors of the study wish to record, however, their personal judgment that, if there had been more enthusiastic encouragement and material support both outside and inside the armed services, the off-duty programs might have reached larger numbers of interested service personnel, and their broad objectives might have been more fully realized. Late in the war, increasing support was given—the change being particularly notable in the Navy—but, for much of the war, the failure of some echelons of command to appreciate fully the broad purposes of the off-duty programs meant that inadequate attention was directed to the implementation of the objectives of the programs.

The second circumstance which has limited this study is that it was undertaken after the war was over. Consequently, the evidence studied and presented had to be secured largely from documentary sources and personal testimony. One major limitation which grows out of this fact is that it has been difficult to study fully the widely varied local programs. In some camps and bases, activities were undertaken which more than met the objectives of the programs. In others, almost nothing was done. Since the study was undertaken after the close of the war, due attention could not be given to actual field practices. Stress had to be placed on the general pattern of organization and operation of off-duty programs with such attention to particular units as could be secured from documentary sources or from the evidence of former participants in the programs.

In compiling the descriptions of the off-duty educational programs of the armed services, the authors relied heavily on and quoted extensively from the various histories compiled by the

Army and Navy. The unpublished "Administrative History of the Bureau of Naval Personnel" was especially valuable in the preparation of the Navy material in the study. Four histories produced by the Army's Information and Education Division were found particularly useful in the preparation of the Army material. These included the "Study of Information and Education Activities: World War II"; the "History of Military Training: History of the Army Education Branch, ASF"; the "History of Military Training: Summary, Information and Education Division, ASF"; and the "Army Orientation." An additional study, "The Army Library Services: A Short History," sponsored by the Special Services Division was used in the preparation of chapter ix which is concerned with the Army Library Service.

The foregoing documents are the best sources extant, and are adjudged by the authors of this volume to be more reliable and authoritative for descriptive and historical purposes than any subsequent survey is likely to be. Accordingly we have taken the extraordinary liberty, with the generous consent of the Historical Division, War Department Special Staff, of presenting the several descriptions of the Army off-duty educational activities [1] in the form of extensive excerpts from the documents named, with very little editorial change and without burdening the reader with the usual device of quotation marks. The materials thus presented are identified by appropriate footnotes in each instance.

While the four authors of this report have worked in close collaboration and made all major policy decisions jointly, each one has assumed responsibility for a particular assignment. Mr. Yale studied the Army programs. Mr. Hamilton studied the work of the Navy, including the Marine Corps and the Coast Guard. Mr. Burr wrote the introduction as well as introductions to the succeeding ten chapters; in addition, he served as executive officer for the study and handled arrangements for the collection of data and the drawing together of the final document. Mr. Houle assumed responsibility for planning the

[1] Some of the agencies and programs involved underwent several changes in nomenclature during the war as a result of reorganization.

study, for outlining its scope and content, for writing the chapter on implications, and for editing the final report.

In the development of this study, the staff turned for assistance to many individuals connected with the off-duty programs during the war, both as civilian consultants and as military personnel. Many of these people gave freely of their time to discuss the programs, to write letters analyzing and describing specific aspects of the off-duty programs, and to verify information included in the study. Many of them listed here by military rank have now returned to peacetime positions in leading educational institutions.

The following personnel of the Navy Department were especially helpful: Capt. L. Ensey, Capt. A. J. Bartky, Commander W. H. Johnson, Lt. Comdr. E. H. Ziegfeld, Lt. Comdr. G. T. Donahue, Lt. Comdr. C. J. Gray, Lt. Comdr. E. J. McGrath, Lt. Comdr. J. B. Lieberman, Lt. J. W. Hurst, Lt. Dudley Johnson, Miss Isabel DuBois, Miss Dorothy F. Deininger, and Dr. James B. MacConnell.

Col. D. J. Kendall and Maj. P. H. Bratten of the United States Marine Corps provided valuable assistance.

Commander E. T. Calahan, United States Coast Guard, aided in the study of the Coast Guard programs.

Mr. H. Stahley Thompson, Manager, Editions for the Armed Services, Inc., was of great assistance in the preparation of material covering the work of his organization.

The following Army personnel provided extensive aid: Maj. Gen. Frederick H. Osborn, Col. Francis T. Spaulding, Col. Walter E. Sewell, Lt. Col. Spencer D. Benbow, Lt. Col. William T. Ramsey, Lt. Col. Lyle M. Spencer, Maj. Irving Liebermann, Maj. Paul E. Postell, Capt. Willard Abraham, Capt. John A. Jamieson, Capt. Robert Quick, Capt. Boyd C. Shafer, Lt. Herbert Goldhor, and Lt. Francis Keppel.

This study has also benefited greatly from the enthusiastic cooperation of the Advisory Committee. The members of this committee who met with the authors of the study, made innumerable constructive criticisms, and read this report to insure its accuracy and its usefulness to adult educators were: Arthur Carstens, director of union programs, University College, the University of Chicago; Grace Coyle, professor of group work, Western Reserve University; Pope Lancaster, director of personnel, Western Electric Company; Ann Ramsey, labor information representative, Division of Labor Standards, U. S. Department of Labor; Ruth Rutzen, assistant librarian, Detroit Public Library; Mary U. Rothrock, specialist in library service, Tennessee Valley Authority; Robert Sharer, chief, Division of Adult Education, Michigan State Department of Public Instruction; M. L. Wilson, director, Agricultural Extension Service, U. S. Department of Agriculture; and G. B. Zehmer, director of university extension, University of Virginia.

Additional assistance in the preparation of the study as a whole was given by: R. M. Bateman, Hugh E. Bell, W. S. Bittner, Frank H. Bowles, Commander Robert H. Connery, Jack C. Elliott, Paul L. Essert, W. L. Evenson, Alvin C. Eurich, Carl W. Hansen, Trimble R. Hedges, F. O. Holt, Peter Krehel, Walter L. Meyer, Leon F. Miller, Capt. H. H. Montgomery, M. C. Mumford, Everett N. Peterson, Paul A. Rehmus, G. W. Rosenlof, William E. Spaulding, John Whitelaw, E. G. Williamson, and Paul W. F. Witt.

The authors are especially grateful to Miss Mabel Swanson who acted as their secretary during the study and was unusually helpful in the final preparation of the manuscript.

CYRIL O. HOULE
ELBERT W. BURR
THOMAS H. HAMILTON
JOHN R. YALE

January 1947

CONTENTS

LIST OF TABLES

LIST OF FIGURES

INTRODUCTION: THE NATURE AND SCOPE OF THE STUDY

At the close of World War II, the twelve million men and women on active duty in the armed services of the United States had available for their use the most extensive adult educational program in our nation's history. Millions had been trained in military skills either for combat or for some service supporting combat. But such training was not enough. A civilian who enters the Army or Navy must accept a kind of anonymity of uniform and serial number. He does not cease to be a man, however, and he still has desires and hopes. Among them is the insistent need, in his own particular way, to fulfill his potentialities and to improve his abilities and his understandings. Consequently, the armed services found it necessary to provide a great variety of voluntary educational opportunities. Millions of men and women were using leisure time in forward areas in training camps, on ships at sea, in occupation areas, and on lonely Pacific outposts to undertake voluntary learning. Here was an experiment in the education of adults without parallel in any civilian undertaking. Never before in history had such a vast program of education and information been made available to a comparable group of American citizens.

In Madison, Wisconsin, the headquarters of the largest school of correspondence instruction in the world had enrolled its one millionth student. The United States Armed Forces Institute, referred to as USAFI, was serving our military and naval personnel in England, on the European continent, in Alaska, Australia, the Philippines, Egypt, India, Hawaii, Puerto Rico, Panama, and New Caledonia. Additional correspondence instruction was available to marines and coast guardsmen through the Marine Corps Institute and the Coast Guard Institute. Some eighty-five American universities cooperated with USAFI in providing correspondence courses. Modern testing methods were developed and made available to service personnel. A cooperative arrangement with civilian schools and colleges made it possible for military personnel to apply for academic credit for all types of service education and experience. Millions of texts were available in a great variety of subjects for classroom use. A stimulating, well-illustrated series of pamphlets was available for off-duty discussions.

Army and Navy library services, with extensive kits of books and magazines, brought new enjoyment and a measure of cultural growth to men and women all over the world, many of whom had never before had much interest in educational and recreational reading. Army newspapers—*Yank, Stars and Stripes, Burma-India Roundup, Persian Gulf Dispatch*—were seen by millions of service men and women each day. Navy personnel throughout the world received the Navy's magazine *All Hands*. Many men were hard at work wherever our forces were stationed, writing, illustrating, printing, or mimeographing thousands of other Army, corps, division, regimental, shipboard, base, and unit papers.

What could not be well said in words was shown in pictures. Some 200,000 copies of *Newsmap,* a graphic description of the progress of the war, the activities in war industry at home, and the problems of the peace were distributed weekly to all services at home and abroad. The motion picture was pressed into service to tell soldiers, sailors, marines, and coast guardsmen the story of the causes of the war, the events leading up to America's entry into it, and the progress toward victory.

The world-wide Armed Forces Radio Service with 177 Army and Navy stations, 54 foreign government and commercial stations, and 149 sound-reproduction systems was a new venture in military and radio history. Each week 77 popular American radio programs were transcribed for the entertainment and information of service personnel. The Army itself, with the help of famous stars of stage, screen, and radio, produced 15 program hours every week. Some 66,000 transcriptions were completed each month and flown overseas for rebroadcast. Transcriptions of radio discussion programs were received enthusiastically. News was broadcast almost every hour wherever there were Americans in uniform. A vigorous effort was made to supply those newspapers and radio stations with accurate, unbiased coverage of the events of the day.

In Army camps and Navy bases, in hospitals, and on ships at sea, off-duty classes were being conducted in a variety of academic and occupational fields. To a large extent, materials were furnished by the United States Armed Forces Institute. Instructors were drawn from local military and naval personnel, and were helped by educators from nearby school systems. Many Army and Navy instructors had been members of secondary school and college faculties. Others had been successful professional men or highly skilled craftsmen in civilian life. A surprising number held advanced degrees. All of them—officers and enlisted personnel alike—offered their services to assist these thousands of men and women in using their leisure time to continue their education. And they taught in every conceivable kind of classroom, welcoming whatever facilities were available.

The end of the war opened up an even wider field for nonmilitary study. Army university centers at Florence, Italy, at Shrivenham, England, and at Biarritz, France, were providing over seven thousand men with full-time courses of study at a high level of quality and with a wide range of subject matter. The Navy expanded its Educational Services centers in the Pacific to provide broader educational opportunities after hostilities had ceased.

The fact that the American Army and Navy were a democratic military force composed to a large extent of "civilians in uniform" meant that throughout the war many service men and women were interested primarily in the prospect of returning to civilian life. This interest stimulated many of them to want information concerning vocational orientation, job training and placement, the relationships of military skills to civilian occupations, and other aspects of living and learning. To meet these needs, the armed services made available on a voluntary basis a variety of vocational counseling materials and the services of qualified counselors in increasing numbers. In this way it was possible to provide interested servicemen and women with help in planning for further education and training while on active duty and after separation.

PURPOSES

Without question this extensive wartime program of service-established adult educational opportunities has had many important values for civilian adult education. While much of the program was developed by civilian educators in the armed services, its very magnitude, its unusual financial resources, the motivation of its students, and its range of educational activities made it unique in adult educational practice. If the implications that these service-operated educational programs have for civilian adult education are to be fully understood, it is important that the programs be studied in broad outline. Analytical studies[1] of particular phases of the programs, which are now being made or are yet to be produced can be appraised more accurately and can be seen in better perspective against a broad, descriptive pattern of the entire range of off-duty education in the armed services. It is the purpose of this study, therefore, to make an inventory of all such programs, to provide a panoramic description of these programs, and to indicate the major implications which are of practical value to civilian adult educators.

ORGANIZATION

This study is one of several undertaken by the American Council on Education when it established the Commission on Implications of Armed Services Educational Programs. After a preliminary study, the members of the Commission marked out various areas within the armed services educational programs which were of particular interest and importance to civilian education and then established each as a separate study. Because the Commission felt that important implications might be discovered in the area of adult education, the present study was undertaken.

The implementation of the adult education study required at the outset a careful analysis of all service-operated off-duty educational programs. Staff members, therefore, studied the off-duty

[1] For a selective, annotated list of items already published, see the Bibliography.

programs at the various service headquarters in Washington. In the Army the major share of responsibility for the program's development was borne by the Information and Education Division of the Army Service Forces. In the Navy the Educational Services Section of the Bureau of Naval Personnel was primarily responsible for the Navy's off-duty educational program. The Marine Corps established an Education Section in its Welfare Division and that section, together with the Marine Corps Institute, conducted the Marine program. A similar, though less extensive, program was established in the Coast Guard. Army and Navy library services served important supplementary roles in the development of these voluntary educational activities.

The early investigations at the headquarters of the services indicated clearly that local modifications had resulted in a great variety of practices which were not included in the historical descriptions of off-duty programs as they had been compiled in Washington. It is indeed understandable that field commanders, under stress of planning and conducting important military operations, sometimes found it difficult to concern themselves with leisure-time educational programs or with detailed reportings of such activities. It is not surprising that little time was available for organizing and conducting evaluation studies, cost analyses, and investigations into the extent of participation in these programs. Many commands were reluctant to assign—from limited reserves—the manpower necessary for the operation of an educational program which had only intangible military results.

Local conditions called for a high degree of local initiative. Field programs reflected the educational philosophy and the administrative ability of individual educational officers. Because of their tremendous interest and enthusiasm, a variety of programs were developed which were far more extensive than those planned in Washington and better adapted to the needs of their own military personnel. It was this initiative and spirit of service which were responsible for a greater part of the success of the programs.

In so far as the programs had to be adapted to an infinite variety of local interests, needs, supplies, and military situations they differed from those which had been planned in Washington. Yet basic policies enunciated in Washington and passed through the military chain of command were adhered to as broad directive guides. This provided a general basis of common procedure and continuity in the programs and has made it possible to develop relatively accurate descriptions from which implications could be determined.

Because of this diversity in the local establishment of programs, the staff felt it desirable to supplement the studies made in Washington with information from a representative cross-section of persons who had been intimately connected, either in uniform or as civilian consultants, with the armed services off-duty programs. The response to personal-letter requests for information has made possible a verification of the information obtained in the Washington studies and has been valuable in providing further insight into the implications for adult education present in this military experience.

A survey of the literature was also made to make certain that all available sources of significant information had been consulted.

There then remained the problem of selecting from these sources of information the descriptive facts and conclusions which would be of greatest significance to adult educators. To assist the study staff in this problem, an advisory committee was chosen. This committee represented seven important areas of adult education including group work, libraries, labor education, corporation training, public-school adult education, university extension, and agricultural extension. The committee's function was to advise the staff in its work to insure the maximum usefulness of the study to adult education. Each member of the committee brought to this task not only a wide background of experience and leadership in adult education, but also fresh insight into the problem of determining the specific implications of the armed services programs for his own work in adult education. Several of the committee members used their professional contacts to acquire additional information of value to the study. The committee has had an opportunity to read and to criticize the preliminary report of the study.

As a final effort to make certain that the study is complete and useful, the report has been read and criticized by a group of other adult educators. The modifications of the report as a result of their suggestions have added a great deal to the value of the present volume.

The report has been organized in three sections. The first consists of the present brief introduction to the study. The second contains the descriptions of the off-duty educational programs. This section has been divided into eleven chapters, each dealing with a specific and significant area of interest, for it was felt that understanding the implications for adult education depended upon an adequate knowledge of the organization and operation of the armed services educational programs. In the eleven chapters, where appropriate, Army, Navy, Marine Corps, and Coast Guard activities have been treated separately and in the order named. The third section is devoted to a statement of general implications.

In several respects, the Army and the Navy handled their problems in a similar fashion so there would be little point in describing the work of both. Therefore, a fairly full description is sometimes given of the activities of one branch of the armed services, and only an abbreviated account is given of the work of the other. It must be recognized that this policy does not seem to take sufficient notice of several worthy programs established by either the Army or the Navy; but the purpose of Part II is not to provide a full and complete history but to give adult educators as concise a view as possible of major accomplishments.

DEFINITIONS AND LIMITATIONS

In planning this study, it became apparent that certain definitions were required and certain limitations of scope were necessary. The criteria set up for limiting the scope of the study were determined in part by the general policies of the Commission after a consideration of the relationships of this study to the other studies which it is conducting. In the establishment of these criteria, an effort has been made to eliminate duplication and overlapping of the content of these and other studies.

For the purposes of this study, adult education has been defined as the conscious effort of the mature individual to improve himself through the acquisition of skills, knowledge, attitudes, understandings, and appreciations. Maturity is not alone a matter of chronological age, and the armed services personnel were forced by the conditions they faced to become old beyond their years. The average age of the men and women in the armed services was less than that in the population as a whole, and the participants in off-duty educational activities varied in this important respect from those who participate in civilian programs. Nonetheless, the Army and Navy programs were basically adult-educational in character.

The off-duty programs referred to in the study include all service-operated educational programs available to service personnel in which participation occurred during leisure time while individuals were not primarily engaged in the performance of some scheduled military duty.

As used here, an implication is a statement of a basic principle or technique used successfully in the off-duty educational programs which has a direct relationship to and importance for civilian adult education. A fuller exploration of the meaning of this term is made in Part II.

The purpose of the study was the analysis of off-duty programs in the armed services to determine implications for civilian adult education. The definition of off-duty programs restricted the study to only those programs in which participation had been voluntary. It was thus necessary to exclude from the study all educational activities in which participation was required by military regulation and occurred on duty time. Even though some of these compulsory military-training programs included study materials which a serviceman might have chosen to study in his leisure time, they were not considered for this study unless offered in a specific off-duty program.

Only such off-duty programs as were operated by the armed services of the United States have been considered. Some civilian agencies, including public schools located near training bases, maintained adult-education programs which were available to service personnel; they also supplied teachers for classes which were service-operated and controlled. These were not service-operated programs and thus were not appropriate for inclusion in the study.

Incidental educational opportunities such as those resulting from travel, from mingling with people of other countries and cultures, and from visiting historical and religious landmarks the world over have not been mentioned because, for the most part, they were not organized, service-operated educational programs.

Except for those programs which started after September 16, 1940, and were completed prior to VJ Day, only those programs which were in active operation on VJ Day, August 14, 1945, have been considered in this and in other studies sponsored by the Commission. The most serious result of this limitation was that it made impossible the consideration of the Navy's program of postwar educational activities which did not get well under way until after the victory over Japan.

Exceptions to these limitations have occurred only when it has been necessary in the interest of completeness to discuss programs which were in part compulsory and in part voluntary. A soldier in the European theater might volunteer for selection and assignment to one of the Army university centers. Once ordered to that center, however, he was on a full-duty status. At the same time, he was free to choose his own courses and was not required to take any courses specifically directed toward the improvement of his military skills. The importance of these university centers in the entire non-training educational program of the Army warranted their inclusion in this study even though they did not satisfy all of the criteria mentioned above.

The Army and Navy orientation programs were also in part compulsory and in part voluntary. At training camps and permanent bases, attendance at orientation lectures was frequently required. Participation in organized forum discussions, attendance at war-information movies sometimes accompanied by lectures on current events, interest in *Newsmaps*, and in keeping up with the news were entirely voluntary on the part of millions of men and women in the service. The publication of service newspapers and magazines was not itself a voluntary off-duty educational activity, but the educational and informational value of these publications cannot be overlooked.

It is also true that library services were not exclusively off-duty educational programs because their basic functions included providing recreation and supplementing the training program. At the same time the availability of books and periodicals in any part of the world where American servicemen were stationed made possible the success of many off-duty programs.

These modifications in the application of the criteria were adopted in order to make the study as useful and as complete as possible.

The inclusion of a description of the Army's and Navy's literacy training programs made necessary another exception to the limitations in scope which had been established. Again participation in the program was almost always compulsory, but the conscious and enthusiastic efforts which servicemen made to develop a functional literacy represented a voluntary effort to improve their basic skills. Also the literacy programs had such particular significance for civilian adult education that it was felt that their inclusion was warranted.

Adherence to these limitations made it impossible to include a description of the nature and use of audio-visual aids because the preparation and development of these devices was included in the programs for training in military skills. Similarly, the unique program of foreign-language instruction was developed for the training of military government and counter-espionage personnel and has been described here only as it was used in the off-duty classes. A description of the teacher-training program used to prepare people without previous teaching experience for instructing adults in Army and Navy training programs would have been interesting to adult educators. But this, too, was outside of the scope of this study. Fortunately, other studies conducted by the Commission on Implications of Armed Services Educational Programs are considering many of the aspects of the armed services programs not possible to consider here.

PLAN OF THE STUDY

Army off-duty programs described in Part I include those activities of the Information and Education Division, Army Service Forces, which could be included within the limitations of this study: the United States Armed Forces Institute (USAFI) and its program of correspondence instruction; the Army Education Program for the post-hostilities period; the Orientation Program; the Army Literacy Program; the off-duty classes; and special staff activities. Attention has also been given to the work of the Army Library Service, Special Services Division, Army Service Forces. The work of the Orientation Branch, Army Service Forces, formerly a part of the Information and Education Division, has been included.

Navy off-duty programs included in Part I are those of the Educational Services Section, Training Activity, Bureau of Naval Personnel. The Navy's orientation activities, its participation in the program of USAFI, and the entire off-duty class program were administered by the Educational Services Section. The activities of the Navy Library Service, Welfare Division, Bureau of Naval Personnel (which also provided library services to the Marine Corps and Coast Guard) and some supplementary activities of other sections of the Training Division have also been included. This centralized control of the Navy off-duty program has made it somewhat easier to describe Navy activities.

Marine Corps off-duty programs were supervised by the Education Section, Welfare Division, Special Services Branch. The Education Section was responsible for the coordination of the services of the Marine Corps Institute with those of USAFI and the organization of off-duty classes in the field. It relied on the Educational Services Section of the Bureau of Naval Personnel for supplies and guidance.

Except for the Coast Guard Institute, the Coast Guard did not maintain an ambitious separate program and instead depended almost entirely on the Navy for off-duty educational opportunities for its personnel.

As has been inferred previously, much of the development of these off-duty programs was charted and implemented by personnel in the field who frequently lacked any close contact with

Washington headquarters. It has been impossible in these brief descriptions to include mention of many local modifications and unique organizational aspects which these field programs might warrant.

Rather than describing each program and activity separately in terms of its place in the internal organization of the Army or Navy, a crosscutting analysis in terms of purpose has been made. The uniqueness of the off-duty programs in the military organization of the armed services makes it essential that one chapter be devoted to an historical account of their development and an explanation of the purposes which made them acceptable in military organization. It is then necessary to describe the place these programs occupied in the organizational framework and the methods by which personnel was selected, trained, and assigned. The programs themselves were then examined in some detail, with a chapter being given to each of the following: correspondence study, direct individual and group education, Army post-hostilities schools, orientation and information, library services, and literacy training. A final group of chapters deals with the methods by which the armed services handled certain pervasive problems, guidance, motivation and recruitment, and investigation and evaluation.

I. HISTORY AND PURPOSES

In 1777, General Washington, on behalf of his army, asked the Continental Congress for a "small traveling press to follow Headquarters." He pointed out that "an ingenious man to accompany this press and be employed in writing for it might render it singularly beneficial." His requests for this and later for another educational program were first tabled and then forgotten.[1]

In World War II the armed services of the United States suffered under no such limitations. During that war, men in uniform aided by civilian consultants were engaged in a never-ending effort to define the purposes of and to develop in the field an extensive program of off-duty educational opportunities. The words of Major General F. H. Osborn, director of the Information and Education Division, Army Service Forces, in writing of the Division's accomplishments during the war years, might well be taken as a summary of the purposes of the entire off-duty educational efforts of the armed services during World War II.[2]

> It has been the purpose of Information and Education that the American Soldier should be the best informed and best educated soldier in any Army. To reach this objective, the following methods were evolved over the past four years: Provision of full and unbiased information; opportunities for free discussion of that information; and the opportunities for formal education in off-duty time or during training prior to discharge.
>
> The value of such an approach for an American Army in time of war has been proved by its broad acceptance in training for combat. In time of peace the practice of these fundamentals of the American tradition will help the Army to maintain public confidence in the type of training given its young men.

ARMY[3]

Until the last months of World War I, the provision of any services to soldiers other than those directly related to training

[1] Philip S. Foner, *Morale Education in the American Army* (New York: International Publishers, 1944), p. 17.

[2] F. H. Osborn, *Information and Education Division.* Privately printed and distributed by the author, October 1945.

[3] This section, with minor editorial changes and some abridgment, is excerpted, with permission, from the manuscript "Study of Information and Education Activities: World War II" (on file in the Historical Division, War Department Special Staff).

or combat was not considered a part of the Army's responsibilities. In every major war in the nation's history, civilian groups had been formed to help the troops by providing for both welfare and morale. In World War I, in accordance with this traditional policy, welfare groups banded together, with the backing of the War and Navy Departments, into the Commission on Training Camp Activities which primarily provided welfare services—recreation clubs, entertainment, and athletic equipment—and cooperated in the distribution of books and magazines through the American Library Association. The Commission was headed by Raymond B. Fosdick and was the outgrowth of his report to Secretary of War Baker on the conditions of the Army on the Mexican border. The Commission was a loose-knit and temporary federation of welfare groups with religious ties (the Knights of Columbus, the Jewish Welfare Board, the YMCA, and the YWCA). These groups had military recognition and cooperation, but depended on public contributions for financial support.

OFF-DUTY EDUCATION BEFORE WORLD WAR II

During World War I, it became clear that the existing arrangement was not satisfactory, and Mr. Fosdick's report to Secretary Baker on June 1, 1919, established a principle of inestimable value to later activities both in welfare and in information and education. It was the principle of public responsibility and financing. Other reports which he made to the Secretary or to General Pershing, including objective analyses of relations of officers and men and of the importance of telling men what to expect and when, were guideposts for the development of later programs to inform and educate officers and men.

During the First World War, the Army had come to recognize the need for assuming a direct responsibility for many activities which were loosely defined as affecting morale. Backing was given to a proposed postwar education program, at the start largely financed by the YMCA. The YMCA education officers were later transferred into an Army Education Corps, and the War Department set up an education and recreation program which was active after the war in the camps in the United States.

Just before the end of the war, a morale branch was established in the General Staff. Its purpose was to coordinate the work of the civilian welfare agencies and to consider and take appropriate action on other factors which influenced the morale of the Army. Experimental studies were undertaken after the war, and other work was begun which might well have had important implications for the military establishment in the years of peace which were to follow. However, the drastic curtailment of appropriations to the Army inevitably struck hard at any unit so recently established.

ORGANIZATION OF THE MORALE BRANCH

Twenty years later, when the Mobilization Regulations of October 28, 1939, were written, morale was defined largely in terms of physical welfare: food, leave, discipline, and recreation. The provisions of these regulations were put into effect in mid-1940, and a Morale Division of the Adjutant General's Office was established. Actually this Division was an administrative office to show movies, hire librarians, and perform other similar services. It had no responsibility to expand into a program of education or orientation.

The Mobilization Regulations of 1939 also provided for the appointment of a committee of civilian and military experts in welfare and community-service activities, to advise the Secretary of War on the relation between the activities of the armed services and those of other governmental and private agencies. Started as a War Department committee in January 1941, it was later expanded at the direction of the President to include the Navy and the Marine Corps, and, in February 1941, became the Joint Army-Navy Committee on Welfare and Recreation. The Committee was not an operating agency, but played a major part in fostering the USO, USO Camp Shows, arrangements between the Red Cross and the Army, and the establishment of educational programs for service personnel. It gave increased prestige to the early Morale Division of the Army and aided greatly in coordinating the work not only of the Army and the Navy, but also of other government and private agencies. The first chairman was Frederick H. Osborn, later director successively of the Special Service Division and the Information and Education Division. The membership of the Committee was made up of men distinguished in education, business, and public affairs.

Public position and personal friendships brought the ideas of these men to the attention of the highest officials of the War Department. Although the most effective backing given Information and Education in its formative years came from the Chief of Staff, General Marshall, the program would never have advanced as far as it did without the interest and formal or informal approval of the Secretary, the assistant secretaries, and of many high-ranking officers of the War Department who were influenced and sometimes guided by the members of the Committee. Even when the program had been made official by War Department orders, the direct and indirect influence of these men continued to be felt at high echelons, for the Committee's members were all officially consultants to the Secretary of War.

Seven months after the establishment of the Morale Division in the Adjutant General's Office, a conference of morale officers was held in Washington. The War Department had instructed the major commands to send their morale officers on very short notice, and an informal poll revealed that over half of them had been appointed within two days before their departure for Washington. Few of them had had professional training or experience in personnel management, welfare work, or recreation, much less the art of informing and educating troops. Many of them had no idea of what their job involved, and most, as one officer put it, "had already taken quite a bit of 'razzing' as morale officers." The formal speeches at the conference put emphasis on leadership as the basis of good morale, but the discussions of things to be done immediately emphasized rapid construction of buildings and other facilities for recreation, and the control and improvement of facilities for soldiers in communities near the rapidly growing posts and camps. Morale theory and practice were far apart.

It had become clear during the months preceding the conference that the War Department's existing machinery was not adequate to do the job of welfare and recreation, or to "enable the

Chief of the Morale Division at all times to know the state of morale of the Army" (as a memorandum for the Chief of Staff stated the problem). Accordingly there was established on March 14, 1941, a Morale Branch of the Army, functioning directly under the supervision and control of the Chief of Staff. Major General (then Brigadier General) James A. Ulio was named Chief of the Branch in addition to his other duties as Assistant to the Adjutant General.

The first organization charts of March and April, 1941, show four major divisions in the Morale Branch, in addition to the normal executive and personnel sections: Welfare and Recreation, Planning and Research, Public Relations, and Services. Under the Welfare and Recreation Division was an education section, whose responsibilities were listed under the titles: Mental, Physical, Moral, Morale Training, Librarians, and Scholarships. Under Public Relations was listed responsibility for camp newspapers and camp radio reception. Under Planning and Research were listed, among other responsibilities: morale information (group and individual), potential morale problems, and studies. Here were the kernels of the future information and education programs. In practice, however, most of the time and attention of the officers of the Morale Branch in the early days of 1941 was taken up with the expansion of recreation facilities in the camps.

At the lower levels of the Morale Branch, however, some of the early planning for information and education was going on with the help of the Joint Army and Navy Committee on Welfare and Recreation. Civilian experts, holding the status of special consultants to the Secretary of War, were made available either individually or in committees and were used by the Army to draw up plans and recommend personnel. Many of these men were later commissioned. The Armed Forces Institute, the research activities on soldier attitudes, and certain radio activities all had their birth in this period. The importance of having men in troops understand the reasons for their service was forced on the War Department by the public discussion of the need for selective service, but the opposition of the public and the Army alike to any program even suggesting "propaganda" made any direct attack on those attitudes difficult.

When General Ulio's illness in August 1941 required his relief from active service for several months, General Marshall recommended the commissioning of Frederick H. Osborn, chairman of the Joint Army and Navy Committee, to the rank of Brigadier General and appointed him chief of the Morale Branch.

GROWTH OF THE OFF-DUTY PROGRAM

Four factors underlay the expansion of the services of the Morale Branch to include mental stimulation and training in addition to recreation and amusement: the intellectual qualities and interests of the new personnel brought into the Branch; the stimulus of public interest and criticism; the objective information on basic factors affecting soldier morale developed by research studies on soldier attitudes; and the needs of the expanding Army, as developed in the field and reported back to Washington.

First, General Osborn's background and interests caused him to select assistants whose training and skills lay primarily in education, information, and social-science research. These men in turn chose younger officers, enlisted men, and civilians of like qualities of mind.

The second factor, the stimulus of public interest and criticism, was particularly evident in August and September of 1941 when the morale of the Army came into the public eye. The civilian members and consultants of the Joint Army and Navy Committee poured in suggestions to the Morale Branch on methods of interesting and distracting men in uniform. The commanding general of the Second Army initiated a lecture program to assist the soldier in having a more coherent understanding of this country and its foreign policies and of the reason for being in uniform. This program received considerable press comment. Reports of a British Army Bureau of Current Affairs with broadly similar purposes were made available. Many offers of service were received from teachers and lecturers who expressed interest in talking to troops about national and international affairs. Private groups, such as the Committee for National Morale, were studying the causes of national confusion and were greatly concerned over the attitudes of troops. It was becoming clearer to the public and to the Army that the attitudes of troops were closely related to those of the public and that morale was a complicated matter.

The third factor, objective information on morale, was the result of the first broad-scale research project begun the day after Pearl Harbor. This study indicated that the success or lack of success of the classification and assignment program played a vital role in the spirit with which soldiers carried out their Army duties. Later reports emphasized these early conclusions, and further studies showed a wide variation in attitudes among men assigned to the various branches and arms of service, among whites and Negroes, and among men with varying lengths of service. Studies of the effectiveness of recreation programs and later of orientation and information programs showed that these had an effect on what was defined as morale, but were by no means controlling factors. This research served to dispel the notion that the Morale Branch could, with the weapons at its command, have any controlling effect on the morale of the Army.

The fourth and most important factor of all was the development of the needs of an expanding Army, which were being reported back to the War Department. Camp newspapers were needing advice and help. There were scattered demands for off-duty classes on nonmilitary subjects, though most commanders thought their troops too busy with military training to permit such activities. There was considerable talk of local camp radio stations.

In response to the new demands and awakened interest the Morale Branch changed its name, established new services, and began implementing its field operations. On January 15, 1942, the name of the Branch was officially changed to the Special Services Branch. The broad lines of the program to provide mental sustenance for the Army also took shape. The short- and long-range purposes of a nonmilitary education program were worked out in some detail in the winter of 1942, and were not substantially changed in the years that followed. The plan was to provide correspondence instruction, and materials and leadership for off-duty voluntary classes. At the same time, preparations were to be made for a large-scale on-duty program after hostilities ceased.

Basic principles governing both the nonmilitary education and the research program were also worked out in the same year. In the case of education it was planned to provide a program closely integrated with analagous civilian activities, based on freedom of choice of the individual as to his course of study and emphasizing the initiative and interest of the student. Wherever possible, materials were to be taken or adapted from the best available civilian sources.

In the case of research, the long-range goal was to study the motivations and reactions of soldiers to obtain information of maximum value to the war effort. The facilities of the research program were put at the disposal of agencies of the War Department which needed help in solving administrative and personnel problems. Complete anonymity for the individual was assured, and materials were not to be collected as the basis for investigations of the type normally associated with the Inspector General.

In mid-February of 1942 the duties of the Information Division of the Special Services Branch were described in the following terms:

> The Information Division encourages and renders necessary assistance and cooperation in the establishment of camp newspapers, and exercises advisory supervision. It prepares news material for release to civilian agencies through the War Department's Bureau of Public Relations, and conducts current studies of the civilian press in its relationship to military morale.
>
> The procurement of photographs and the reviewing of current newsreels are also functions of the Information Division. The personnel of the division considers ideas for posters, stimulates interest in art and cartooning and concerns itself with radio promotion in the Army from the morale standpoint. To date some 250 radio stations are affiliated with a mythical network known as the "Red, White and Blue Network." Material of interest to these radio stations is furnished at regular intervals. The proper functioning of radio programs emanating from Army camps comes within the scope of this division.

Soldiers in camps in the United States depended on normal civilian sources for their news. It was not until some time after the first troops landed at overseas bases that the Army undertook the responsibility of providing and effectively servicing newspapers and radio stations. Its natural hesitancy to enter a field fraught with political danger (even despite reports such as that of Wendell Willkie, whose round-the-world trip showed him that soldiers overseas were not getting enough news) meant that in 1942 and 1943 the information program overseas did not meet the needs of the men. In general, Special Services Branch in the winter, spring, and summer of 1942 limited its information program to matters of particular and peculiar interest to troops. *Yank,* for example, which was planned in the winter and spring of 1942, was described as a weekly by soldiers about soldiers, for distribution only to soldiers.

It was natural that the officers of the Information Division should, therefore, have been particularly interested in the orientation program which was at that time being conducted by the Bureau of Public Relations and which was designed to explain to troops the causes of the war and to tell them of its progress. Discussions had been held with the Signal Corps even before Pearl Harbor about making a series of films to explain to soldiers why they were in uniform. By the time the orientation program was transferred to the Chief of Special Services Branch in June 1942, a staff had been assembled and was at work making a series of films on the background and causes of the war to replace the lectures which formed the orientation part of the basic training of all troops. As a part of the transfer, *Newsmap,* a weekly poster illustrating the current developments of the war in graphic form, was also made a responsibility of the Information Division. Experimental work with recordings in early 1942 had led to the establishment of a small radio section, which later became the world-wide Armed Forces Radio Service (AFRS). Guidebooks to foreign countries, starting with the *Guide to Great Britain,* were in the planning stage. The three major media for the information of troops—press, film, and radio—were therefore available before the over-all policy governing Army information services had been established.

Despite this activity in what was to become the Information and Education Program (I and E), the greatest Army and public interest was still devoted to the welfare and recreational activities. The Army Motion Picture Service, the USO Camp Shows, and the recreation clubs were growing into big business and required a large part of the energy of the Chief of the Special Services Branch and all of the time of the recreation officers in the field. Field visits by officers of the Special Service Branch evinced an acute need for training recreation officers, who were only occasionally experts in similar work in civilian life, and accordingly there was established a School for Special Service, the first class starting on March 1, 1942.

In the general War Department reorganization of March 9, 1942, Special Services was made a part of the Services of Supply and was placed under the Chief of Administrative Services. Five months later, in a reorganization of the Services of Supply, Special Services was assigned to the newly established Assistant Chief of Staff for Personnel, and the name changed to Special Service Division under a director rather than a chief.

In the summer of 1942, with the addition of orientation, there developed within the Special Service Division itself a natural separation of interests, in which recreation and welfare were grouped on one side and information, education, and research on the other. The greatest expansion in headquarters took place in the second group.

A similar expansion did not, however, take place in the field. The directives which were issued were phrased almost entirely in terms of welfare and recreation, and the training school only gradually increased the time allotted to "mental training." The revision of MR 1-10 dated October 1942 defined the duty of the Special Service officer as "assisting commanding officers in all matters pertaining to morale, recreation, and welfare." The director in speaking to the classes attending the School for Special Service in the summer and fall of 1942 spoke often of the need for "mental and physical stamina" and of the need of enlarging the soldiers' conception of the significance of the war and his place in it. What actually reached the Special Service officers on duty with troops, however, were buildings, bats, and entertainment; only the exceptional officer paid any attention to his responsibilities as the consultant to the commander on basic morale factors, or the officer responsible for information and education programs for the troops.

Within the Division itself, a variety of opinions developed in 1943 as to the Army's responsibility for the morale of troops through mental training. Three main lines of thought can be distinguished and are here stated, perhaps in oversimplified form. Actually one opinion shaded into another, and common agreement was found on many topics.

The first opinion was that the Army at war had the right and duty to use every medium at its command—film, radio, newspapers, posters, orientation lectures, and discussions—to keep the soldier's mind focused on the basic issues of the war, on his own responsibility, and on the enemy's strategy and power. Carefully designed campaigns using all media were recommended. The aim was a professional fighting man, eager to close with the foe.

A second opinion was that no Army in a democracy had the right to select news on behalf of its personnel—even if every word was true—but that it rather must as far as possible provide every side of every issue, must sedulously avoid any effort to make up the soldier's mind for him, must give him a chance to talk freely on any subject—war or peace, military tactics or architecture—and encourage him to prepare for civilian life.

The third opinion was most disconcerting. It pointed out that a soldier's attitudes toward the issues of the war, toward his own civilian future, and toward the enemy and the ally were only minor factors in the composite of the soldier's motivations. Far more important were his job assignment, his attitudes toward his noncommissioned and commissioned officers, his faith in the integrity of the Army's plans, and his own chances for advancement. If Special Service was held responsible even to some degree for the morale of the soldier, it should worry about the major issues, not the minor.

Many considerations, therefore, plus the most cogent fact of all—that a good recreation officer was not necessarily or even usually a competent orientation officer—caused a complete review in the fall of 1943 of the purposes and organization of the Special Service Division. Several important steps were taken in this period to improve field operations, culminating in directives of October and November of 1943 providing for a mandatory discussion hour on duty time for all troops, and authorizing the addition of a full-time orientation officer functioning in regiments and separate battalions, and in all posts, camps, and stations having a minimum population of two thousand.

On October 14, 1943, the Research, Control, Information, Education (less Library), Orientation, and Training Branches of Special Service were transferred to the jurisdiction of the Director of Military Training, ASF. There was also established a Director of Morale Services, similarly attached to the Director of Military Training, and the welfare and recreation activities retained the name "Special Service" and were assigned to the Director of Personnel, ASF.

On October 25, there was established within the office of the Director of Training an Army Education and Information Division, consisting of the Education, Information, and Orientation Branches. The Director of Morale Services (General Osborn) continued in a separate capacity, directing the activities of the Research Branch, and maintaining a supervisory relationship to the new Army Education and Information Division.

This arrangement lasted only a few weeks, and on November 10 both parts of the office of the Director of Military Training, ASF, were combined and reassigned to the jurisdiction of the Director of Personnel, ASF, with the name of the Morale Services Division. Not until the spring of 1945 was "I and E" separated from Special Service and established independently in the European theater.

THE ARMY LIBRARY SERVICE [4]

In 1940, the Army Library Service was expanded along with the many other functions of the Army. When the Morale Division of the Adjutant General's Office was organized in July 1940, the Library Branch was established in that Division to super-

[4] This section is excerpted, with permission, from the manuscript, "The Army Library Service: A Short History" (on file in the Historical Division, War Department Special Staff).

vise the Army Library Service. The Library Branch underwent a number of reorganizations and, finally, in April 1945, it was given the status of a branch in the Special Service Division.

DEVELOPMENT OF I AND E ACTIVITIES

The separation of I and E from Special Service permitted concentration on developing unified overseas I and E operation, and improving services to these operations. In 1944, for the first time, a complete staff of trained officers and men including experts in the major aspects of orientation, education, and information were sent as a unit in response to a request from the southwest Pacific. Visits of the director and his senior staff members helped to integrate overseas operations which had previously been scattered throughout several staff groups in the command. The newspaper, the edition of *Yank* (for administrative purposes), the research team, the branch of USAFI, the radio activities—all were combined under one head and one policy direction. The news services, radio, *Yank,* and branches of USAFI had expanded overseas independently in 1943 and had tried, for understandable reasons, to maintain a separate status from the entertainment and recreation activities.

Almost from the start of their activities, *Yank,* USAFI, AFRS, and Research had established overseas branches or units and supplied them with specialized personnel. The Education Branch had provided education officers to the service commands in the United States, as well as to overseas theaters, to initiate off-duty programs and to prepare for the post-hostilities period. Thus there were going concerns in operation all over the world, except in regard to orientation. Here, despite two years of effort, there was inadequate understanding of the purposes of the program by commanders, and there was insufficient trained personnel in smaller units.

The appointment of full-time orientation officers in late 1943 and early 1944 gave impetus to the orientation program, however, and required both increased material for use in supervising the weekly discussion hour and improved training facilities to prepare both the officers and their enlisted staffs for their work.

A twenty-eight-day course for orientation officers at Lexington,

Virginia, was inaugurated in early January 1944 as a part of the School for Personnel Services after several months of experimentation with a ten-day course. Over three hundred officers were enrolled, and the start of an I and E program planned by a skilled staff, sanctioned by Army regulations, and supervised in the field by men selected and trained to lead discussion, can be dated from that class.

By March 1944, the Morale Services Division had established its major activities and was busily engaged in a rapid expansion overseas. New editions of newspapers and of *Yank* appeared on the continent of Europe and in the Pacific, radio stations were being added almost daily, USAFI enrollment and the number of USAFI branches grew rapidly, and research teams were appearing at all but one major overseas theater. The Division, almost to its surprise, found itself directing the largest program of its type ever attempted in American history. The program rivaled and surpassed the great civilian press associations, radio networks, and adult-education projects.

Integration with the Navy was achieved in many activities (in USAFI and later in AFRS, involving coordinated operations as well as policies) and extended still further the influence of the Division's work. The earlier, more academic discussions of purpose, mission, and methods became matters of public importance, requiring prompt decision and affecting the affairs of millions of men. The Research Branch undertook studies of men's attitudes toward a fair method of demobilization, and it was the Morale Services Division which, on the basis of the results obtained from these studies, laid the basis for the point-score system later put into effect.

Preparations for the post-hostilities period took definite form in the spring and summer of 1944; the plans that started in 1942 were turning into a huge program for duty-time courses to start after the end of the war. Millions of textbooks were chosen and ordered, and shipments started to Europe in the fall of 1944. Films were nearing completion. Posters were being printed. Teaching aids were put in final form. The program as a whole came of age with astonishing rapidity after it had been separated from its childhood associates.

In August 1944, the name of the Division was changed to the Information and Education Division, and shortly thereafter all staff officers in field units were similarly designated. The responsibility for soldier morale, so long the source of confusion and debate, had been narrowed and defined. A detailed circular setting forth the duties of I and E at all echelons, and prescribing the personnel to carry out these duties, was issued a month later in War Department Circular 360. The gradual application of its provisions throughout the Army served to unify operations and cause higher quality officers to be asigned to I and E work.

The effort to define an operating philosophy for the information and orientation program and to establish machinery and methods to carry out this philosophy still continued. The three diverging conceptions described earlier were in part combined and rationalized, and were originally set forth in a memorandum to guide the teachers at the School for I and E Officers in October 1944; later they were woven into the text of a technical manual for Information and Education officers in July 1945. The following quotation from the memorandum summarizes the position taken:

> 2. First, as to selection: Information and Education Officers should be men who hold two basic beliefs:
>
> (*a*) Belief in the essential integrity of the individual. This belief is basic to the American tradition. It is both a religious and an ethical concept, and in its practical application is the basis for the American way of life.
>
> (*b*) A belief in democracy; that democracy is practical; the belief of Lincoln in the soundness of the majority opinion of the common man when properly informed. This again is a concept basic to American life.
>
> We would not be justified in graduating from our school officers who did not hold these two beliefs, nor would Congress and those in authority be satisfied that men lacking these beliefs should instruct the soldier in the meaning of the war and the meaning of citizenship.
>
> 3. Second, as to training: The Information and Education Officer should be so trained that he will distinguish clearly among the following different fields of ideas, and will vary the handling of his subject in accordance with what is proper in each of these fields.

I. *Ideas which are basic to the American Tradition.* Belief in the integrity of the individual, and belief in democracy. Also, ideas which flow inevitably from these beliefs, such as: Freedom within the law is essential to our way of life; except at the price of freedom, peace is preferable to war; toleration of race and religion is essential to freedom.

As to these, the Information and Education Officer must have an outspoken and affirmative attitude, for these are the fundamentals on which all else we do is based. They are presupposed in the American tradition, and in the acts of democratic government which have given us our national character by which we take our stand. As to these, the Information and Education Officer will energetically present the soldier a concluded opinion. These fundamentals should inform our whole approach to more specific ideas and subjects.

II. *Policies and Commands of the Government.* (Congress and the War Department.) These represent, in the case of Congress, the majority decision of the American people, and in the case of the War Department, the unified command necessary to the success of an army. Lend-lease is an example of Congressional decision; strategy of the war, or the required behavior toward our Allies, examples of Command.

In such matters, the Information and Education Officer has his explicit conclusions; he should lead the soldier to them and encourage acceptance of them. The unity which is essential to success in war can be obtained only by cheerful obedience to commands which, in the orderly processes of American government, derive their authority from the will of the majority.

III. *Current Issues.* All fields of thought and subjects appropriate to an informed man, whether civilian or soldier; these include matters which will be resolved politically through the franchise. These the Information and Education Officer does not resolve for the soldier, but carefully gives him the facts, pro and con, as they are available.

In time of war, discussion of current issues is more appropriate to off-duty periods with voluntary attendance than to mandatory on-duty orientation. However, mandatory discussion may be necessary in the case of issues in which apathy, ignorance, prejudice and misunderstanding may interfere with the efficient accomplishment of the military mission, and where a balanced presentation of the facts may be used to effect uninformed or extreme attitudes injurious to morale.

4. All armies now recognize the need for training the soldier's mind in order to protect his morale. The enemies of the United States believe that the regimented mind is the best mind for a soldier. The United States holds the very opposite belief, that the soldier's mind should be free, informed, judicious, able to protect itself from sophistry and falsehood, alert, and understanding of the problem of command.[5]

[5] *The Information–Education Officer,* War Department Technical Manual 28-210 (Washington: Government Printing Office, July 1945), pp. 6-9, Sec. III, par. 7-9.

There now developed a series of special programs to prepare soldiers to meet special circumstances. On these matters there was no hesitation either within the Division or in the higher echelons of the War Department. Everyone agreed that men should be mentally prepared for the invasion of Europe in June 1944, and later for the landings in the Philippines. Reinforcements going east or west obviously would benefit from orientation in the reason for their assignment and preparation for what lay ahead. Research results had emphasized that uncertainty of what lay ahead—immediately ahead, such as what happened in replacement depots—was a disturbing factor for the soldier, and the materials used had therefore to be kept up to date and judiciously handled. Specially trained officers were assigned for permanent duty with the transports, and efforts were made to coordinate the program with the orientation work in the overseas theaters to which the replacements were assigned.

Experimental studies by the Research Branch indicated that soldiers learned rapidly when they felt that the information was of immediate and personal use, but the studies did not show any marked or immediate changes in attitude as a result of the efforts made simultaneously to impress the man with the underlying causes of the war and the contribution of the Allies. There was not sufficient evidence to show whether this was the result of poor materials, poor presentation, bad timing, or some more fundamental factor of motivation. The end of the war terminated some fundamental studies of the effects of the orientation program and the discussion group which might have helped to make them more effective, or cause them to be abandoned as impractical.

The fall of 1944 and the winter of 1945 saw also the completion of the staff plans and supply operations for the redeployment period. To explain the redeployment plan and the whole concept of "two down and one to go" a special program to start on VE Day was prepared, using films, pamphlets, posters, and radio. Overseas theaters supported this plan with materials of their own, and efforts were made, particularly in Europe, to have the books and the teachers for the unit schools and the universities all ready for the Army Education Program. The Information program to explain redeployment was more immediately successful, since there were already in operation established and dependable distribution methods for newspapers, for *Yank,* for pamphlet material, for radio broadcasts, and for film distribution. The on-duty Education program, with a need for immense numbers of trained personnel and extensive supplies and without the benefit of gradual expansion during the war, was slower in establishment. The Mediterranean theater was the first to start unit schools and the first to open an Army university center. The inevitable confusion attendant on the category method of redeployment limited the scope of the program in the European theater until the late summer. Nevertheless, despite great complications and difficulties, it was generally agreed that the various aspects of I and E activities, first in Italy and later in the European theater following VE Day, and in operation in the Pacific, combined to make the most successful and useful special program ever undertaken by the Division. These activities were a considerable factor in maintaining the morale of the Army during a difficult period.

NAVY [6]

Prior to World War II the Navy had done little in the way of an off-duty educational program. Following World War I, Secretary Josephus Daniels had instituted a compulsory educational plan for naval personnel. For various reasons, it was short-lived.

At some stations, commanding officers, and more frequently chaplains, encouraged men to use commercial correspondence facilities, to make use of the educational opportunities of the area, or to pursue a planned reading program. But these were isolated examples and not integrated by a policy which applied to the Navy as a whole.

In February 1941, at the direction of President Roosevelt, the Navy joined with the Army to form the Joint Army and Navy Committee on Welfare and Recreation. The Navy was slow in starting a program to meet the objectives of the Committee. It was not until May 1942 that naval attendance at meetings

[6] Use has been made throughout this section of the "Educational Services Section," "Administrative History of the Bureau of Naval Personnel," (MS on file in the Office of Naval History, U. S. Navy Department).

of the Committee led to the preparation of a tentative program to be administered by the Officer Training Unit of the Training Division of the Bureau of Naval Personnel. This tentative program was given the title of Navy Voluntary Wartime Education. The program was announced on May 27, 1942, in a memorandum listing the five following objectives:

1. Improvement of in-service efficiency of officers and men.
2. Training to supplement skill in Navy rating to prepare enrollees for related work in civilian life.
3. Continued indoctrination in war issues and American ideals.
4. Preparation for civilian life after the war.
5. Improvement of morale.

Shortly after this, an officer from the Bureau of Naval Personnel went to the naval station at Guantanamo Bay, Cuba, to look into the possibilities of installing some sort of an off-duty educational program there. The station was ideal for such an experiment, having at the time a large number of personnel with relatively little to do in their off-duty time. The lack of facilities or any program was creating a considerable problem in morale. Returning to the States, the visiting officer reported what he had found and secured permission to take another officer and as much pertinent material as could be gathered in a short time back with him. The so-called "Guantanamo Experiment" was inaugurated officially on October 2, 1942, and was an outstanding success from the first. An abandoned schoolhouse was reclaimed for an educational center, word was circulated that applications for classes in spoken Spanish would be received, and, on the first day, 275 men appeared to enroll.

In certain respects, the center at Guantanamo established a pattern for the entire Educational Services Program. From the very first, classroom instruction was conceived to be the core of the off-duty program. In the early days of the program, most of the courses offered were designed to provide a background for Navy work. The first courses at Guantanamo included such subjects as blueprint reading, Spanish, shorthand, Morse code, and English. The classes usually met five nights a week for hourly sessions. Suitable texts were obtained by means of requisitions to the Bureau of Naval Personnel which purchased them in the commercial field.

The experiment at Guantanamo was sufficiently successful so that the commanding officer there wrote a letter endorsing the project to the Chief of Naval Personnel; and, with this encouragement, a unit which was called the War Education Unit proceeded to assign officers to other outlying bases.

Not all of the impetus for an off-duty educational program emanated from Washington. At various bases, officers who were worried about the problem, primarily as it related to morale, were encouraging the establishment of similar projects, unrelated to the Bureau's efforts. Thus, at San Juan, Puerto Rico, the chaplain was sponsoring in-service educational training as early as the summer of 1942, while the Welfare Division under the Alaskan Sea Frontier was shortly to undertake a more extensive project of the same kind.

EDUCATIONAL SERVICES

During this same period, an event occurred which gave added motivation to the establishment of an organization in Washington to coordinate the various types of off-duty education. The Army had established, in April 1942, the Army Institute at Madison, Wisconsin, to serve as a headquarters of its correspondence course program. In August of 1942, an interchange of letters took place between the Secretaries of War and Navy; as a result, the Army Institute made its courses available to the other services. A letter to all ships and stations, dated October 27, 1942, announced this fact to the Navy; and, in December 1942, the first naval personnel were enrolled in correspondence courses. As a result of these various activities, which indicated that the need for an off-duty educational program was present, it was finally agreed by the Bureau of Naval Personnel to establish such a coordinating agency. On January 7, 1943, a memorandum was issued, officially creating a War Education Section within the Training Division of the Bureau of Naval Personnel. A week later the name was changed to the Educational Services Section, and on February 3, 1943, this Section, the organization which was to develop and coordinate the Navy's off-duty educational program, was officially established.[7]

The establishing letter explained that the Bureau of Naval Personnel "is expanding and developing opportunities for voluntary in-service education of Navy personnel, which action is of particular interest to everyone in the Navy who has a real desire to continue his education when the war is over and wishes to improve his position for obtaining employment upon discharge. Such a program was the express desire of the President when he approved the 18–19 year draft law." This same letter set forth the original content of the Educational Services Program as, "(*a*) establishment of Educational Service Centers under the direction of qualified supervisors on United States shore establishments and overseas bases . . . . (*b*) on stations where it is not feasible to establish voluntary educational centers because of the small number of personnel involved or the type of course desired, correspondence and self-teaching courses will be used . . . . (*c*) steps are being taken to enable educational institutions to evaluate the total educational experience that men and women will receive during the term of their military service . . . ."[8] The letter which established the Educational Services Section in 1943 indicated that the program was to be available on a Navy-wide basis wherever requested by commanding officers.[9]

A letter written in August 1945 contemplated the great extension of voluntary education by the establishment of additional Educational Services billets at naval stations with 2,000 or more personnel, and the working out of procedures for establishing similar billets aboard battleships and aircraft carriers. The last three paragraphs of this letter describing duties and methods represent the Navy's thought about this program at the end of the war:[10]

[7] U. S. Navy Department, Bureau of Naval Personnel, *Circular Letter No. 12-43,* February 3, 1943.

[8] *Ibid.*

[9] U. S. Navy Department, Bureau of Naval Personnel, *Circular Letter No. 236-45,* August 11, 1945.

[10] While not released until August 1945, this letter and the policy it enunciated had been many months in preparation.

5. Educational Services Officers have two major duties:
(a) Informational—to keep Naval personnel informed concerning the war.
(b) Education—to offer opportunities for personnel on active duty to continue their education while in the service.

6. The information function is accomplished through a program of orientation, designed to increase the effectiveness of naval personnel by keeping them informed regarding the background and progress of the war, the nature of our enemies and our allies, and the causes for which the war is being fought. The program is further designed to develop pride in the Navy, to demonstrate to each man what his contribution is toward the successful prosecution of the war, and to show him what his responsibilities will be during the post-hostilities period. The methods used in attaining these objectives vary according to the ship or station to which the Educational Services Officer is attached. They include such activities as: Distributing maps, pocket guides, pamphlets, and other informational materials; showing films on various aspects of the war; broadcasting news over P.A. systems; organizing and directing discussion groups on subjects of current interest; preparing articles for ship and station papers; arranging lectures by authorities on the war and related subjects.

7. The educational function is to make available at high school, technical school and college levels three methods of study: (a) Voluntary classes in subjects of interest to personnel taught by volunteer instructors. (b) Correspondence courses available through enrollment in the United States Armed Forces Institute (USAFI) including courses from 85 cooperating colleges and universities. (c) Self-study through the local issuance of texts to interested individuals or by enrollment with the United States Armed Forces Institute. Fundamental to the educational aspect of the program are: (a) Counseling, directed toward assisting naval personnel to formulate their educational and vocational plans and to undertake steps in attaining them; (b) Accreditation, . . . whereby naval personnel are assisted in making application to civilian schools and agencies for credit for their military training and experience.[11]

This expansion of the Navy's off-duty educational program, long planned and sought by those immediately concerned, undoubtedly was facilitated by the fact that in February 1945 the Secretary of the Navy made a tour of inspection through the Pacific in the course of which he observed and commented favorably on the work being carried on at various Educational Services centers. In March 1945, a special representative of the Secretary, sent to the Pacific in connection with welfare activities, also

[11] U. S. Navy Department, Bureau of Naval Personnel, *Circular Letter No. 236-45*, August 11, 1945.

took occasion, in his official report, to speak further words of praise for these centers.

Some speculation as to why the off-duty educational program was not more enthusiastically received by the Navy is perhaps in order. Objections most commonly followed one of four lines. First, some of the older officers had a not too pleasant memory of World War I experience with a compulsory academic training program within the Navy. This criticism was hardly apt, since the new program was being conducted outside duty hours and entirely on a voluntary basis. Secondly, there was a widespread belief that men were not interested in education after they had been freed from their day's duties. This argument proved to be a total misconception of the nature of the personnel in the Navy during World War II. Equally fallacious was the third argument that the working schedule at any station allowed insufficient time for off-duty education. On the contrary, it was the very excess of leisure time at many overseas establishments which created the need for the program in the first place. Finally, it was often stated that teachers were not available. Yet Educational Services officers found this one of the easiest of all problems to solve, since every station could supply a surprisingly large number of officers and enlisted men who were not only willing, but also were qualified to offer their services for classroom instruction.

As has been indicated, great expansion of the Educational Services program was contemplated when the war came to an end. It had been planned that Educational Services officers and enlisted personnel to assist them would be assigned to capital ships. While this program did not get very far, the end of the war found Educational Services officers (ESO's) aboard the *Iowa, New Jersey, Alaska, Guam,* and *South Dakota.*

In spite of some difficulties the program was extensive in scope and took into its various programs a large number of naval personnel. Table 1 which gives a cumulative total of its activities to December 31, 1945, indicates the tremendous number of people who were touched by this program before the peak of its development was reached after VJ Day.

TABLE 1

EDUCATIONAL SERVICES PROGRAM—SUMMARY OF ACTIVITIES ACCUMULATED TO DECEMBER 31, 1945

	OVERSEAS	CONTINENTAL	HOSPITALS	TOTALS
Total number of classes	4,744	1,664	1,361	7,769
Total enrollment in all classes	77,934	28,744	21,211	127,889
Counseling interviews	128,428	149,336	430,819	708,583
Total servicing visits to ships	9,512	7,483	....	16,995
Individual instruction to hospitals	....	....	....	59,819
USAFI correspondence and college extension courses	....	....	....	387,586
Total requests for interviews by ESO's at separation centers	....	....	....	167,900
Total requests for accreditations	....	....	....	36,881

The above figures are based only on official reports from Educational Services offices. Since much of the program was carried on by collateral-duty officers, the Bureau of Naval Personnel made the following estimate of participation based on both reports and on informational survey during the three years of the Educational Services Program:

a) Informational program
1. Orientation film showings........................ 100,000
2. Orientation lectures and discussions.............. 48,000
3. Orientation pamphlets distributed............... 1,500,000
4. *Newsmaps* distributed.......................... 2,500,000
5. *NavWar Maps* distributed....................... 75,000

b) Educational program
1. Classes.. 50,000
2. Enrollment in classes.......................... 750,000
3. Individual instruction......................... 350,000
4. USAFI enrollments at headquarters and branches.. 350,000
5. Counseling interviews.......................... 1,613,600
6. Number of ships serviced....................... 60,000

The following sampling of the program at various places will indicate the scope and diversity of the Navy off-duty programs.

At the recruit training center at Sampson, N. Y., 164 courses were being offered in the summer of 1945. Of the 312 men enrolled in the formal evening classes at Mare Island Navy Yard in July and August of 1945, 134 obtained high school credits. At the same station in September, formal graduation exercises were conducted at which 67 students were awarded high school diplomas. In addition, one man obtained his college degree by completion of requisite credits through USAFI correspondence courses. Some of the centers outside of the continental limits of the United States conducted educational programs which would have taxed the facilities of a large university. In August 1945, 9,446 men were under instruction in 424 classes in the 14th Naval District alone. During July and August of 1945, 94,016 texts were distributed to the 14th Naval District, to fleet Marine forces, and to ships, while some were retained for use at the Pearl Harbor center. Although the program of the 14th Naval District had been in existence less than two years, cumulative figures show that about 60,000 officers and men had attended off-duty classes at high school and college levels, while 35,000 had enrolled in correspondence courses and 50,000 had received counseling service.

Pearl Harbor was the largest of the overseas centers operated by the Educational Services Section, but as the following figures indicate, very extensive operations were undertaken at other local points in the advanced areas:

Pearl Harbor Center	
Total number of classes to November 1, 1945	505
Class enrollment	14,375
Saipan	
Total number of classes to January 1, 1946	244
Class enrollment	4,015
Midway Island	
Total number of classes to November 1, 1945	243
Class enrollment	4,747
Advanced Base Reshipment Depot—Pearl Harbor	
Total number of classes to January 1, 1946	132
Class enrollment	3,332
Naval Air Station, Kanehoe, Oahu, Territory of Hawaii	
Total number of classes to November 1, 1945	113
Class enrollment	2,731
Naval Operating Base, Guam	
Total number of classes to November 1, 1945	107
Class enrollment	2,364

It is not possible to estimate the extent of the educational facilities made available through collateral duty ESO's since they did not submit official reports, but the scope of the program was certainly greatly extended by this means. By the autumn of 1945, approximately 110 centers had been established in the 11th Naval District alone at activities where no specially trained ESO's were stationed. These programs were handled on a collateral duty basis by education officers, personnel officers, chaplains, and training officers. With the exception of a few large ships, the Educational Services program afloat was entirely entrusted to ESO's functioning on a collateral basis. Aboard the U.S.S. *Wakefield,* for instance, the Chief Quartermaster took over this role. With a ship's company of 800, personnel were enrolled in classes as follows, in the summer of 1945:

Classes	Enrollment
English	14
Celestial navigation	26
Seamanship	70
Business law	70
French	17
Algebra	11
Plane geometry	7
Basic mathematics	19
Total	234

The collateral duty Educational Services officer aboard the U.S.S. *Fanshaw Bay* had enrolled 20 percent of the ship's company of 400 in the off-duty educational program.

It was the policy of the Educational Services Section to encourage Educational Services officers to adjust to the local situation. The center at Adak had an excellent course on the geology of the Aleutians. In Trinidad, a course was organized in citrus fruit-growing. At the air station in Kahutul, various authorities from the region were brought to the station to give lectures on the culture and problems of the Hawaiian Islands. At Pearl Harbor, an enlisted man who was a well-known professor of economics at a leading university gave a course in the economics of warfare.

At some bases, hobby shops were set up and informal training was carried on in arts and crafts. Naval Operating Base, Midway, and Naval Construction Battalion Training Station, Davisville, R. I., both had outstanding shops of this kind. At Midway the shop managed to procure discarded materials which were used by the men in making gifts and trinkets of all sorts. At San Juan, a "View-Finders Camera Club" was organized by the ESO. All pictures were developed and printed in the Educational Services' photographic laboratory.

Informally, many of these Educational Services centers were given names by the men themselves, which emphasized the regional aspect of the program. Some of these designations were: University of Midway, College of the Admiralties (Manus), College of the Aleutians (with branches at the various bases in the Aleutian chain), Trinidad Tech, University of New Hebrides (Espiritu Santo), Saipan University, NavPac U. (Pearl Harbor), Magellan University (Philippine Islands), and SNAF-U (Guantanamo).

While not within the scope of this study, it should be mentioned that after VJ Day the Navy's program experienced a great expansion. In the Pacific area a great number of Educational Services Study Centers [12] were established. By March 1, 1946, 2,279 classes with a total enrollment of 46,838 men were in operation at these centers.[13] A description of one of these centers is quoted below:

DEWEY UNIVERSITY
Naval Base, Manila, P. I.

Classes began in October, 1945. Reports up to 1 March 1946 show that 28 officers, 9 enlisted men, and 1 civilian taught 106 classes in 76 different subjects, including high school and college mathematics, physics, and English; French, Spanish and Italian; business, farming, and technical courses. Of the instructors, 10 officers and 1 enlisted man had B.A. degrees, 7 officers and 1 enlisted man had B.S. degrees, 4 officers had M.A. degrees, 2 officers had M.S. degrees, 1 officer had an LL.D. degree, 1 enlisted man had a Ph.D. degree. Also 1 officer had B.B.A. and LL.B. degrees; 1 officer had a C.E. degree, and 18 of the 38 instructors had previous teaching experience

[12] The term "Educational Services Study Center" was used by the Navy to designate an Educational Services organization existing in an area of more than usual personnel concentration which provided organized classes based on popular demand augmented by a counseling and testing program.

[13] U. S. Navy Department, "Educational Services Study Centers in the Pacific Area" (MS on file in Office of Naval History, U. S. Navy Department), p. 1.

totalling 91 years. The enrollment in these classes totaled 1,107 officers and enlisted men.[14]

THE NAVY LIBRARY SERVICE

The Navy, from its beginning, has used books as a means of increasing the skill of its officers and men. For many years, shipboard libraries have been maintained by an appropriation called "Libraries for Ships of War," a part of the regular appropriation for instruments and supplies. Books were considered as instruments of equal importance with compasses and other navigational equipment.[15]

Until World War I, the Navy lacked professional library leadership. Prior to that period, there had been money allotted for books, but no professional librarians were provided for large shore stations and the program in general was directed by untrained staff members. As a result of the Library War Service organized by the American Library Association during World War I, a program was initiated within the Navy to modernize its program for furnishing books to its personnel. By 1925, the Navy's library program had been professionalized, and it remained in much the same form until the attack on Pearl Harbor.

The Navy was fortunate in having its library program directed by the same civilian professional librarian between the two wars and through the second one, thus giving a continuity not found in the other Navy activities treated in this study. The wartime role of the library was one of expansion and not inauguration. To be sure, ingenuity had to be exercised to provide for the greatly increased demand, but the organization, the trained leadership, and the experience were available.

It should also be pointed out that the library program was accepted as a valid one by naval authorities long before World War II. There was no need to use valuable time trying to get a basic policy approved. The personnel could thus devote their energies to making the service effectively meet the needs of naval personnel.

[14] *Ibid.*, p. 2.
[15] Isabel DuBois, "Navy Libraries," *The Library Journal*, LXVII (May 15, 1942), 444.

Even though reading was a popular off-duty pursuit in the peacetime Navy, its expansion during the war period was remarkable. In 1941 it was estimated that Navy men read about 2,000,000 books a year. The Navy in the same year purchased 114,000 new books. By way of contrast, in the first quarter of the fiscal year of 1944 the Navy bought 2,000,000 new books, a ratio of about 70 to 1. During the war period libraries increased from 500 to 9,000. Table 2 shows the war-year amounts of congressionally appropriated funds.[16]

TABLE 2

WARTIME EXPANSION OF CERTAIN FUNDS APPROPRIATED FOR THE NAVY LIBRARY SERVICE

FISCAL YEAR ENDING JUNE 30	FOR COMMISSIONING LIBRARIESFOR NEWLY CONSTRUCTED SHIPS	FOR UPKEEP
1940	$300,000	$ 136,000
1941	400,000	148,000
1942	500,000	380,000
1943	500,000	2,711,000
1944	700,000	2,853,000
1945	920,000	3,050,000

It has been observed that libraries were first used for the training of personnel in Navy-used skills. With the establishment of the present library organization in 1925, this purpose was retained and integrated with the new one of providing recreation and education. The Navy's Library Service, in contrast to the Army's, is aimed at supplementing the training program as well as providing recreation for leisure time. While the limits of this study preclude that aspect of the library program which has to do with training for Navy skills, it is important to remember that the program has a dual purpose.

The basic philosophy of the Navy's Library Service is a forceful one, held to so tenaciously by the personnel of that service that it seems to permeate the entire organization. The librarian who directs the Navy's library programs has stated this philosophy in the following words:

[16] U. S. Navy Department, Bureau of Naval Personnel, "Library Section," "Administrative History of the Bureau of Naval Personnel" (MS on file in Office of Naval History, U. S. Navy Department).

We believe that reading is a necessary part of everyday existence; that it is as foolish to live without printed matter as it is to live without food. In other words, that one must feed the mind as well as the body. It is by making books readily accessible and always at hand that we think we accomplish this, at least in part.[17]

INFORMATIONAL SERVICES

The Navy paid far less attention to the problem of information of a general nature than did the Army. In point of fact, the Navy did not get anything comprehensive under way until the war was over. There are, however, two exceptions to this general statement: the magazine which finally came to be called *All Hands,* and the Educational Services' *War Orientation Bulletin.*

In the autumn of 1922, there first appeared a small publication known as the *Bureau of Navigation News Bulletin.* A two- or three-page mimeographed affair addressed to commanding officers, its purpose was to explain directives issued by the Bureau of Navigation. It appeared at fairly regular monthly intervals in this form until October 1928, when a heavy paper cover was added. With this edition came the statement that the bulletin was published to disseminate general information of probable interest to the service.

Shortly after this the title was changed to read *Bureau of Navigation—Information for Naval Personnel,* and the number of pages was increased until the total reached fifty or sixty; but the document was still mimeographed. The range of information was gradually expanded to include more news items and special features. In April 1941, it was announced that for the duration of the emergency the bulletin would include the material formerly included in the *Naval Reserve Bulletin,* which was then discontinued. At this same time the name was changed to *Bureau of Naval Personnel Information Bulletin.* During the early part of the war, not much attention was paid to this publication, but, in May 1942, the circulation had increased to such an extent that it was decided to multilith the bulletin and include pictures.

[17] Letter to the author from Miss Isabel DuBois, April 1946.

The publication got another boost in 1942 when an administrative survey of the Bureau of Naval Personnel was made, and the report recommended the assignment of a qualified, full-time individual as editor. There still seemed to be a lack of consistent policy as to what the magazine was to be, but its circulation continued to increase. By the autumn of 1942, 5,000 copies were being multilithed. In October, the printing of the magazine was authorized, and the first printed issue ran to 6,500 copies. The magazine in this new form was very popularly received. In November 1942, 15,000 copies were printed; after that, the run gradually expanded. By November 1943, 150,000 copies were being distributed; and in December 1943, 180,000. In 1944, the magazine was made available to the general public through the Superintendent of Documents, and soon afterward there were over 27,500 private subscribers. By the end of the war, the total circulation was 390,000. In June 1945, the name was officially changed to *All Hands*.

In 1943, as a part of the War Orientation Program in Educational Services, a mimeographed *War Orientation Bulletin* was prepared and distributed to all Educational Services officers. This was a semi-official publication carrying world news stories and background information on the various theaters of hostilities. Its publication was stopped in 1944 shortly before the establishment of the Informational Services Program. It was widely used by Educational Services officers throughout the Navy in conducting war orientation discussions.

MARINE CORPS

At the time of World War II, the Marine Corps had a history of over twenty years of furnishing correspondence courses of a nonservice-connected type to its personnel. The Marine Corps Institute had been organized in 1920 in order to promote ". . . the general efficiency of the United States Marine Corps and to offer educational facilities as an aid in obtaining promotion and to help raise the general education level of the individual." [18]

[18] U. S. Marine Corps, *Education for Marines* (Washington: The Marine Corps Institute, Marine Barracks), p. 9.

The Marine Corps Institute purchased study materials from a large commercial correspondence school until the fall of 1944. Early in 1944 material to supplement the courses purchased was prepared by the Marine Corps Institute staff. These supplements consisted of review lessons and examinations. Complete revision of the curriculum was inaugurated in July 1944. The new courses are based on standard texts supplemented when advisable by additional study and explanatory material. All lesson questionnaires and final examinations are prepared by the Marine Corps Institute staff of Marine instructors.[19]

As early as July 1944 the Commandant of the Marine Corps had authorized the assigning of marines to the educational phase of the Navy's hospital rehabilitation program. These Marine officers were instructed to maintain the same relationship with the Educational Services Section of the Navy as did naval officers involved in the same work. They were to report to the Bureau of Naval Personnel on Navy forms and have their work in general supervised by the two Navy bureaus concerned, Personnel and Medicine and Surgery. Supplies, with the exception of a few Marine Corps training materials, likewise came from the Navy.

The Marine Corps had operated an information program for some months before it was given the sanction of organizational recognition in February 1945. At that time the Education Section was recognized as an organizational entity of the Welfare Division. According to those in charge of the program the Section had as its purpose the coordination of the services of the Marine Corps Institute and the USAFI; it was to organize off-duty classes in the field and to establish and send to the field policies and administrative and operational procedures for the program. Broadly stated the organization was " . . . to make available a voluntary, off-duty, on-the-spot education and information program for the personnel of the Marine Corps."[20]

[19] Letter from Col. Donald J. Kendall, USMC, Director, United States Marine Corps Institute, June 20, 1946.

[20] Education Section, USMC, *Catalog No. 1* (Washington: Education Section, Welfare Division, Special Services Branch, Headquarters, U. S. Marine Corps, June 1945), p. 2.

COAST GUARD

The Coast Guard's off-duty educational program dates from 1928, the year in which the U. S. Coast Guard Institute, an institution offering correspondence courses, was established at Groton, Connecticut. With World War II the Coast Guard's program expanded along with that of the other services. It entered into the activities of both USAFI and the Navy's Educational Services plan when these were initiated. Because of the Coast Guard's wartime place in the Navy, it tried to adapt other programs to fit its particular needs, supplementing them where necessary.

The purposes of the Coast Guard in offering off-duty educational opportunities are best stated in the directive [21] which is concerned with the appointment of educational officers:

> It is urged that care be exercised in selecting the best possible persons for these duties, which include organizing and promoting educational programs and counseling personnel regarding continuation or completion of their education, as well as trying for advancement in rating. The educational officer should devote especial attention to younger persons who have entered the Coast Guard without graduating from high school, to urge that they complete their high school work while in the service and to render them all possible assistance in so doing. He should also be prepared to work in close cooperation with other officers assigned to advise personnel on postwar problems and with education and other civilian groups dealing with the return of military personnel to civilian life.

[21] U. S. Coast Guard, *Personnel Bulletin No. 27-45,* 16 March 1945.

II. PERSONNEL AND ORGANIZATION

THE SUCCESS of the off-duty educational program in the armed services depended to a large extent on the degree to which those responsible for its development in the field understood its mission, possessed a genuine enthusiasm for its potential contributions to the welfare and morale of military personnel, and were resourceful in using the facilities available to them. Effective selection and training of personnel for duty in these educational programs was the most satisfactory method of insuring success in the field. Early in the development of off-duty educational opportunities, attention was directed toward determining sound criteria for the selection of personnel with appropriate educational background and leadership qualities. Efforts were made to establish training programs in which personnel could be given the necessary orientation and which would stimulate that enthusiasm which field experience had demonstrated to be essential. The administrative organization, regarding off-duty programs as merely a minor division of the welfare, recreation, and special service activities, made it difficult in the early days of the war to set up adequate selection and training procedures. As the off-duty programs developed in scope and in popularity and as the services made additional personnel available for nonmilitary purposes, the programs achieved greater prominence in the headquarters organization of all branches of the services. Although at the war's end an increasing number of carefully selected, qualified personnel were being trained and assigned to educational activities throughout the world, local execution of these programs often remained in the hands of the unselected and untrained.

ARMY [1]

Scattered through Army regulations and particularly in the *Basic Field Manual* are many statements concerning principles of

[1] This section, with minor editorial changes and some abridgment, is excerpted, with permission, from the manuscripts, "History of Military Training: Summary, Information and Education Division," "Study of Information and Education Activities: World War II," and "History of the School of Personnel Services" (on file in the Historical Division, War Department Special Staff).

leadership which illustrate the desirable end product for an educational worker. For example, the *Field Manual* states:

> The environment and education of the average American soldier have laid great emphasis on his value as an individual; in order to get the most out of him, you must treat him as such. Make it your business to know the name, habits, peculiarities, and social background of every man in your organization. Let all your direct dealings with him be influenced by this knowledge.[2]

And in another part is the statement:

> In all phases of administration, training and operations, make every effort to keep your men informed. Nothing irritates American soldiers so much as to be left in the dark regarding the reason for things.

Thus the I and E officers, as well as the Army librarians, had important tasks to do. It was not easy, however, for such information-giving personnel to function at top efficiency until much organization and reorganization had been accomplished. Until nearly the end of the war the effectiveness of the off-duty programs was hampered because of their relatively lowly positions in the Army's organization. While the I and E Division was one of a number reporting to the Director of Personnel in the Army Service Forces, it had difficulty in establishing programs in the Ground Forces and Air Forces, which not unnaturally looked askance at receiving orders from such an obscure source. Only when the I and E Division was at the Special Staff level was it in a position to develop the type of field organization which it needed.

From the early days of the I and E Division, it was clear that success depended basically on an understanding of its mission by officers at all echelons. Efforts were made, particularly after 1943, to describe the program to large numbers of officers, and the director and the deputy director devoted much time to educating the staff officers of the War Department in the purposes of the Division. It was not until a considerable group of officers and men had been specifically trained for I and E activities in units or in posts, camps, and stations that there were any effective orientation or education programs in the field.

[2] U. S. War Department, *Morale,* Basic Field Manual, MB-1-10 (October 1, 1939), Section I, par. 5a.

INFORMATION-EDUCATION PERSONNEL

Duties of I and E officers

The responsibilities of the off-duty officer fell into three categories: orientation, off-duty education, and miscellaneous tasks.

In the orientation program a minimum of an hour per week was to be devoted during duty time to discussing the news and the topic of the week. War information centers containing maps and displays were to be maintained. In the off-duty education program, the Information-Education officer was required to analyze educational needs, enroll individuals in USAFI courses, supervise individual and group study, and arrange for accreditation. Under miscellaneous tasks came cooperation with the Army librarian in making reading material easily available, publicizing the I and E program, and introducing training aids to other officers.

School for Personnel Services

The School for Special Service, later called the School for Personnel Services, was established at Fort George G. Meade, Maryland, on February 15, 1942, for the broad function of instructing and training Army personnel in the approved purposes, doctrines, materials, methods, and operative procedures in all phases of the duties and responsibilities of the Special Service Branch; and instructing and training Army personnel in morale, recreation, and theatrical functions. The specific purpose of the school was to train recreation officers in "devising, planning, and supervising practicable recreation and welfare activities for combat troops in theaters of operations, domestic and overseas."

Nearly a year after its founding the school was moved to more commodious quarters at Washington and Lee University, Lexington, Virginia. By April 1943, the eleventh class at the school had begun. Many of the earlier problems of organization had been solved and a revised curriculum of 192 hours of instruction, divided into two categories—one a basic course for Special Service officers, and the other a specialized course for Special Service company commanders—was in force, as follows:

Department	Hours Basic	Hours Specialized
Information and education		
Research in Special Service	5	3
Military psychology	3	0
Information to troops	16	14
Army education	11	6
Military geography	3	0
Methods of instruction	4	4
Miscellaneous	4	1
Total	46	28
Athletics and recreation		
Athletics	13	10
Soldier shows	6	4
Soldier music	4	0
Recreational games and crafts	4	0
Field operations	12	0
Miscellaneous	4	2
Total	43	16
Technical training		
Organization for Special Service	5	4
Funds	7	0
Property	5	0
Facilities	9	0
Special Service Kits	5	5
Miscellaneous	6	3
Technical operations	0	7
Total	37	19
Military training and tactics		
Staff functions and procedures	4	0
Exercise of command: close order drill	8	0
Military leadership: courtesy and discipline	3	0
Individual preparation for overseas duty	1	0
Problem and critique	2	0
Unit training	0	16
Leadership	0	9
Hygiene, sanitation, first aid	0	5
Clothing and equipment	0	4
Company administration and logistics	0	18
Tactics	0	26
Marksmanship	0	6
Miscellaneous	0	3
Total	18	87

Department	Hours Basic	Hours Specialized
General school administration		
Ceremonies	6	6
Inspections	4	4
Written tests and critiques	6	6
Applicatory exercises	12	12
Processing and deprocessing	10	10
Reserved for commandant	10	4
Total	48	42
Total number of hours	192	192

Prior to the opening of the thirteenth class, a quota for enlisted men was established and again it was deemed practicable to revise the curriculum. The basic and specialized courses were combined, and specialized hours of instruction were arranged for both officers and enlisted men. The process of arranging the curriculum to meet current needs had been so well systematized during the reorganization period that the new changes were readily accomplished in the minimum time allotted.

In September 1943, a memorandum from the Chief of Staff directed that two Special Service officers for each regiment or equivalent organization be provided. One of these officers was to be qualified and trained for the staff supervision of athletics, recreation, and welfare activities; the other was to be qualified and trained for staff supervision of orientation and indoctrination activities. An orientation officer in grade of not less than captain would be assigned to each post, camp, and station having a troop population of two thousand or more, and, in the case of large installations, the number of orientation officers could be increased when considered appropriate by the responsible commander controlling the allotment to the particular activities concerned.

In view of this need, the Director, Special Service Division, recommended the establishment of the ten-day orientation-officers' course, as follows:

Subject	Hours
Military psychology	
Mission of Army orientation	1
Morale and leadership	1
Mission of orientation officer	1
Ideas as weapons	6
Morale factors	7
Total	16

SUBJECT	HOURS
Army orientation and education	
Global war	1
Why we fight	4
Orientation: introductory phase (films)	8
Film critique	3
Introduction to foreign populations	3
Radio	2
Army newspapers	1
Films	1
Education	5
Orientation: current phase	10
Total	38
Methods and materials	
Methods of instruction	2
Group leadership	8
Military correspondence	1
Staff organization and functions	4
Orientation and education	4
Total	19
Physical conditioning	4
Operations	
Inspections, comprehensive examinations, and research activities	3
Total number of hours	80

Before the end of the fourth course it was evident that ten days was too short a period in which to impart the training required. Criticism was made by both students and graduates that the course was too academic in character. It was, therefore, decided to extend the course to four weeks.

The fifth course, which opened January 5, 1944, was of four weeks' duration and consisted of the following:

SUBJECT	HOURS
Morale services	
Orientation	5
Military psychology	29
Total	34

Subject	Hours
The Army orientation course	
Causes of the war	19
Course of the war	22
Procedures and techniques	37
Total	78
The Army education program	
Mission, philosophy, organization activities and materials	17
Information media	
Facilities and materials	4
Military training	
Staff procedure	5
Staff study	14
Drill and ceremonies	10
Total	29
Physical training	
Progressive conditioning program	22
School administration	
Test, exams, questionnaire	4
Total hours in course	188

No major changes in program content were made through the twelfth course. For the thirteenth course a revised program of instruction was approved. Benefiting from the experience and the operations of the first twelve courses and in order to place more emphasis on procedures and techniques, a realignment of subjects and emphasis was recommended. The changes, for the most part, were brought about by decreasing time devoted to theoretical courses and increasing time devoted to procedures and techniques as illustrated in Table 3.

Field operations included such subjects as briefing the company officer, I and E at redistribution centers, field expedients, fiscal procedures, organizing the duties of the I and E officer, preparation of news bulletins and summaries, and problem-solving conferences.

Course Fifteen became effective December 20, 1944. It called for twenty hours of elective supplementary activities provided

TABLE 3

SCHOOL FOR PERSONNEL SERVICES—CHANGE IN NUMBER OF HOURS ALLOTTED TO COURSES

SUBJECT	HOURS		INCREASE	DECREASE
	Course Ten	Course Thirteen		
Orientation	5	4	....	1
Military psychology	31	23	....	8
Causes of the war	20	24	4	....
Course of the war	24	22	....	2
Army education program	17	14	....	3
Staff study	8	7	....	1
Military correspondence	2	0	....	2
Malaria control	4	0	....	4
Mission and scope, A and R	6	3	....	3
Field operations	0	20	20	....
Total	117	117	24	24

to increase the flexibility of the program and to adapt it to the individual needs of the students. These elective hours gave the students reasonable opportunity to select instructional activities according to individual needs and interests. The elective supplementary activities established were collateral reading and research, preparation of staff reports, educational-vocational counseling service, foreign language instruction, special skills conferences, and preparation of original materials.

Instruction was given by means of lectures, conferences, demonstrations, group performances, applicatory exercises, and examinations. Of the total of 192 hours, approximately 80 hours were devoted to lectures, 60 hours to conferences, 10 hours to demonstrations, 30 hours to group performances and applicatory services, and the remainder were given over to examinations and administrative procedures. Group-discussion classes where the students put into practice the principles they had learned at previous conferences and demonstrations present an example of applicatory exercises. All examinations were composed of multiple-choice questions.

The Information and Education Department of the school obtained its instructors from several sources: a few graduates of the Information and Education course whose talents and academic achievements qualified them to act as instructors;

Information-Education officers who had had field experience, particularly overseas, and whose wide knowledge was valuable to the Information and Education program at the school; and graduates of officer-candidate schools who had been previously trained in the Information and Education course at the school and whose civilian experience or military experience as enlisted men warranted such an assignment.

The prerequisites for students attending this course were stated officially as follows:

> Officers and enlisted personnel selected for training in this course should possess a deep conviction concerning the justice of the cause for which we fight, and the importance of the role of the individual in winning the war; the ability to grasp, interpret, and express ideas effectively, both orally and in writing, and to assist others in doing so. It is desirable that they be college graduates with backgrounds of training and experience in such fields as teaching, educational administration, government, international relations, law, journalism, creative writing, public speaking, advertising, personnel management, radio-script writing, and broadcasting. Officers should have had experience in handling troops.[3]

Table 4 shows the number of military personnel (commissioned and enlisted) who were enrolled, withdrawn, failed, and graduated in the Information and Education Department, School for Personnel Services, Classes One to Thirteen inclusive, October 27, 1943, to November 8, 1944.

The twenty-first Information and Education course at the Lexington school was completed August 14, 1945. Total students since the start of the I and E programs had been 5,500 with the average size class of 350.

Ordinarily officers and enlisted personnel attending Information and Education courses were returned to their station on completing courses. In order to make officers immediately available for assignment, particularly in theaters of operations, a replacement pool was established at the school. On completion of courses, I and E officers were usually placed on temporary duty with the service commands for on-the-job training. No training center was established to which enlisted men were assigned. Arrangements were made, however, whereby a few

[3] Program of Instruction for I and E Personnel. Approved Oct. 3, 1944.

TABLE 4

SCHOOL FOR PERSONNEL SERVICES—CLASS ONE TO THIRTEEN INCLUSIVE
(October 27, 1943, to November 8, 1944)

Class Number	Enrolled		Withdrawn		Failed		Graduated	
	Officers	Enlisted Personnel	Officers	Enlisted Personnel	Officers	Enlisted Personnel	Officers	Enlisted Personnel
1........	154	0	1	0	15	0	138	0
2........	187	0	4	0	20	0	163	0
3........	177	0	6	0	21	0	150	0
4........	168	0	3	0	12	0	153	0
5........	304	0	22	0	18	0	264	0
6........	265	13	10	4	28	1	227	8
7........	209	18	7	2	16	0	186	16
8........	310	19	27	1	19	0	264	18
9........	183	32	6	1	9	1	168	30
10........	200	25	13	1	17	0	190	24
11........	217	36	10	1	17	0	190	35
12........	193	55	7	3	19	1	167	51
13........	179	215	15	15	17	15	147	185
Total...	2,746	413	131	28	228	18	2,387	367

selected enlisted men were carried on a detached-service basis, pending assignment to theaters of operations.

Officers selected for assignment as education officers were given specialized training before being placed on temporary duty for on-the-job training. When the number of education officers graduated from a particular class was small, it was the practice to bring them to Washington on a few days' temporary duty for briefing. During this period they met officers of the Division, read field reports, and attended meetings at which the following subjects were presented: Army Education Branch, Special Projects Branch, United States Armed Forces Institute, procurement and distribution of educational materials, radio in education, foreign-language materials, the *G.I. Roundtable,* USAFI movie trailer, and related matters. When classes were too large for the Washington trip to be practicable, the same program was conducted at the School for Personnel Services. After completing the temporary duty period in Washington or at the school, education officers were sent to USAFI Headquarters for temporary duty of from fifteen to thirty days. The Commandant, USAFI, scheduled a series of meetings for them, and in addition to this they sat with the officers in the various sections and observed the actual conduct of the work being done.

In response to requests for the training of I and E officers in overseas theaters, schools were organized in the North African Theater of Operations of the United States Army, and in the Central Pacific Area. The NATOUSA school opened at Naples, Italy, on May 10, 1944. The staff was composed of four officers on temporary assignment from the School for Personnel Services. Informal liaison was effected with the American Red Cross, Allied Military Government, Psychological Warfare Branch, British Area Education Office, and Base Censorship. Each course offered by this school covered a period of six days of eight hours' instruction each. The original program employed at the School for Personnel Services was used, with certain adaptations: two hours on allied military government and one on the Negro soldier were added. Seven courses were conducted at the Naples school and 485 officers attended. The school terminated July 1, 1944.

The CPA School was opened in Honolulu on May 21, 1944. The staff consisted of seven officers from the School for Personnel Services and from the Information and Education Division in Washington. The course lasted ten days and included eighty hours of instruction. The program included Army orientation, the orientation mission and materials, ideas as weapons, background of the war, Army education, Army information, Army research, field operations, and staff studies. Six courses were conducted at the CPA School, and over five hundred officers attended. The school terminated August 10, 1944.

A Pacific Ocean Area Mobile Information Unit was organized in September 1944 with a faculty of seven officers, two of whom were on temporary duty from the School for Personnel Services. Of the five other officers, three had formerly been members of the School for Personnel Services staff. The mission of the unit was to inform military personnel concerning the aims, need, and operation of the Information and Education program and to conduct training conferences and demonstrations for Information-Education personnel. During the first month of its existence the unit operated in Oahu and Kauai, Hawaii, and instructed some 1,200 officers and men. Between September 23 and November 15, it reached 23,000 officers and men in New Caledonia, Espiritu Santo, and Guadalcanal.

It became apparent in 1943 that a training program was required for officers and enlisted men who were to constitute the Armed Forces Radio Service, the mission of which was to inform, orient, and entertain troops overseas by means of radio broadcasting. The first class, in which were enrolled five officers and twenty-four enlisted men, all selected on the basis of commercial broadcasting experience, opened early in December 1943 and continued for four weeks. Because of the increasing demand for trained personnel in this field, it became essential to establish the school officially rather than to conduct it on an informal basis. Consequently the Radio Program and Broadcasting School was organized as part of the Los Angeles, California, Branch Office of the Morale Services Division. A maximum capacity of nine officers and thirty-five enlisted men was authorized. The first class at Los Angeles, comprised of four officers and twenty-four enlisted men, opened April 1, 1944. The second, with nine officers and twenty-four enlisted men, opened May 22, 1944. The subsequent course was given until December 4, 1944. The training program at the Radio Program and Broadcasting School was as follows:

Subject	Instructional Hours
Broadcasting	
First-day processing	8
Commanding officer's time	5
Welcome address	2
General orientation and policies	2
Program Section, Armed Forces Radio Service orientation, practical work, and conferences	45
Short-wave operations	6
Study and research, Broadcast Distributing Section	4
Study of overseas American Expeditionary Stations	10
Technical study broadcast equipment	10
Orientation Armed Forces Radio Services, general	6
Information Section	2
Simulated operations of American Expeditionary Stations at Camp Irwin, California	20
Examinations on course	4

Subject	Instructional Hours
Military Subjects	
POM-POE, instruction and checks	4
Malaria control	4
Safeguarding military information and censorship	4
Articles of war and relation to American Expeditionary Stations	2
Field fortifications, camouflage, and gas chamber	7
Carbine familiarization and firing	7
Anti-aircraft familiarization and firing	2
M-1 familiarization and firing	7
Infiltration course	4
Physical training and drill	27
Total hours in course	192

Graduates of these courses subsequently operated radio stations and supervised the broadcasting of programs beamed to troops on New Guinea, Espiritu Santo, Guadalcanal, New Zealand, New Caledonia, Bougainville, Hawaii, Guam, Tarawa, Saipan, Makin, Eniwetok, and Kwajalein.

Reports from officers who had extensive opportunity to observe the operations of the Information and Education program under field conditions indicated that the training given to Information-Education personnel at the School for Personnel Services and at field schools resulted in a more effective program. The fact that active theaters of operations requested the setting up of Information and Education schools in their theaters is proof of the value attached to trained Information-Education personnel overseas. Both in the continental United States and in overseas areas, it was generally demonstrated that school-trained personnel did a better and more comprehensive job than personnel who had not had the advantage of school training.

I and E training materials

A considerable number of training and in-service materials were prepared for the guidance of I and E officers. The *I and E Digest,* a pocket-size monthly magazine, provided professional articles on a wide variety of topics. The mission of the *Digest* was "to define the wide horizons of information and education in the armed forces, to encourage good operation, and to lead through the counsels of collected experience." An extensive handbook entitled *The Information-Education Officer* was developed as a basic professional tool. This book gave clear directions concerning duties, materials, and program planning, all directed to the I and E officer.

The *Guide to the Use of Information Materials* gave facts on controversial questions and guidance in the use of facts in building understanding and morale. Other materials took up the questions of absence without leave and the fighting qualities of the Negro soldier. For the Army Education Program an extensive instructional manual entitled *Army Education Program for Inactive Theaters* was prepared.

NAVY

EDUCATIONAL SERVICES

Throughout its entire history the Educational Services Program was placed at headquarters in the section of the Bureau of Naval Personnel which had to do with training. Figure 1 shows this organization near the end of the war.

In the spring of 1943, authorization was given to procure 100 Educational Services officers. The figure was increased to 150 shortly thereafter. All were designated for duty in the field.

As of May 1945, and before the peak of development was reached after VJ Day, officers assigned to full-time duty in the Educational Services Program numbered 391—of whom 125 were WAVES and 20 were Marines. Table 5 shows how this personnel was distributed.[4]

A one-time officer-in-charge of the Educational Services Section wrote as follows concerning this personnel:

> Before selecting the [first] one hundred and fifty officers to be placed in charge of the program on the various stations and bases, the records of over a thousand men were examined. They were drawn almost exclusively from administrative or teaching positions in secondary schools and colleges. Of these, 24 percent hold the degree of Doctor of Philosophy and 50 percent the Master's degree from recognized graduate schools. Others have professional degrees in specialized fields, such as engineering and the law. Almost all of them have had extensive teaching experience, the average for the group being ten and a half years. Since the duties of Educational Services officers are primarily administrative, previous experience as a dean, school

[4] U. S. Navy Department, Bureau of Naval Personnel, "The Educational Services Program" (MS on file in Office of Naval History, U. S. Navy Department), p. 7.

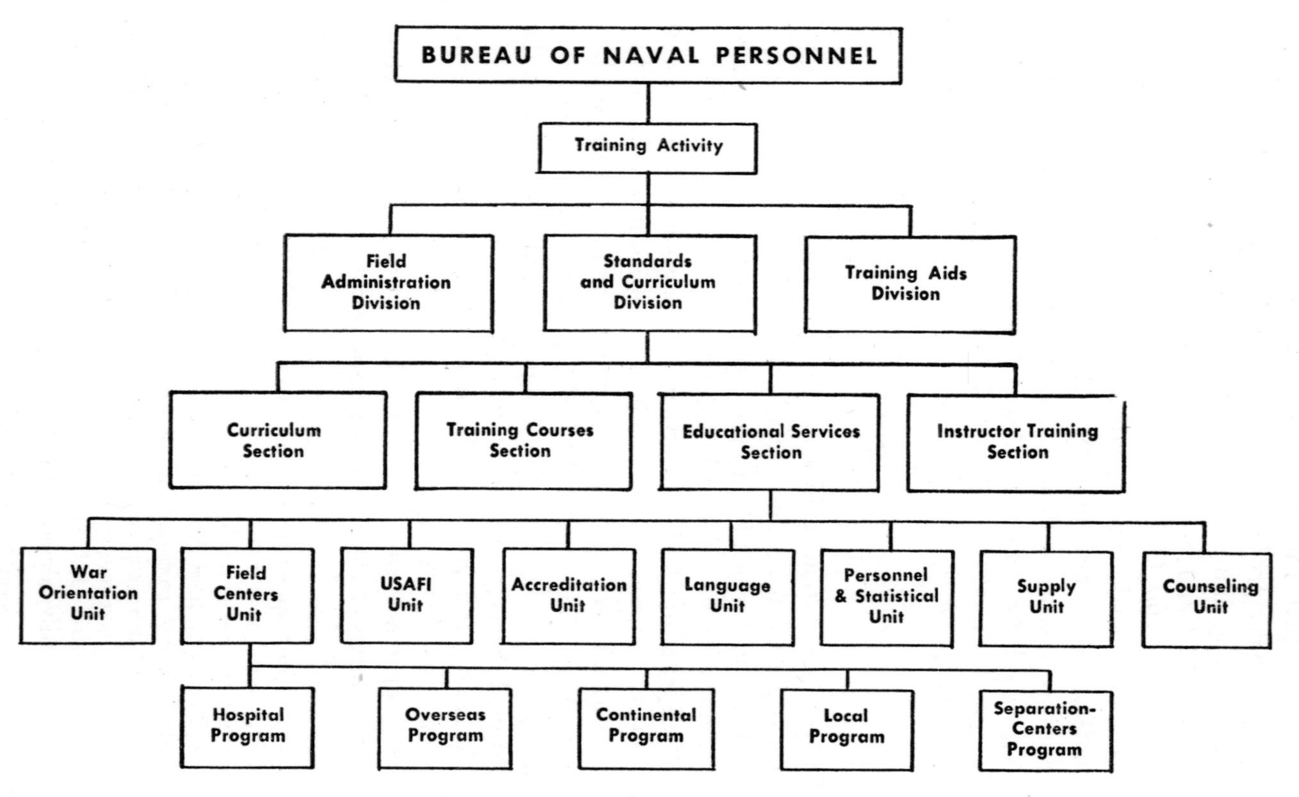

FIG. 1.—Organizational Status of the Educational Services Section as of August 1945

TABLE 5

EDUCATIONAL SERVICES PERSONNEL
(May 1945)

	ALL PERSONNEL	WAVES	MARINES
Overseas			
Educational Services centers	79	2	0
District headquarters	9	0	0
Overseas hospitals	6	0	0
USAFI branches	7	0	0
Advanced base units	23	0	0
Total	124	2	0
Continental			
Educational Services Section, BuPers	18	4	0
Educational Services centers	41	12	0
District headquarters (1–3–4–5–6–8–9–11–12–13)	19	6	0
USAFI, Madison and Seattle	11	3	0
Continental hospitals	169	96	20
Total	258	121	20
Temporary duty			
BuPers, temporary duty under instruction	9	1	0
Grand total	391	124	20

superintendent, or other administrative officer, was given considerable weight in the selection of these officers. In intelligence, education, and experience, Educational Services officers compare favorably with the faculty members of the average college.[5]

Officers selected for the Educational Services Program were, in most instances, brought into the Bureau of Naval Personnel in Washington for an indoctrination period. The period of this training varied considerably, but finally came to be standardized at approximately six weeks. The following is the view of the Educational Services Section as to the purpose of this indoctrination:

The six-weeks indoctrination period is planned with the object of turning out well-informed, confident, enthusiastic officers to direct the program at Naval Stations around the globe. During the indoctrination period, officer-trainees receive specific information concerning the purpose and nature of the Educational Services Program, as well as the background, history, and organization of the Educational Services Section; information on the par-

[5] Earl J. McGrath, "Navy Off-Duty Education and Post-War Educational Re-Adjustment," *Harvard Educational Review,* XIV (March 1944), 95.

ticular duties which he is to perform, and methods of performing them.

Educational Services Officers who returned from the field also participated in the indoctrination period. Their observations and recommendations have formed the basis for discussions concerning methods of organization, administration, and solution of problems.[6]

In connection with this period of indoctrination, it is important to note that it was the policy of the Educational Services Section not to impose any one set of detailed procedures upon the officers assigned to set up new centers. Instead, the Section took the position that these officers should analyze the local situation and, in cooperation with the commanding officer, adapt their program to conform to the personnel and facilities which were available. The following outline indicates the content of the indoctrination course as it existed at the war's end.[7]

OUTLINE FOR ORIENTATION OF TEMPORARY-DUTY OFFICERS

I. *Introduction:*

You have been brought to BuPers for temporary duty in the Educational Services Section, Standards and Curriculum Division. The purpose of this outline is to give you an overview of what you will be doing while you are here, and what matters will be discussed as your orientation period progresses.

Since you will be on your own after you are detached from temporary duty in the Bureau, it is suggested that careful notes be kept on the policies and other information which will be covered in the class sessions and which you will need at hand as an Educational Services Officer on the job. Your success on the job depends on your knowledge of the program. It is assumed, therefore, that each officer will exert himself to the utmost in preparing himself to assume the responsibilities of an Educational Services Officer.

II. *The Orientation Program:*

The following outline indicates the matter that will be covered during organized class sessions. The sessions and topics will not necessarily follow the order of the outline.

A. Introduction to Educational Services

1. What the Educational Services Program provides

a) Educational opportunities

[6] "The Educational Services Program," p. 8.

[7] U. S. Navy Department, Bureau of Naval Personnel, "Educational Services Section Information for New Officers Reporting Aboard" (MS on file in Office of Naval History, U. S. Navy Department), pp. 2-9.

   b) War information
   c) Related services

2. The need for the program in the Navy
3. Development of Educational Services
4. Personnel in the program
5. Recent and probable future developments

B. Organization of Educational Services
1. Office and field organization
   a) Of BuPers
   b) Of Educational Services Section
   c) Of Educational Services centers

2. Nature and scope of Educational Services Program
   a) Development by type of station
   b) Development by function of Educational Services Officers

3. Navy policies regarding operation of Educational Services Program
   a) Relation to other military organizations: Education Branch, ASF, War Department, Marine Corps Special Services Branch, Coast Guard Institute, Welfare Activity, Demobilization Division
   b) Relation of program to civilian educational policies and institutions

4. Operating procedures
   a) Regarding personnel and materials
   b) Regarding correspondence
   c) Regarding *Newsletter* or other information releases

C. Organization of off-duty voluntary classes
1. Procurement of instructors
2. Advertising of the class
3. Classrooms
   a) Projection screen, maps, and miscellaneous material

4. Necessary gear for student use
   a) Education manuals
   b) Work experience kits
   c) Materials purchased or prepared locally

5. Development of a curriculum
6. Instructor responsibility
7. Class records
8. Testing results
9. Scheduling of classes

10. Recognition of students and instructors
11. Special classes
12. Use of educational facilities in area
13. Factors influencing success of class program

D. The United States Armed Forces Institute

1. What the U. S. Armed Forces Institute is
2. Why men take USAFI courses
3. Organization of USAFI
4. The USAFI curriculum
    a) Institute courses
    b) University extension courses
5. Materials which the Educational Services Officer needs relative to the USAFI curriculum
6. Examination of one or more correspondence and self-teaching courses
7. Factors in helping an applicant select the right USAFI course
8. Instructions for filling out USAFI applications, and discussion of common errors
9. Variation in enrollment policy and fees with respect to Army, Navy, Marine Corps, and Coast Guard
10. USAFI Information Service: What it includes and material used
11. USAFI Testing Service
    a) Kinds of tests—end-of-course, subject examinations, and General Educational Development tests
    b) Purpose and use of various kinds of tests
    c) Examination of one or more end-of-course tests
12. Certificates of completion
    a) USAFI vs. voluntary class certificate
    b) Recording course completion and test results on service record
13. Accreditation
    a) Old and new procedures
    b) USAFI Form #47
    c) American Council on Education handbook
    d) Discussion of a number of actual accreditation cases
14. USAFI statistics
15. Plans and outlook for the future

E. War Orientation Program

1. Objectives of war orientation
    a) To inform naval personnel on:

(1) The background of the war
(2) The progress of the war
(3) The objectives of the war

b) To help naval personnel answer these questions:
(1) Why are we fighting?
(2) With whom are we fighting?
(3) Against whom are we fighting?
(4) Where are we fighting?
(5) For what are we fighting?

c) To instill:
(1) Pride in the Navy
(2) Pride in the individual's role in the Navy
(3) Confidence in the American way of life
(4) A sense of the responsibility of citizenship

2. History of war orientation
a) Early examples
b) Use of orientation by Axis Powers
c) Britain's ABCA (Army Bureau of Current Affairs)
d) Orientation in ETOUSA
e) The Army's program
f) Orientation in the Navy, Marine Corps, and Coast Guard
3. Typical programs of war orientation
a) Recruit training station
b) District headquarters
c) Advanced base
d) Continental station
4. Techniques of war orientation
a) Oral
b) Visual
c) Written
d) Map displays
5. Materials of war orientation
a) Films
(1) *Why We Fight*
(2) *Background of War Areas*
(3) *Know Your Ally*
(4) *Know Your Enemy*
(5) *Progress of the War*
(6) *How We Fight*

b) Maps
(1) *Newsmaps*
(2) *NavWar Maps*

(3) Theatre-of-war maps
(4) Atlases

c) Discussion materials
(1) *G.I. Roundtable* series
(2) Army talks
(3) Other

d) Pocket Guides to foreign countries
e) Pamphlets
f) Reprints
g) *Digest, "Pony" Time, N. Y. Times Overseas Weekly*

6. Correspondence and report forms

F. The procurement and use of films and other visual aids
1. Procurement
a) From local sources:
(1) Navy: Usually under the cognizance of an audio-visual aids officer
(2) Army: Many Army outfits regularly receive films which officers are glad to share with naval activities on a give-and-take basis
(3) Civilian agencies: Includes state educational institutions

b) From other sources:
(1) Navy: Through official channels, from the appropriate BuPers training aids section, or libraries set up by BuAer to serve air activities
(2) Army: Through official channels, from the appropriate Army Service Command
(3) Civilian agencies: By official letter, from headquarters, branch offices, and depositories of foreign government ministries, U. S. Government departments and offices, and commercial firms. (Costs on the last-named are more than nominal.)

2. Use
a) Effective utilization is more important than a large quantity of aids, including films:
(1) Examine or screen before use
(2) Plan instructive comment to accompany aid, including introductions to films and discussions afterwards
(3) Organize presentation to avoid mechanical difficulties and to make use of aid effective
(4) Stow or return aids in good condition after use

- *b*) Extend use of visual aids to all aspects of the program:
  - (1) Make them available to teachers of classes
  - (2) Give individual students access to them
  - (3) Incorporate them in war orientation

G. Film Program

1. Films will be selected to illustrate these aspects of the program:
   - *a*) The use of training films
   - *b*) The Army and Navy Educational programs
   - *c*) The Army reconditioning program
   - *d*) Psychiatric and educational rehabilitation in the Navy
   - *e*) Vocational training
   - *f*) The British orientation program
   - *g*) Aspects of the Navy orientation program
     - (1) Why we fight
     - (2) How we fight
     - (3) The enemy
     - (4) Progress of the war

H. District Educational Services Officers

1. Typical district organization, showing administrative and consultative relationships of the district Educational Services Officer
2. Functions of the district Educational Services Officer
   - *a*) Providing for needs of local area
   - *b*) Maintaining a district supply depot to meet local demands, as well as emergency needs of the district
   - *c*) Preparing and disseminating information about the program, in order that all activities of the district may be aware of the opportunities available to naval personnel
   - *d*) Contacting ships, informing officers and crews of program, and supplying materials (in situations where applicable)
   - *e*) Working cooperatively with activities of the district to facilitate the functioning of Educational Services throughout the district
   - *f*) Preparing reports to Educational Services Section, BuPers
   - *g*) Organizing and maintaining office routine
3. Relations with other divisions of district headquarters
   - *a*) Distribution (formerly personnel), including classification
   - *b*) Civil readjustment
   - *c*) Recreation and welfare
   - *d*) Redistribution of surplus materials

I. Continental centers

1. Brief description of program

2. Statement on administrative relationships within districts and commands
3. Case studies on six major aspects of the program
    a) War orientation
    b) Correspondence courses
    c) Self-study books
    d) Off-duty classes
    e) Testing and accreditation
    f) Educational, vocational, and professional counseling
4. Forum period
    a) Operating procedures
    b) Publicity
    c) Miscellaneous

J. Overseas centers
1. Reporting to a new station
2. Necessary gear, housing, and personnel
3. Source of supplies
4. The program
    a) Voluntary classes
    b) USAFI correspondence courses
    c) Educational and vocational guidance
    d) War orientation
    e) Special language programs
    f) Services to ships and outlying areas
5. Special services offered by some Educational Services centers
    a) Training courses
    b) Literacy programs
    c) Hobby shops
    d) Classes in "Know the Local Area"
6. Suggested office procedures
7. The Educational Services center as an "Information Bureau"
8. Problems peculiar to centers in different geographical areas
9. Highlights in reports from overseas centers
10. What personal gear to take along
11. Collateral duties

K. Hospital centers
1. Administrative set-up in naval hospitals
2. Cooperation with other hospital personnel
3. Cooperation with other agencies; use of community resources
4. Special problems in counseling the handicapped
5. War orientation program from the hospital point of view

6. Special devices and training aids
7. Filmstrip on St. Albans

L. Language-instruction program
1. Objectives of the Navy's language-instruction program
2. Methods and materials used
3. Demonstrations of proper procedures
4. Availability of language materials
5. Distribution policy
6. Problems encountered in setting up a language-instruction program
7. Relation of the language unit in Washington to the Educational Services Officer in the field

M. Reporting forms and procedure
1. Purpose of Educational Services reports
2. Frequency of submitting reports
3. The various forms that constitute the current reporting system
4. Number of copies of each form to be prepared
5. Detailed instructions as to preparation of each form
6. Common errors to be avoided in preparation of reports
7. Use of the course enrollment card

N. Supplies
1. Materials available
a) Education manuals
(1) Types
(*a*) Self-teaching
(*b*) Standard reprints
(*c*) Small business series
(*d*) *G.I. Roundtable* series
(*e*) Languages
(2) Selection by editorial staff
(3) Selection by Educational Services Section
b) USAFI correspondence courses
(1) A and B centers
(2) Original stock
(3) Replenishments
c) Supplementary books
(1) For group classes
(2) For reference
d) War orientation materials
(1) Pamphlets

(2) *Newsmaps*
(3) Posters

e) Guidance kits
f) Office supplies and equipment
g) Miscellaneous supplies
h) Materials of other bureaus and divisions
(1) BuPers special devices
(2) Navy training courses and progress tests
(3) Projectors—training films—training aids
(4) Official manuals
(5) Surplus V-12

2. Basic Kits
a) Organization
b) Shipment
c) Back orders

3. Requests for additional supplies
a) Method of making the request
b) Sources of supply
c) Shipments from Washington
(1) Methods
(2) Back orders
(3) Delivery times required

d) Materials not distributed by Educational Services Section

4. Distributions
a) New items
b) Special items

O. Counseling and advisory program
1. Counseling objectives
a) Introductory
(1) The need for a counseling program as part of Educational Services
(2) The kinds of problems, educational and vocational, that Educational Services Officers encounter

b) Objectives
(1) To develop a philosophy basic to good counseling
(2) To develop techniques and a facility in handling counseling problems

2. Counseling materials
a) The *Occupational and Related Information File*
b) The *Dictionary of Occupational Titles,* Parts I, II, and IV

- *c*) The interview
- *d*) The counseling record form
- *e*) Tests
- *f*) Vocational forms
- *g*) Occupational information films
- *h*) Work experience try-outs
- *i*) Special devices

3. How to advise a man who wants to complete his high school education
   - *a*) Requirements for high school graduation
   - *b*) Planning high school programs
   - *c*) Choice of courses
   - *d*) Follow-up

4. How to advise a man who wants to attend college when he is discharged
   - *a*) College entrance requirements
   - *b*) Evaluation of background in terms of college entrance requirements
   - *c*) Choice of courses
   - *d*) Follow-up

5. How to advise a man who wants to supplement his Navy training
   - *a*) How men are rated
   - *b*) Requirements for various rates
   - *c*) Choice of courses allied to rates
   - *d*) Follow-up

6. How to assist a man who does not know what civilian occupation he wants to enter after discharge
   - *a*) Information on the counselee
     - (1) Personal
     - (2) Civilian education and work experience
     - (3) Navy education and work experience
     - (4) Test scores and their interpretation
     - (5) Miscellaneous
   - *b*) Conversion of information on the individual to job fields
   - *c*) Use of occupational information
   - *d*) Making a choice
   - *e*) Making a plan to arrive at an objective
   - *f*) Choice of courses
   - *g*) Follow-up

7. War Manpower Commission occupational analysis training

8. Use of other agencies in counseling
   a) Physical fitness and medical officers
   b) The chaplain
   c) Recreation and welfare officers
   d) Education officers
   e) Others—civil readjustment

9. Counseling the physically handicapped
   a) As in item 6 above
   b) Use of physical-capacities and physical-demands technique
   c) Manuals for placement of physically handicapped

10. Cooperation with other agencies
   a) The Veterans Administration
   b) The Veterans Employment Service
   c) Selective Service
   d) The Red Cross
   e) State rehabilitation programs
   f) Civil Service Commission
   g) Local schools and colleges

P. The foundations of national power

1. The role of power in politics
2. The elements of national power
   a) Physical elements—size and strategic location, population, agricultural and industrial resources, military establishment
   b) Social elements—political and economic organization, national unity, international appeal, the will to power
   c) International elements—commercial and political relations among states and their effects on national power

3. The power position of Britain, the Commonwealth and the Empire
   a) Physical and social elements of British power
   b) International elements—Britain's role in world politics

4. Europe
   a) Bases of power in Europe—a general view
   b) Why Europe is divided

5. The power position of France
   a) Physical and social elements of French power
   b) International elements—France's role in world politics

6. The Mediterranean region
   a) A general view of power in the Mediterranean region
   b) The power position of Italy

7. The power position of Germany
   a) Physical and social elements of German power
   b) International elements—Germany's role in world politics
8. The power position of the Soviet Union
   a) Social elements
   b) International elements
9. The Far East
   a) The power position of China
   b) India
   c) The East Indies area
   d) The power position of Japan
      (1) Japan's role in world politics
10. Latin America
11. The power position of the United States
   a) Physical elements
   b) Social elements
   c) International elements—the role of the U. S. in world politics
12. National power and the problem of world order
   a) The causes of war
   b) The organization of power in support of world order

A series of special evening lectures will be held on the dates specified in the schedule of classes. These lectures form an integral part of the course, and attendance is required. Time off during the day is ordinarily given to compensate for the time required for attendance at the evening sessions.

THE NAVY LIBRARY SERVICE

After a varied organizational career which found the Library Section at the end of World War I in the Sixth Division of the Bureau of Navigation [8] and later in the Training and Morale Divisions, a reorganization in October 1942 placed the Section in the Welfare Division under the cognizance of the Director of the Division. In July 1944, the Welfare Division became a major function of the Bureau of Naval Personnel and was re-christened the Welfare Activity. The organization for libraries became the Library Section of the Special Services Division of that activity. Actually these organizational changes made little

[8] Now known as the Bureau of Naval Personnel.

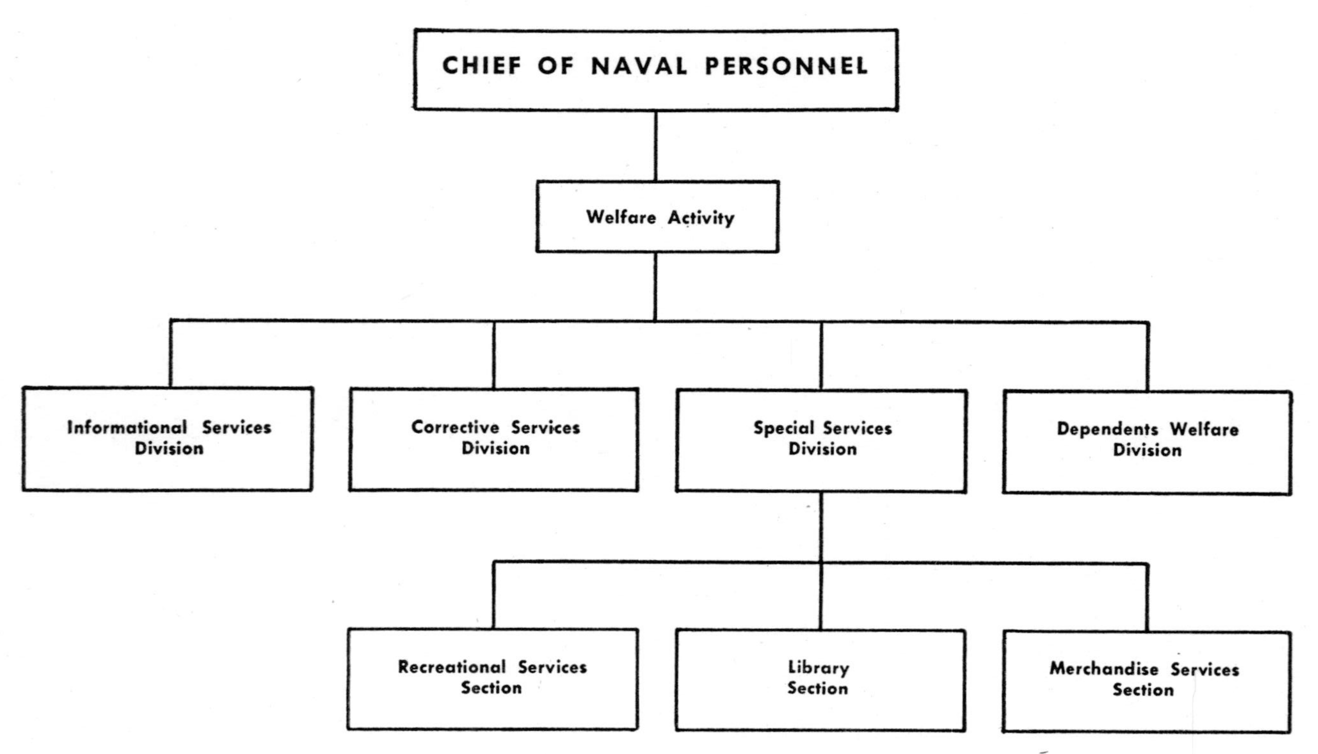

FIG. 2.—Organizational Position of the Library Section as of July 1945

difference in policy or administration. Figure 2 shows the organizational position of the Library Section as of July 1945.

The personnel of the Navy's library service was civilian and professional. To be sure, professional librarians could not be furnished to advanced bases and ships, but the large continental libraries were administered by trained civilians. In 1939 the Library Section was staffed by a Director of Libraries and one clerical assistant. In August 1943, an assistant head, six professional assistants, four yeomen, and seven civilian clerical assistants had been added. In the field a professional librarian was assigned for Navy and Marine Corps shore stations of two thousand or more personnel and for hospitals of five hundred beds or more, with assistants as required. At the end of the war the professional library personnel of the Navy totaled over four hundred.

Authority over this professional group of librarians was centralized in Washington. The authority placed in the office of the Navy Library Section of the Bureau of Naval Personnel included the authorization of positions as well as the authority to make appointments. This system had many advantages. It permitted ready exchange of personnel, a promotion system free of organizational blocks, easy structural readjustments, and the growth of an *esprit de corps* by considering the library service as a unit rather than as a collection of isolated entities. These advantages might well have been impossible to attain had each librarian been simply attached to the station to which he was appointed.

MARINE CORPS

As has been indicated earlier, the Education Section was a part of the Welfare Division which in turn was a part of the Special Services Branch. Figure 3 shows the way in which this Section was organizationally related to other functions of the Special Services Branch in the headquarters of the Marine Corps.[9]

This organizational structure also was followed rather carefully in the field. Figure 4 shows the structure at the division level. The rank of commissioned officers called for by the table

[9] Adapted from charts contained in *Organization of Special Services,* Special Services Branch Personnel Department, Headquarters, U. S. Marine Corps.

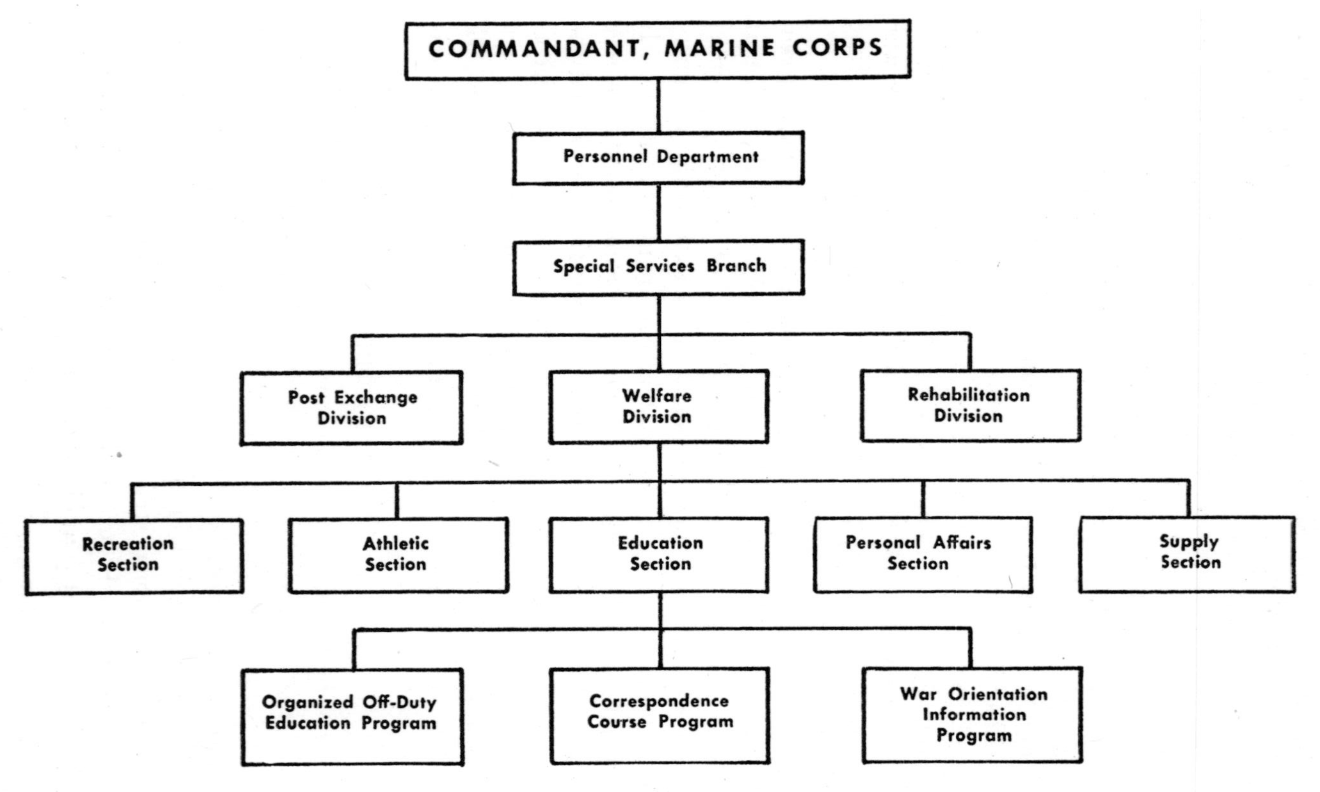

FIG. 3.—Headquarters Organization for Special Services

of organization has been inserted. Twenty enlisted men were authorized for Special Services at the level of the division.[10]

The duties of the Marine Corps Special Services officers were less specialized than those of the Navy's Educational Services officers. In the smaller units such an officer was responsible not only for the education program but for recreation, athletics, dependents' welfare, and supply as well. If a table of organization did not allow for a Special Services officer, the function was assigned to an officer in addition to his regular and primary duties. Only if the personnel of a unit numbered more than 3,000 was an officer assigned exclusively for educational duty.

Marine officers were assigned to the naval hospital program in the ratio of one for the first three hundred Marine patients and one for each additional five hundred Marine patients. As has

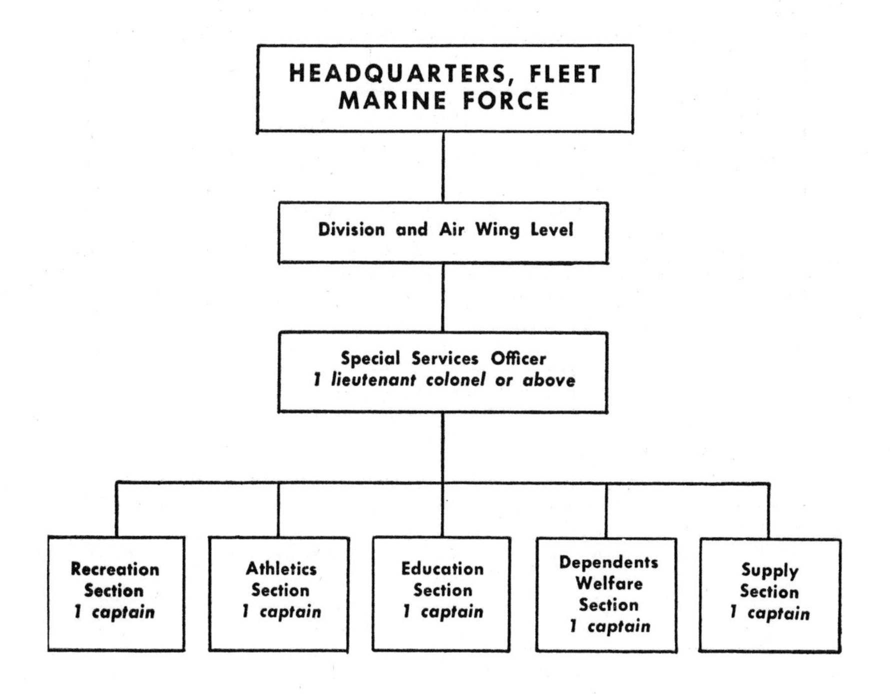

FIG. 4.—Organization for Special Services in the Field

[10] *Ibid.*

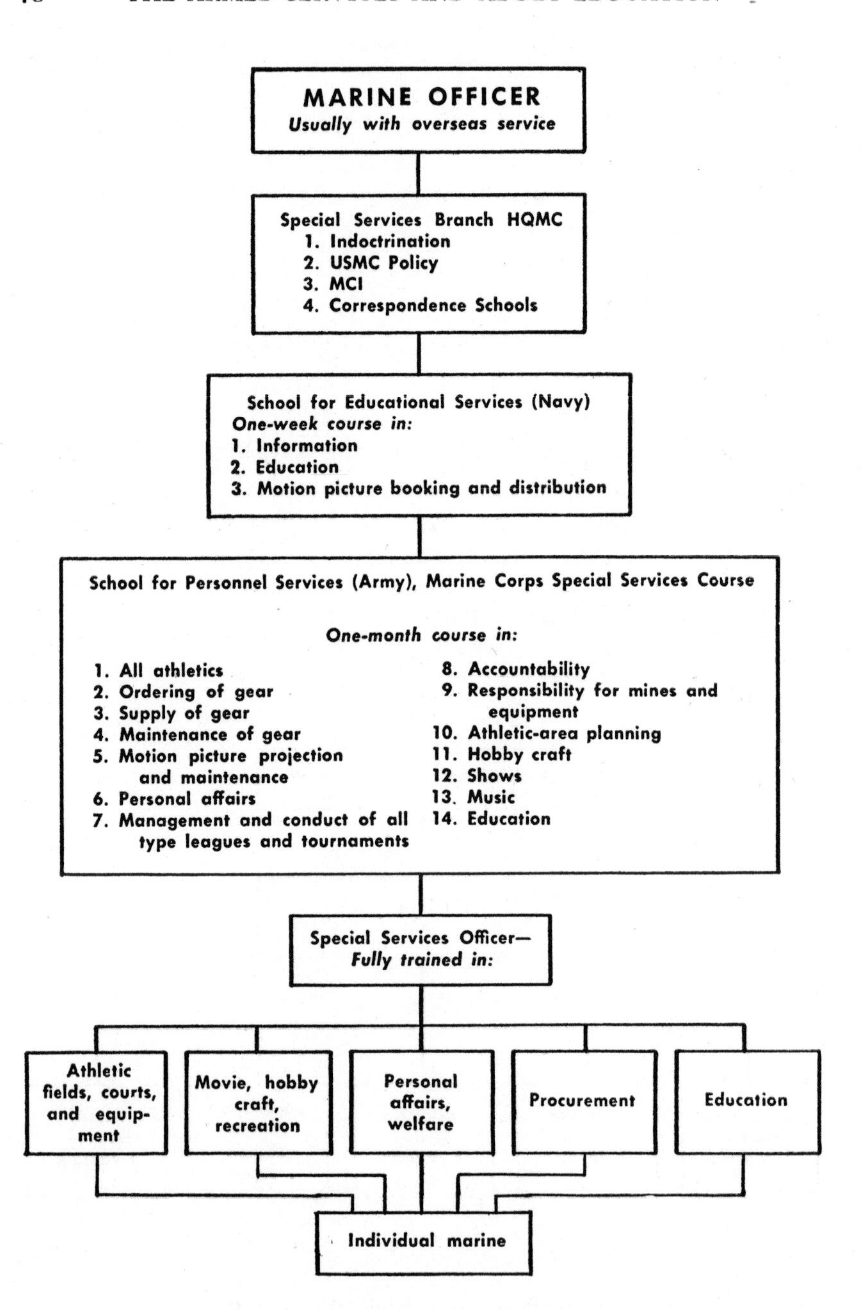

FIG. 5.—Training of a Special Services Officer

been indicated above, these officers were trained by the Navy and functioned as an integral part of the Navy's program.

For the most part, the selection of Special Services officers was a highly decentralized process. Each commanding officer was simply directed to appoint such a functionary or, in the case of smaller units, to designate the function as collateral duty for an existing billet. It is safe to assume that there was thus no uniformity of either professional background or quality of performance. In the case of the selection of officers for key Special Services duties (i.e., headquarters, divisions, and large units), the personnel department at headquarters took the initiative. Again, however, there is little pattern of professional background. Considering the breadth of competence expected of such officers, it is perhaps fortunate that overspecialization was avoided.

In general, the selection of Special Services officers did not stress a background in education. The Commandant of the Marine Corps listed desirable qualities as qualities of leadership, interest in the individual marine and his problems, a background of participation in athletics, or experience in coaching or physical education. Also listed as important was the possession of ". . . the necessary cultural and educational background to equip him for supervision of entertainment and musical programs. He should have initiative, organizational ability, and an understanding of, and sympathy with, the welfare problems of the enlisted personnel." [11]

The training of Special Services officers was jointly done by the Marine Corps, the Navy, and the Army. The initial stage of the training was conducted in Washington, D.C., after which the student was sent to the Army School for Personnel Services at Washington and Lee University, Lexington, Virginia. Not all of the Special Services officers received this training. In general, it was confined to those designated for the key duties as described above. Figure 5 gives the Marine Corps presentation of this training process and its end result.[12]

[11] *Commandant of the Marine Corps to all Commanding Officers* (DGS–493–eh, March 3, 1945).

[12] Adapted from charts contained in *Organization of Special Services, op. cit.*

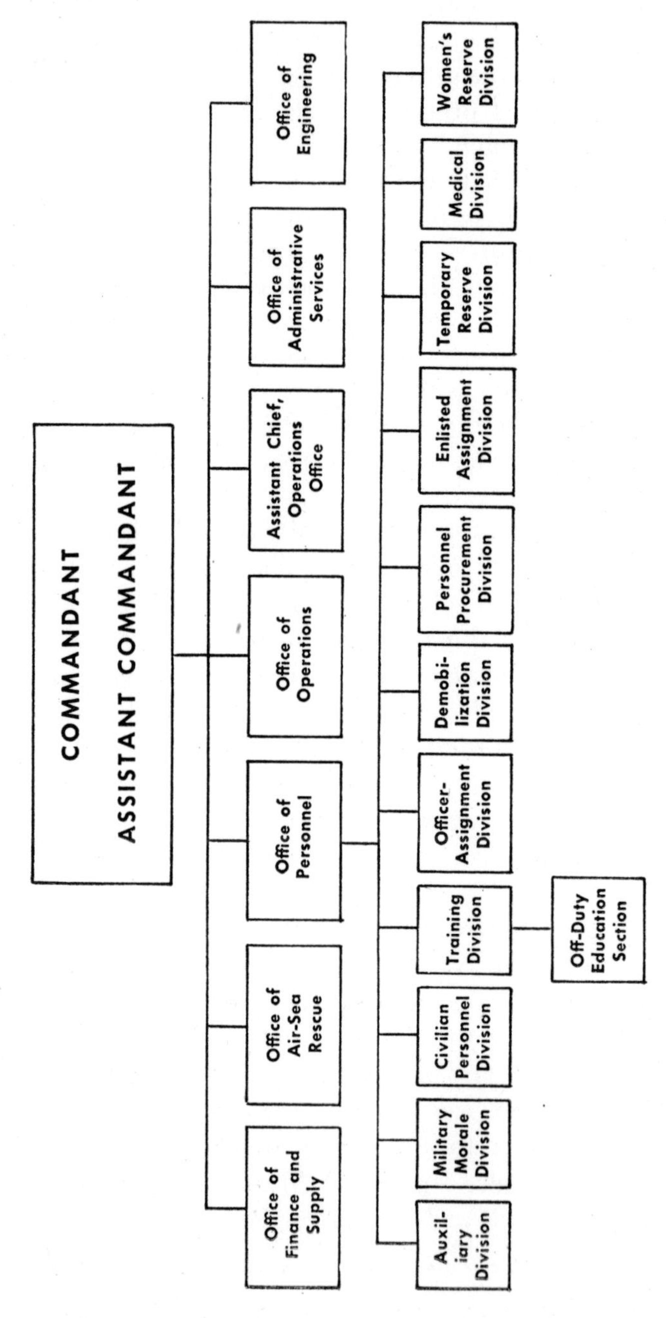

FIG. 6.—Coast Guard Headquarters Organization

COAST GUARD

The duties of supervising the off-duty educational program in the Coast Guard were made a collateral responsibility of the education officer who was also charged with the service-training function. In cases where there was only one commissioned officer attached to a unit, the education officer could be a warrant officer; if there were no commissioned or warrant officers, the senior petty officer was designated as educational officer. In all other cases the billet was filled by a commissioned officer.

As might be expected, these educational officers did not have a consistent pattern of civilian background. Such officers were selected primarily for their ability to cope with service training. No effort was made to procure men especially skilled in educational techniques. The range in terms of education attained extended from the Ph.D. to one or two years of high school.

The headquarters organization which supervised the off-duty educational program was a section of the Training Division of the Office of Personnel. Figure 6 shows this organizational relationship as of June 5, 1945.

III. CORRESPONDENCE STUDY

SINCE ITS FIRST development in the latter part of the nineteenth century, correspondence instruction has been chiefly used as an adult educational method. Its great flexibility and availability has made it peculiarly suitable as a means of meeting the needs of mature people, who are motivated to study and who often have no other means at hand. It is not surprising, therefore, that the armed services used correspondence instruction very extensively in their off-duty programs. When those responsible for such programs first began to recognize the magnitude of the task of serving men who were scattered all over the world and who had widely varying interests, they found themselves placing a heavy reliance on correspondence instruction. The Marine Corps and the Coast Guard had operated correspondence schools of modest size ever since the twenties, but the program of World War II greatly extended the facilities available by that method.

It is not hard to understand why correspondence study fitted so well the needs of the armed services. Correspondence courses can be taken at any place in the world that is served by postal service. They can be taken by individuals or by groups and can be started at any time. They let each student progress as rapidly or as slowly as his desires and abilities permit. Although there is no direct personal contact between instructor and student and therefore the teaching of values and insights may be somewhat limited, a well-designed correspondence course taught by a conscientious and able teacher is superior to the resources available in many civilian communities or military stations. The range of subjects which may be taught is extensive although some courses are difficult or impossible to offer because of the kinds or the diversity of instructional materials required.

By far the largest program of correspondence instruction in World War II was undertaken by the United States Armed Forces Institute, in which both of the major branches of the service cooperated. Most of this chapter will deal with USAFI, therefore, with brief mention also being made of the programs of the Marine Corps and the Coast Guard.

UNITED STATES ARMED FORCES INSTITUTE[1]

The United States Armed Forces Institute, known everywhere as USAFI, was one of the largest enterprises of the Education Branch, Information and Education Division. The story of its development, its problems, and its accomplishments bears telling in detail because of the large numbers of individuals in both the Army and Navy who were in one way or another connected with USAFI. In high schools and colleges for years to come its influence will be felt.

USAFI's wide range of activities stemmed largely from the broad requirements of its extensive correspondence-study program. USAFI found it necessary, for example, to procure, to adopt, to stock, and to distribute a variety of textbooks and materials for self-study and correspondence instruction. This activity resulted in the assignment to USAFI of responsibility for supplying materials for the post-hostilities Army education program. Effective guidance was needed to insure the success of students in the USAFI program. As a result, USAFI distributed the Army Vocational Information Kit. The interest which USAFI's students had in gaining academic credit for correspondence instruction led the Institute to establish, with the assistance of civilian educators, a formal accreditation program covering not only correspondence study and self-study but the whole range of military experience.

ESTABLISHMENT OF USAFI

The Army Institute, the predecessor of the United States Armed Forces Institute, was brought into being at Madison, Wisconsin, on April 1, 1942. As a result of changed conditions created by the declaration of war, earlier plans for operation of the Institute entirely by military personnel were modified to make all possible use of civilian personnel in the administration

[1]This section, with minor editorial changes and some abridgment, is excerpted, with permission, from the manuscript, "History of Military Training: History of the Army Education Branch" (on file in the Historical Division, War Department Special Staff).

of the correspondence-course program. Instructional service in connection with noncredit courses offered directly by the Institute was provided by the University of Wisconsin under government contract.

After the Army Institute was formed, it became evident that self-teaching and test materials would be needed in addition to the normal type of correspondence courses. In April 1942, the Chief of Special Service requested that the Subcommittee on Education of the Joint Army and Navy Committee take the necessary steps to provide such materials. The Subcommittee appointed a group of experts as an advisory committee on the Army Institute to recommend administrative procedures for the development of the education program and to work with staffs handling testing and teaching materials. Later, as the Advisory Committee for the United States Army Institute, this group continued to review the Institute's educational program and to plan for accrediting educational work in the Army.

At first the Institute's services were available only to Army enlisted personnel. In August 1942, however, the Secretary of the Navy requested the Secretary of War to make the various facilities developed in the Army education program, including the services of the Army Institute, available for use by the Navy. In September, the War Department agreed to the proposed arrangements. A Navy registrar was assigned to the Army Institute and enrollment in Army Institute courses was opened to Navy, Coast Guard, and Marine Corps personnel. The cost of materials and services in connection with Navy enrollments was charged to the Navy Department. Under this cooperative arrangement, the Navy increased its staff of officers at Institute headquarters and assigned enlisted WAVES for clerical service. It also assigned personnel for overseas branches. On February 3, 1943, the Army Institute was officially renamed the United States Armed Forces Institute. At that time USAFI facilities were made available to Army commissioned personnel.

Because USAFI was designed to serve the needs of individuals, its activities were made directly accessible to them. Military personnel were encouraged to write to the Institute in the expectation of receiving personal attention as well as information and help related to their own educational problems. The publication of the Army catalog *What Would You Like to Learn?* in October 1942 and its wide distribution helped further to establish a policy of personal service. Other editions of the catalog were later issued to present new USAFI courses for military personnel and to provide users with more complete information about USAFI courses and services.

Fees for USAFI services were kept to a minimum and were a token of serious intent on the part of the enrollee rather than a substantial payment toward the actual cost. Prior to July 1943, a two-dollar fee was charged enlisted men for each Institute course taken. After that date, enlisted personnel paid only a registration fee of two dollars for the first enrollment in USAFI courses. No additional fee was to be required for additional courses so long as satisfactory progress was maintained. Because the education program was financed by Welfare of Enlisted Men funds, commissioned, warrant, and flight officers were required to pay fees covering costs of courses and services.

Distribution of textbooks to students was originally a simple process calling chiefly for the mailing of books and lesson materials to individuals in the United States. With the expansion of overseas forces, however, the shipments of texts to supply overseas personnel became a difficult problem. Educational supplies were stocked at ports of embarkation, and overseas requisitions were filled from port stocks. This method, however, was found to be impracticable. In early 1944, the function of book distribution was transferred to USAFI at Madison, Wisconsin. Overseas theaters were to be supplied through USAFI overseas branches. The new arrangement was expected to keep overseas branches adequately stocked and to facilitate distribution of educational materials.

Until February 1944, USAFI was operated by commissioned and enlisted personnel of the Army and Navy. Enlisted Army personnel were then gradually replaced by civilians. Many of the enlisted men were assigned to overseas branches of the Institute.

ESTABLISHMENT OF USAFI OVERSEAS BRANCHES

In July 1942, the Commanding General of the Hawaiian department requested the establishment of a USAFI branch within that department. Necessary materials and equipment were provided for establishing such a branch. One officer and three enlisted men were assigned to the Hawaiian department to assist in organizing and administering the branch. Later this branch was designated the Central Pacific Branch. Lesson service was provided by the University of Hawaii. The Navy assigned an assistant commandant and a registrar.

As time went on, overseas branches were requested by other theaters. By the end of the war there were branches in London, Rome, Anchorage, Brisbane, Manila, Cairo, New Delhi, Puerto Rico, Panama, and New Caledonia. The establishment of these overseas branches reduced materially the long waiting period between the serviceman's application for a particular USAFI course and his receipt of the materials. One of the greatest problems that USAFI found in 1944 and 1945 was that of getting the requested courses to the men in their military installations throughout the world.

GROWTH OF USAFI

The Army's off-duty education program grew greatly during the last six months of 1944, requiring a re-study of services afforded to individual applicants and to groups. USAFI had been writing a large number of advisory communications to individual applicants in response to their questions about courses, preparation for occupations, possible study programs, and the like. Many of these letters, requesting detailed information about college entrance requirements and training for particular occupations, frequently required a good bit of investigation and research. It was vastly more of an undertaking than USAFI had anticipated. Due to the greatly increased numbers of these letters and applications, it became more and more difficult to render this individual service. To relieve this situation, forms of various types which could be checked and returned to inquirers, were developed to replace the letters.

By the end of 1944 eleven million education manuals had been procured, and were stocked at Kansas City, Missouri, and Jersey City, New Jersey, in addition to Madison, Wisconsin. As the volume of supplies being stored for overseas shipment grew, it became necessary to arrange for additional warehouse space. Adequate facilities were finally obtained in Salt Lake City, Utah, and Wilmington, Delaware, and newly purchased items were shipped to these new depots. Plans were made to abandon the space at Kansas City and Jersey City.

Individual enrollees were instructed to place their applications for enrollment in the Institute through their local Information-Education or education officer, thereby obtaining more personal guidance and advice. This acted as an impetus to other phases of the education program for more off-duty classes were organized as local Information-Education officers became aware of the interests of their men.

Posters, advertisements in soldier newspapers, fact sheets, and articles describing the education program were produced by the program-promotion section of the New York branch office. Particular emphasis was placed on planning and producing copy and art for graphic material to be used in publicizing the Army education program. This artwork was furnished to the theaters for local reproduction.

In addition to facilities in this country and overseas, a program was instituted for troops while aboard transports. An information and education transport kit was developed after increased inquiries indicated the need for such a program. This included USAFI catalogs, application blanks, and samples of self-teaching texts. Officers were selected in the ports of embarkation and given a special three-day training course in information and education work. Study through USAFI self-teaching texts was recommended while aboard ship.

EDUCATION FOR PRISONERS OF WAR [2]

In January 1944, personnel of the United States Armed Forces held as prisoners of war were permitted to become mem-

[2] This section is excerpted, with permission, from the manuscript, "Supplement II, History of the Army Education Branch, 1 January to 30 June 1945" (on file in the Historical Division, War Department Special Staff).

bers of USAFI without payment of fees. By June 1945, over 100,000 education manuals and 13,000 USAFI correspondence courses had been furnished War Prisoners Aid of the YMCA for distribution to American POW's in Europe, and 3,000 education manuals and 2,000 correspondence courses for POW's in Japanese camps. In addition, hundreds of individual requests from American prisoners of war for USAFI materials were filled.

The Geneva office of War Prisoners Aid established what was known as the Geneva branch of USAFI. Records were kept of materials sent to individual American POW's and of bulk shipments to appointed education officers (American Army personnel) within the camps. Directions for keeping records of individual achievements of POW's were also sent to education officers. Every effort was made to route these achievement records through Geneva so the serviceman would have certified records of his studies to submit to educational institutions in this country for accreditation.

USAFI INSTRUCTIONAL MATERIALS [3]

When the Army Institute was opened in April 1942, two types of instruction were offered: correspondence courses offered directly by the Institute, and correspondence courses offered through seventy-five cooperating civilian schools and universities.

In order to expedite the procurement of original Institute courses, it had been necessary to purchase all text materials from the civilian source having available the most complete offering of correspondence courses. All the original sixty-four Army Institute courses were purchased from a large private correspondence school. Most of these courses were at the high school level. The curriculum was limited to fields of English, social studies, mathematics, science, business, mechanics, electricity, and technical subjects. These sixty-four correspondence courses proved inadequate to meet the needs of military personnel. Arrangements were made in late 1943 to increase the Institute curriculum

[3] This section, with minor editorial changes and some abridgment, is largely excerpted, with permission, from the manuscript, "History of the Army Education Branch," and "Supplement II, 1 January to 30 June 1945" (on file in the Historical Division, War Department Special Staff).

to include some 250 courses at high school, college, and technical school levels. More than 125 of the best available courses offered by leading universities were purchased by USAFI and were offered as USAFI correspondence courses.

Some individuals, however, wanted the opportunity to take work directly with the college or university of their choice. University extension correspondence courses were helpful for Army personnel so located that they could communicate easily with the civilian educational institutions in the United States. In December 1941, therefore, the Subcommittee on Education supplied officers of the Special Service Division with a list of colleges and universities judged well equipped to furnish correspondence study instruction of high standard to men in the Army. Contracts were drawn up in March 1942 with more than seventy institutions. This number was later increased to eighty-five.

Even before the Army Institute was established, it became apparent that the wide geographical distribution of Army personnel and the great range of their intellectual capacities would necessitate off-duty instructional materials which would be: fully self-teaching, so that even the most isolated soldier might study without the personal assistance of a skilled teacher; briefly and compactly organized to insure the most economical use of the student's time; as clear and accurate as they could be made, to insure comprehension in the self-teaching situation; varied in educational level to meet the range and intellectual capacity of Army personnel; and selectively planned to contain only useful subject matter and emphasize only that most urgently needed by military personnel.

Instructional materials which would meet these requirements were not available. The standard texts used with correspondence courses were bulky, not suited for individual study, and difficult for mailing purposes. Experience had demonstrated the need for materials for men who wished to study a particular course but did not want to send in correspondence lessons. A well-written textbook together with sufficient instructions for study, opportunities for self-evaluation, and simplified explanations of the text were needed to keep servicemen interested in their study. It was essential that all of this self-study material be included in one bound volume for ready use when time could be taken from pressing military obligations, and that it be distributed locally as well as on application to a USAFI branch or headquarters.

In April 1942, the Subcommittee on Education recommended that a staff of school and college teachers be established for the purpose of selecting and developing adequate materials for self-teaching courses in the Army Institute. This staff was organized at Indiana University late in May 1942. Financial support was provided in a contract, dated May 25, 1942, between the War Department and Indiana University. The staff's work was supervised by a special Advisory Committee appointed by the Subcommittee on Education. During four months members of the staff produced partial or completed manuscripts in arithmetic, algebra, bookkeeping, typewriting, English, and radio.

Although limited by contractual arrangements, the experience of the staff at Indiana University was valuable in indicating the most suitable procedures for subsequent work. Two principles were confirmed: first, that suitable instructional materials should be obtained as far as possible through the selection and adaptation of existing materials; and, second, that an editorial staff for this purpose should be set up conveniently near the Army Education Branch in Washington.

In September 1942, with the approval of the Subcommittee on Education, new arrangements were made for the development of the necessary materials. Under contract with the War Department, the American Council on Education established at American University a special editorial staff for USAFI, selected from the staffs of leading educational publishers and nominated by officers of the American Institute of Textbook Publishers. Working in cooperation with the Army Education Branch, this staff was directed to select the most suitable existing textbooks in various fields and enlist the cooperation of publishers in making them available for Army use.

Through cooperation with the authors and publishers of books selected for Army use, the editorial staff was able to obtain special editions of widely used textbooks, revised to suit Army needs. Initially these special editions were simply identified as USAFI textbooks. In September 1943, approval was granted for the publication of selected textbooks as a new series of War Department education manuals. The editorial staff selected or prepared adaptations of textbooks in the major fields of instruction from the fifth-grade level up to the second year of college.

In selecting educational materials, the Army Education Branch indicated the subjects and types of material needed. The editorial staff then submitted inquiries to outstanding educational authorities who were familiar with the subjects under consideration and with the use of instructional materials in civilian schools and colleges and requested them to make recommendations. By this process, the books recommended by the editorial staff to the Army Education Branch for purchase had won wide acceptance in civilian education and were judged practicable for Army needs. If suitable materials could not be found, the editorial staff made special arrangements with individuals or organizations to produce the needed materials.

As a basis for preparing certain college-level materials, the assistance of a joint committee of the American Council on Education and the Association of American Colleges was requested to outline a suitable curriculum in general education covering the eleventh and twelfth grades of the secondary school and the first and second years of the usual college course. Final recommendations of this committee were published in June 1944, in an American Council on Education report entitled *A Design for General Education*.[4]

As soon as *Education Manuals* were distributed to the field, servicemen studying correspondence courses which relied heavily on the more formal standard texts began to ask education officers for permission to substitute self-teaching manuals for the textbooks. Not infrequently an education manual had been developed from the standard text already in use in the correspondence course. The USAFI Advisory Committee indicated the desirability of using education manuals as texts for correspondence courses. Since many such manuals were already available in quantity, it was pointed out that they could be made excellent

[4] Committee on a Design for General Education, *A Design for General Education* (Washington: American Council on Education, 1944).

correspondence-course materials by the addition of guides or syllabi for students. Such use of *Education Manuals* would also greatly simplify the Army's problems of stocking and distributing instructional materials. The USAFI editorial staff was requested, therefore, to prepare correspondence-course syllabi to be used with certain of the *Education Manuals*.

Beginning in February 1945, procurement of approximately 10,700,000 education manuals was initiated to meet further needs in the European and Mediterranean theaters and anticipated requirements in Pacific Ocean areas. Subsequently, upon advice from the European theater that the post-VE program requirements for VE Day plus twelve months could be filled from stocks already on hand in the theater, orders for approximately 2,500,000 education manuals were cancelled. Roughly 5,500,000 manuals were on hand in the United States awaiting shipment to the Pacific, and an additional 8,000,000 were being procured for delivery before January 1946. This total of manuals included about 350 titles.

Early in 1943 the Army Education Branch had begun to formulate tentative recommendations for an Army education program to be conducted in inactive theaters following cessation of hostilities. This phase of the program became known as the Army Education Program or the AEP.

Early in 1944, the USAFI editorial staff was assigned the task of selecting textbooks for vocational courses. In early planning of the Army Education Program, it had been assumed that the fullest possible use should be made of existing Army instructional materials. It had been expected that syllabi and other instructional materials developed and proven in Army specialist schools should be used in the AEP schools. It was found, however, that the Army's training courses were not suitable for the AEP because service operations in the Army in wartime are necessarily different from those in civilian occupations in peacetime. Thus if the vocational instruction and training offered Army personnel in the AEP were to prepare them for readjustment to civilian occupations, the instructional materials used must be obtained from civilian sources. The USAFI editorial staff, therefore, was authorized to select textbooks for these courses according to its established policies in cooperation with civilian consultants and educational publishers.

In response to a widespread demand for vocational information materials, a comprehensive kit of such materials was assembled and issued as an Army Vocational Information Kit. This kit was designed to supply officers and enlisted personnel with job information that would help them adjust to postwar civilian work. When completed, the kit consisted of six standard texts and over four hundred pamphlets, arranged in seventy-three major fields. It was contained in a large wooden box about the size of a file drawer, which could be used as a convenient filing case. Ten thousand Vocational Information Kits were purchased and distributed by the end of 1945.

Approximately 1,300,000 textbooks for use in the Army Education Program were obtained as surplus from the Army Specialized Training Division. Five thousand AEP Reference Library Kits were procured. Each kit contained about fifty volumes for use by students and instructors in AEP schools. Instructor's course outlines for some eighty education manuals for use in the AEP were prepared.

In August 1944, the USAFI visual-aids department initiated the planning and preparation of graphic-chart materials for use as instructional aids in the AEP. Graphic-chart kits were developed to implement texts and course outlines supplied for AEP courses, and to make possible more effective instruction. Each chart kit included a manila envelope with an identifying label and simple instructions on the outside, a set of one or more colored charts emphasizing important topics in the course, and a sheet of utilization notes indicating to the instructor the relation of each chart to the text and the course outline it accompanied. Individual charts measured 19 x 24 inches and were printed on both sides.

TESTS AND ACCREDITATION

It was recognized at the time the Institute was first established that the education program of the Army would not be complete unless military personnel could readily transmit for appraisal of civilian educational institutions reliable evidence of their educational achievements and abilities.

In April 1942, a special committee of the American Council on Education recommended to the Subcommittee on Education of the Joint Army and Navy Committee on Welfare and Recreation that success in the Army Institute correspondence courses be appraised in terms of skills, attitudes, and knowledge achieved by the students; that the Army Institute provide opportunity for soldiers, not registered in courses but with comparable training experience, to take appraisal tests and receive proficiency ratings if they could achieve a satisfactory standing in such tests; and that carefully constructed appraisal tests be used to determine the educational significance of skills acquired through various types of war experiences. Through the executive secretary of the Subcommittee on Education, the special committee's report and recommendations were transmitted to the Director of the Special Service Division, who concurred in the recommendations and authorized the Subcommittee to set up a group to develop the necessary tests through circular agencies. The cost was to be borne by the War Department.

A contract was entered into with the University of Chicago in May 1942 to establish a special examinations staff for the Army Institute (later USAFI). This staff engaged in developing three major types of examinations: (1) end-of-course tests for USAFI courses; (2) examinations to be used in determining a student's proficiency in a special field of study, such as mathematics, physics, or American history; and (3) general educational development examinations to determine the educational level at which a student might resume work on his return to school or college.

In February 1943, the American Council on Education published the bulletin, *Sound Educational Credit for Military Experience*. It recommended to schools and colleges the use of reports on USAFI examinations of the second and third types described above, rather than "blanket credit" or the insistence on records of time spent in classes, as a basis for awarding academic credit to returning service personnel. The wide circulation of this bulletin, the issuance of similar publications by the National Association of Secondary School Principals dealing with problems of secondary school credit, and effective leadership by officers of both of these organizations led to the acceptance of the basic recommendations by regional accrediting associations, and by virtually all secondary schools and colleges.

The USAFI Advisory Committee at first recommended that the United States Armed Forces Institute at Madison, Wisconsin, serve as a central clearinghouse which would receive from armed forces personnel applications for credit to be transmitted to educational institutions. Such a clearinghouse would assemble accurate descriptions of service training courses and other types of educational opportunity available in the services to be transmitted with credit applications. After some months of experimenting with these recommendations, it became evident that the accreditation service was so acceptable to schools that the special clearinghouse would become unwieldy. It would undoubtedly become so widely used as to require a very large operating personnel at the Institute. Much time was involved in correspondence about academic credits, particularly for applicants stationed overseas.

Revisions in accreditation forms and procedures used in the USAFI program were undertaken, therefore, by representatives of the Advisory Committee, the Department of Secondary School Principals of the National Education Association, the American Council on Education, and the appropriate organizations of the armed forces. These revisions enabled applicants for credit to send directly to schools or colleges certified transcripts of records of their education, training, and job assignments in the military service, and to receive from educational institutions official reports of credit granted and recommendations for continued education.

In order to interpret educational records transmitted by applicants for credit, it was necessary for educational institutions to have conveniently at hand adequate descriptions of training courses and educational training programs in the armed forces. To meet this need and also to provide educators with authoritative recommendations concerning the granting of credit, the American Council on Education in December 1943 established a project for the development of a handbook for school and college officials. The Army Education Branch and the comparable organizations in the Navy, Coast Guard, and Marine Corps assisted the American Council in obtaining official descriptions of training-school programs in their respective services. Descriptions of these courses, together with credit recommendations from competent civilian authorities, were made available in a handbook entitled *A Guide to the Evaluation of Military Experiences in the Armed Forces,* published in loose-leaf form by the American Council on Education.

It was apparent that many civilian educational institutions wished to use the USAFI General Educational Development Tests and other USAFI accreditation examinations for admission for veterans returning to their campuses. The American Council on Education arranged, therefore, to obtain equivalent forms of USAFI accreditation examinations and to make them available to civilian secondary schools and colleges. These tests were distributed by the Coperative Test Service and Science Research Associates.

NUMBERS INVOLVED IN USAFI COURSES

On July 1, 1942, the Institute's total enrollment in correspondence courses was 1,255; by July 1, 1943, these enrollments had increased to 40,804. After that time, however, with the establishment of overseas branches and with a great shortage of staff personnel, the growth of the Institute's service wholly exceeded its capacity to assemble accurate current data on its services to individuals. It is known, however, that enrollments in correspondence courses in June 1944 numbered some 250,000 while attendance in locally organized classes was more than twice that number. Total enrollments in June 1945, were 866,000. Enrollments in the Army alone in August 1945 indicated that there were 575,000 individuals active at that time. Considering locally organized classes, probably over 2,000,000 members of the armed forces made use of study materials distributed by USAFI and by the Navy, while individual enrollments in correspondence courses and self-teaching courses totaled more than 1,250,000 including Navy, Coast Guard, and Marine Corps.

In both the Army and Navy about 10 percent of registrants completed courses undertaken. Bookkeeping and accounting, auto mechanics, American history, algebra, and arithmetic were the most popular courses. Table 6 is the best summary available to September 30, 1945.

TABLE 6*

UNITED STATES ARMED FORCES INSTITUTE
CORRESPONDENCE ENROLLMENTS AND COLLEGES UTILIZED IN LESSON SERVICE†
CUMULATIVE TO SEPTEMBER 30, 1945

THEATER OF OPERATIONS	AGENT FOR LESSON AND TEST SERVICE	ENROLL-MENT	LESSON SERVICE	ENROLLMENTS IN 85 CO-OPERATING SCHOOLS‡
Continental United States	University of Wisconsin, Madison§	367,367	943,890	100,684
Alaska	University of Washington, Seattle	7,754	20,102	....
Antilles	University of Florida, Gainesville	299	447	....
Central and South Pacific	University of Hawaii, Honolulu	56,176	102,087	....
European Theater	Battersea Polytechnic Institute, London	85,487	167,815	....
India, Burma	University of Calcutta, India	15,519	24,853	....
Middle East	American University, Cairo	15,026	25,921	....
Mediterranean	University of Rome	27,306	38,857	....
Panama	University of Florida, Gainesville	2,493	4,542	....
Southwest Pacific	Sydney Technological College, Australia; later G. I. Faculty, Manila	70,802	164,823	....
Total		648,227	1,493,337	100,684‖

* This table is excerpted, with permission, from the manuscript "History of Military Training; History of the Army Education Branch" (on file in the Historical Division, War Department Special Staff).

† Includes lessons graded and returned.

‡ War Department records contain no data relative to lesson service or correspondence courses with civilian colleges and universities offering correspondence courses through the United States Armed Forces Institute.

§ Provided some overseas lesson service.

‖ Enrollments in courses offered by cooperating schools are transferred from branches to headquarters, Madison.

Upon return to civil life of the first 7,000 veteran applicants for accreditation, 98 percent obtained some high school credit, with 28 percent being awarded diplomas. Out of every 100 applicants for college credit, 95 obtained credit, with 20 receiving diplomas.

THE NAVY AND USAFI[5]

After the Navy was admitted to participation in the Army Institute (later USAFI) in the autumn of 1942, the policies of the center at Madison became nominally the joint concern of the Educational Services Section in the Bureau of Naval Personnel and the Education Branch, Information and Education Division, Army Service Forces. In actual practice, though, USAFI continued to develop along the lines originally laid down for the Army Institute, with the naval representatives charged with the responsibility of seeing that the Navy's interests were adequately met.

The Navy unit at Madison was eventually expanded to a complement of eleven officers and sixty enlisted personnel. The head of the Navy unit served dually as assistant commandant under the Army commandant of USAFI and as officer-in-charge (later commanding officer) of the Navy unit.

In spite of the Navy's emphasis on voluntary classes, naval participation in USAFI was high. Approximately 35 percent of all USAFI enrollees were Navy. In the case of college and university extension courses this figure approached 50 percent with only about 25 percent of the enrollments in self-teaching courses being accounted for by naval personnel. It should be noted, however, that each Educational Services officer was given a considerable stock of self-teaching courses which he distributed directly to personnel on his ship or station. These were not included in USAFI totals.

In the quarter October-December of 1942 only 36 of the Navy's personnel were enrolled in USAFI correspondence and extension courses. For the same quarters in 1943 and 1944 the figures had increased to 10,686 and 30,274 respectively. As of September 30, 1945, naval enrollment in USAFI correspondence courses was 140,001, and for college and university extension courses, 46,766.

[5] Use has been made throughout this section of "Educational Services Section," *Administrative History of the Bureau of Naval Personnel* (MS on file in Office of Naval History, U. S. Navy Department).

MARINE CORPS INSTITUTE

The catalog of the Marine Corps Institute in use during the last days of the war indicated that 159 courses were available. These were distributed as shown below[6]:

Subjects	No. of Courses Offered
College courses	
Foreign service studies	5
Business administration	2
Language and literature	12
Foreign language	5
Mathematics and natural science	5
Others	3
Total	32
High school courses	
Mathematics	7
English	7
Foreign language	6
Science	5
Social science	9
Business and clerical	13
Physiology and health	1
Total	48
Technical courses	
Automobile	4
Aviation	15
Building trades	12
Diesel and gas engines	5
Civil engineering	4
Electricity	5
Radio	4
Air conditioning and refrigeration	6
Industrial	12
Total	67
Special courses	
Investigations and security	6
Others	6
Total	12
Total of all courses	159

[6] U. S. Marine Corps, Marine Corps Institute, *College, High School and Technical Courses* (Washington: Marine Corps Institute, Marine Barracks), pp. 2-7.

The Marine Corps also used the services of USAFI, but, loyal to its own organization, set up rules which prevented USAFI from taking away the function of the Marine Corps Institute. No marine could take a course from USAFI if that course was offered by the Marine Corps Institute. Courses offered by the Marine Corps Institute were free, and upon successful completion of the course the textbooks became the property of the student.

Table 7 indicates the activity of the Marine Corps Institute during the war years.

TABLE 7

WARTIME ACTIVITY OF THE MARINE CORPS INSTITUTE

Year	New Enrollments	Enrollment at End of Year	Average Activity Percentage*
1942	4,797	6,419	20.0
1943	17,291	20,336	20.0
1944	38,820	55,289	13.5
1945	55,483	48,304	20.2

* Active students as a percent of enrollment.

Inasmuch as the Marine Corps Institute was the first organization of its kind in any branch of the armed services, its influence was somewhat out of proportion to the size of its clientele. MCI assisted in the organization of the Coast Guard Institute in 1926, and for some twelve months in 1926-27 Coast Guard personnel were attached to MCI for training. The original Army Institute incorporated many of the organization plans of the MCI.[7]

THE COAST GUARD INSTITUTE

The Coast Guard Institute was established in 1928 at Groton, Connecticut, to provide training for Coast Guard personnel by means of correspondence courses.[8] The primary emphasis of these courses is on the professional training of personnel. Such training is outside the scope of this study. However, there are a few courses labeled "academic and preparatory" which meet

[7] Letter from Col. Donald J. Kendall, USMC, Director, United States Marine Corps Institute, June 20, 1946.

[8] U. S. Coast Guard, Coast Guard Institute, *Institute Courses for Coast Guard Personnel* (Groton, Conn.: U. S. Coast Guard Institute, September 1945), p. 1.

the present criteria. All courses offered by the Coast Guard Institute are available to both officers and enlisted personnel and are issued without charge with the exception that officers are charged the cost of nonreturnable textbooks.

Of the total of ninety-one courses listed as available, only sixteen were of the classification "academic and preparatory." The distribution of these included: English, three courses; mathematics, six courses; social studies, three courses; business, four courses. At the outbreak of World War II, there was some inclination to expand the academic offerings of the Coast Guard Institute, but the establishment and expansion of USAFI during the war made such a change unnecessary.

IV. DIRECT INDIVIDUAL AND GROUP INSTRUCTION

IN THE MINDS of many educators, the most interesting features of the armed services off-duty educational programs were to be found in leisure-time classes, in the methods of teaching spoken foreign languages, and in Army and Navy discussion groups. Men and women in uniform would use their free time to attend classes of their own choice, frequently held in crude classrooms lacking adequate materials and under the leadership of one of their own number. Classroom programs were set up entirely on the basis of student interest.

The possibilities inherent in a program of leisure-time educational activities for adults are increased by the use of language recordings and a teaching emphasis on spoken foreign language attractively prepared discussion guides (such as those produced in the *G.I. Roundtable* series) to stimulate effective discussion groups. Utilization of local facilities in the development of a broad educational program for adults is desirable.

ARMY[1]

The Army provided many opportunities for study in off-duty classes. Local class programs depended upon the initiative of interested individuals and upon the availability of suitable instructional materials. Local off-duty study programs increased rapidly as education officers were assigned to headquarters and to local posts and units, and as specially selected textbooks and other materials for group instruction were made available through USAFI. In some organizations where personnel were sufficiently permanent to warrant their enrollment in local classes, the offerings of off-duty schools were comparable in scope and variety to those of outstanding civilian institutions.

[1] This section, with minor editorial changes and some abridgment, is excerpted, with permission, from the manuscript, "History of Military Training: History of the Army Education Branch" (on file in the Historical Division, War Department Special Staff).

LOCALLY ORGANIZED CLASSES

At Fort Monmouth, New Jersey, for example, in April 1943, evening classes were conducted by soldiers who had been teachers in civilian life. Courses there were given in such subjects as mathematics, English, French, Spanish, German, history, government, accounting, shorthand, typing, public speaking, and music appreciation. Courses were offered at both secondary-school and college levels and were organized in one-month units. Students were awarded certificates of proficiency upon satisfactory completion of their work.

Experience gained and patterns developed in class programs in the United States were subsequently used in developing similar local programs overseas. As soon as overseas troops received necessary quarters and utilities, and had developed certain organized daily routines, locally organized classes and schools sprang up in large numbers. In New Guinea, for example, an engineer battalion organized its own GI Jungle University, using its own personnel for administration and instruction and USAFI materials as texts.

With the appointment of additional Information-Education officers and education officers, and with the increased distribution of educational materials through USAFI, there was a parallel expansion of locally organized off-duty classes and schools. No accurate enrollment figures can be given because such reports were not required. The number was indicated, however, by the large quantity of materials sent out from USAFI and its branches, together with occasional reports sent in voluntarily from the theaters. Where feasible, some classes were organized in connection with nearby civilian educational institutions.

Particularly in areas where combat organizations were temporarily inactive, locally organized schools proved to be effective solutions for problems of morale and discipline and satisfying avenues for maintaining the active interest of military personnel. A school established in Italy by a unit of the Twelfth Air Force was one of the first comprehensive schools of its type in the Mediterranean theater. It originally offered some thirty-five courses. A few classes were taught by competent teachers without texts. In other classes USAFI textbooks were used. Observers testified to the interest shown by the students and the ability of their instructors. The interest of students in their classes was reflected in the fact that class attendance fell off less than the attendance of team members in athletic games. It was further indicated by the increase in voluntary reference reading in the library. The school was useful also in that it became the nucleus of a whole network of community activity.

Another example of locally organized classes in operation was the program at the ATC Base in Accra, British West Africa, early in 1944. At first, courses included algebra, analytic geometry, art, arithmetic, differential calculus, French, German, plane geometry, and trigonometry. Later, courses were added in college algebra, English, Fanti (a West African dialect), music appreciation, shorthand, and Spanish. Subjects were determined by a questionnaire sent to each man at the base. Results showed that interests lay in mathematics, languages, technical courses, and cultural subjects. Three hundred students started in these classes, and enrollments continually increased until about four hundred were attending classes regularly.

The program flourished from the start in spite of the many problems that had to be met. Among these, the following five were outstanding: (1) inadequate facilities and a slowed-up building program, making it necessary to use tents, storerooms, and other odd places as classrooms; (2) an almost complete lack of textual material; (3) a high turnover in personnel; (4) duty schedules which were continually shifted to meet changing conditions; and (5) tropical climatic conditions not conducive to voluntary work.

In June the commanding officer turned over to the school an officers' barracks and classes were moved from the varied assortment of meeting-places into seven new classrooms, properly lighted, well-screened, and fitted with writing armchairs, blackboards, and other facilities. The GI college took a new lease on life. Plans were formulated for a broadened program. The student body grew to over five hundred, with twenty-five instructors in charge.

The standards of the GI college were high. Cooperation was wholehearted and disciplinary problems were few. The improved physical facilities included a large office, two large classrooms, four smaller classrooms, a laboratory, two storerooms, and three washrooms. One of the rooms was used as a music studio and was equipped with a piano. Classrooms were well-equipped. The school had a movie projector, a record player, and a slide projector.

By November the enrollment had dropped to 250 because of the removal or transfer of men. Some of the classes started in January had ended. The school had added classes in Latin, physics, Hebrew, organic chemistry, abnormal psychology, and advanced Spanish. Twenty-three classes were maintained, with fifteen instructors. Several competent instructors had been lost by rotation and transfer. The work moved on, however, with completed classes closing out and new ones being started periodically.

A typical example of a well-organized off-duty education program in the United States was "Crowder University" at Camp Crowder, Missouri.[2] "Crowder University," known officially as the Army Service Forces Training Center Off-Duty Education Program, was organized in April 1944. A few instructors offered eight courses, and forty students enrolled in the original program.

In June 1945, the opening registration for a midsummer term was announced. Instruction was offered in fifty-eight classes by forty-five instructors, with an enrollment of more than eight hundred. The most popular subjects were bookkeeping and accounting, psychology, Spanish, German, and auto-mechanics, but the classes also included such diverse fields as criminology, aeronautics, statistical analysis, logic, and radio production.

Qualified teachers were available as instructors, and both enlisted and commissioned personnel were used. For example, a class in abnormal psychology was taught by an Army private who held a Ph.D. from Columbia University. He had studied at Oxford as a Rhodes scholar, and had formerly taught in an American university. A class in radio production was taught by a private and a noncommissioned officer, both of whom were

[2]This item is excerpted, with permission, from the manuscript, "Supplement II, History of Army Education Branch, 1 January to 30 June 1945" (on file in the Historical Division, War Department Special Staff).

radio production men with years of experience. This subject was conducted as a laboratory course in which students had an opportunity to help write and stage programs.

THE FOREIGN-LANGUAGE PROGRAM[3]

The armed forces overseas needed facility in the use of foreign languages for interrogating and handling prisoners of war, for conducting civil affairs, and for use in daily contact with allied troops and friendly civilians. This need required the development of self-teaching materials for instructing troops to converse in a number of languages.

In April 1942, the Education Section of the Welfare and Recreation Division was asked to assume responsibility for the preparation of foreign-language supplements to the information manuals on foreign countries prepared by the Information Division. These language materials were to provide overseas troops with usable phrases of the language of the country in which they were stationed. It was believed that such instruction in languages would improve the morale of troops by enabling them to converse, however slightly, with local inhabitants. It was also believed that language study would provide valuable educational activities for troops in transit.

In May 1942, a special consultant was employed to develop language materials for an initial list of twenty-six foreign languages. These materials were to include phonograph recordings which would be fully self-teaching. The recordings were to include words or phrases in English and their foreign-language equivalents spoken by a native speaker, along with suggestions for the learner presented in English. Small handbooks were also prepared, presenting all of the content of the phonograph records, with the foreign-language content printed in a newly developed phonetic script easily read by American soldiers. At first this material was included as a supplement to the Information Branch's *Pocket Guides to Foreign Countries.* Later the language materials became so popular in the Army generally that it was decided to print them separately.

[3]This section, with minor editorial changes and some abridgment, is excerpted, with permission, from the manuscript, "History of Military Training: History of the Army Education Branch" (on file in the Historical Division, War Department Special Staff).

In 1943 the Director of the Special Services Division was made responsible for the preparation of foreign-language materials. These projects now included the language guides and accompanying phonograph recordings in a total of thirty-seven foreign languages, military phrase books in thirty-one languages, military dictionaries in twenty-two languages, and general-purpose dictionaries in nine languages. The development of these materials was assigned to the Education Branch.

Preparation of language guides and records was coordinated with that of the military phrase books which contained emergency expressions and military terminology in a form usable for interrogation of prisoners of war or for enlisting the cooperation of friendly civilians. More advanced materials were required for members of the armed forces who wished to acquire a basic knowledge of a language for their military duties or as general educational background.

In December 1942, the assistance of the American Council of Learned Societies had been obtained in the development of more advanced language courses. By early 1943, experimentation in these materials by the Council and the Education Branch had progressed to such a degree that a basic pattern could be established.

Although the Education Branch was to exercise supervisory and editorial control over the preparation of these various courses, the experimentation and writing involved in their preparation and publication was to be in cooperation with D. C. Heath and Company and the American Council of Learned Societies. A special edition of each course was to be published as a War Department *Education Manual* for the USAFI.

The basic course *Education Manuals* and accompanying sets of phonograph recordings were to contain a total vocabulary of 1,000 to 1,500 words presented in ordinary conversational situations. These self-teaching basic-course manuals were designed to be used either with phonograph recordings or with a native speaker as a guide. A special manual for the guide accompanied each basic course.

At the request of the Director of Military Training, the preparation of a language guide, phrase book, and basic course in

English for the instruction of members of Italian service units was undertaken. These so-called "reverse" materials were developed by the same method as the corresponding instructional materials in Italian for American troops. Subsequently, "reverse" basic courses for Spanish and Portuguese speakers were prepared for the Department of Commerce.

In a release prepared by the Education Branch in early 1945, descriptions of the purposes and uses of the foreign-language materials were given as follows:

> As a child learns to talk by imitating the sounds he or she hears, so members of our armed forces are taught to imitate the sounds of frequently used words and phrases. Children talk before they can write and can make themselves understood verbally even though an attempt to transfer their words to paper results in a meaningless series of words. American soldiers are learning to speak useful phrases in many languages in exactly the same way.
>
> No one can learn what a language sounds like from a printed page; therefore, the main emphasis is on an instructional phonograph record. To supplement what the learner can get through the ear, key words and phrases of the foreign language which is to be learned are printed in a phonetic or simplified spelling. Examples are given of the sound values or vowels and consonants.
>
> The soldier on foreign duty is provided with a *Language Guide,* and his organization is provided with instructional phonograph records, of the language spoken in the country where he is ordered. For most languages there are two double-faced twelve-inch records, which can be played on any phonograph. For some of the Arabic dialects there are three records. The material is entirely self-teaching, and it is possible for groups of men of 100 or less to learn everything on the records—some 150 phrases—in from six to ten hours. The records first give the English equivalent of a phrase, then twice give the phrase in the foreign language, spoken by a native speaker, with a pause each time while the learner repeats, imitating as closely as possible the pronunciation and intonation of the speaker. At the same time the learner refers to the *Language Guide,* which contains the exact text of the record. In this way, the learning is through two senses instead of one.
>
> By listening to the records six or seven times, the soldier can learn to understand and pronounce all the phrases. At the same time he learns exactly what sounds the letters of the simplified, phonetic spelling stand for, and is in a position to use the additional material at the back of the *Language Guide.* This additional material, which is not on the records, consists of some more useful phrases and a number of "fill-in" sentences—sentences

containing blanks and a list of key words which can be put in the blanks.

For those soldiers who may come into contact with speakers of any of several languages, sometimes dangerous contact, sometimes friendly, *Phrase Books* are available. These use the same means of writing the foreign language as do the *Language Guides,* but are different in some other ways. The content is designed to cover many different types of emergency, from "Halt or I'll fire!" to questions as to how much weight a bridge will carry. The questions are so worded that a native speaker can reply satisfactorily with "yes" or "no," or by signs rather than by a lengthy flow of words. The contents are arranged topically and the same arrangement holds in all the different *Phrase Books.* If a soldier has had experience with one of them, he will be able to use another efficiently since the books follow the same pattern.

Rather than turn such soldiers out on their own with nothing but the language "shot in the arm" which the various introductory materials will give them, more extensive courses are being prepared in many of the more widely used languages, to be called "Spoken French: Basic Course," and so on. These courses are designed to take up to 150 to 200 hours of working time, but are so organized that the soldier who drops out sooner will have learned something useful, and will not have wasted his time.

The basic method is the same as with the *Language Guides*—listening to phonograph records of a native speaker, or, wherever possible, to a native himself, and following with the eye the simplified spelling given in the printed material. The native speaker who is used when possible is called the Guide. A "Guide's Manual" is supplied, written in the Guide's own language. This tells him what to say and when to say it. Thus, with a few hand signals, even a native speaker who knows no English can be helpful.

There are twenty-four twelve-inch double-faced phonograph records, which accompany a little more than the first third of the Basic Course. Even when a native speaker is available, the records are useful as a second example of the language being studied, and can be listened to at odd times when a Guide might not be on hand. By the time the phonograph records have been studied thoroughly the learner's habits of pronunciation are sufficiently fixed that he can manage easily with just the written materials from then on.

The materials are self-teaching; a group can work under the direction of someone who knows nothing at all about the technique of teaching a language or a single soldier can work on his own. However, when a more experienced teacher is available he can use the same material and supplement it from his own experience.[4]

[4] U. S. War Department, Army Service Forces, Information and Education Division, "Language Goes to War" (Mimeographed; Army Education Branch, February 17, 1945).

G.I. ROUNDTABLES

The discussion technique, as a means of education, was used extensively in off-duty programs. As early as December 1942 an informal survey of educational activities in the first four service commands revealed a considerable number of active discussion groups. Such groups needed good materials for carrying on their programs. Reports from overseas emphasized a similar need for discussion materials.

Early in 1943, a canvass of available discussion materials was made. Examination of the results indicated that a modification of a monthly booklet being distributed to civilian groups by *Reader's Digest* more nearly met the needs of military personnel than anything else then available. The publishers of the *Digest* offered to provide a special edition of this discussion booklet for trial use within the Army without charge. One edition of this experimental booklet entitled *Camp Talk* was distributed in March 1943 to appropriate officers in four service commands. Officers receiving this booklet had agreed in advance to supervise its use, and had been given special instructions for reporting the reaction of military personnel. Their reports showed widespread approval of both the form and content of the publication. Because of the uncertainties regarding the consequences of offering discussion materials which probably would present at times very pungent or very controversial points of view, it was decided to discontinue this project.

Later developments in the preparation of discussion materials waited, therefore, until the summer of 1943, when reports from overseas again emphasized the need for them.

In October 1943, the Education Branch concluded arrangements with the American Historical Association, according to a plan approved by the Secretary of War, for the preparation of a series of pamphlets to be used in off-duty discussion. When the first of these pamphlets were ready for publication in the late spring of 1944, it was decided to issue them under the title *G.I. Roundtable*.

Off-duty discussion, utilizing *G.I. Roundtable* pamphlets, was a voluntary educational activity conducted in accordance with the desire of commanding officers concerned. In establishing policies for the conduct of voluntary discussion groups, attention was drawn to the fact that partisan efforts to promote special causes were not in harmony with the objectives recommended for discussion programs. These objectives were to strengthen morale by assisting the men to recognize, analyze, and understand problems about which they felt concern; to furnish background facts which would permit intelligent consideration of such problems; and to offer opportunity for orderly exchange and adjustment of individual opinions. Voluntary discussion groups, having these objectives, were recommended to all Army units operating educational programs.

G.I. Roundtable manuals were made available with the suggestion that discussion leaders and members of voluntary discussion groups read them and use them for reference. The *Guide for Discussion Leaders* was the basic manual and listed objectives of the program; it suggested techniques of organizing and administering discussion groups; and it described methods of selecting discussion leaders, choosing subjects, and conducting forums, informal discussions, panel discussions, symposiums, and debates.

Each of the other *G.I. Roundtable* discussion manuals contained objective, accurate information presented in a clear and direct style, covering a subject of personal, community, national, or international importance. Subjects of current interest dealt with in these pamphlets were suggested by the Education Branch on the basis of reports from the Research Branch and other data indicating the interests of military personnel.

Suggested subjects approved by the Director of the Morale Services Division were submitted to the American Historical Association. The required manuscripts were then prepared by the Historical Service Board, a special editorial board set up for the purpose. The method of preparing discussion pamphlets followed this sequence: subjects were suggested to the Historical Service Board by the War Department; drafts of manuscripts were prepared by authors chosen by the Board; manuscripts were submitted to the War Department for acceptance and official approval; artwork was prepared; the pamphlets were published and distributed to overseas branches. At the peak of the program, usually two hundred thousand copies of each pamphlet were being printed. Later this number was reduced slightly, as overseas theaters printed their own copies from proofs or type which was sent to them.

Publication of *G.I. Roundtable* discussion pamphlets on current controversial subjects developed two special problems during the last half of 1944. The pamphlet *Shall We Have Universal Military Training?* was not distributed, because decision was made that it would be unwise to circulate a discussion pamphlet on a controversial subject on which the War Department and the national administration had adopted a definite policy. *Can War Marriages Be Made to Work?* was printed in only 100,000 copies and circulated only in continental United States, because discussion of the subject might injure the morale of troops overseas.

Early in 1945 the Chief of the Army Education Branch returned after several weeks overseas and expressed concern over the unfavorable impression many American troops were receiving of the peoples of some European nations. About the same time, various newspapers carried articles on the disturbing situation developing as a result of misunderstanding between American troops and the people of certain countries, particularly France. It was decided, therefore, that discussion pamphlets be prepared on various foreign countries.

Altogether, twenty-seven *G.I. Roundtables* were prepared and distributed. Their titles are as follows:

Guide for Discussion Leaders
What Is Propaganda?
What Shall Be Done about Germany after the War?
What Shall Be Done with War Criminals?
How Can We Prevent Future Wars?
How Shall Lend-Lease Accounts Be Settled?
Is the Good-Neighbor Policy a Success?
What Has Alaska to Offer Postwar Pioneers?
Will There Be Work for All?
Why Co-ops? What Are They? How Do They Work?
Do You Want Your Wife to Work after the War?
Can War Marriages Be Made to Work?
Shall I Build a House?
What Will Your Town Be Like?
Shall I Take Up Farming?

Does It Pay to Borrow?
Will the French Republic Live Again?
Our British Ally
Our Chinese Ally
The Balkans—Many Peoples, Many Problems
Australia: Our Neighbor "Down Under"
What Future for the Islands of the Pacific?
Our Russian Ally
G.I. Radio Roundtable
What Shall Be Done with Japan after Victory?
Shall I Go Back to School?
What Lies Ahead for the Philippines?

A discussion of the techniques used to make the discussion program effective will be found in chapter v.

NAVY[5]

VOLUNTARY CLASSES

As has been mentioned before, the heart of the Educational Services program was classroom instruction on a voluntary, off-duty, tuition-free basis. The method by which an Educational Services officer was to organize these voluntary, off-duty classes is described in the *Educational Services Manual* which was distributed to all ESO's.[6] This manual was issued late in the war and was not as useful to Educational Services officers as earlier publication would have made it. These steps in establishing the voluntary class program seem worth summarizing here.

(1) *Determine educational interests.* The success of a voluntary class program will depend largely upon offering classes in which the men are interested; if possible, therefore, a preliminary survey of educational interests should be taken before organizing the program. The best way of taking such a survey is to distribute a questionnaire to all hands; this may list a number of possible classes so that men may check those they would like to attend and also provide space for men to write in classes not listed. The questionnaire may also ask how many hours a week the men would like to spend in the class program, and for other information which would help to determine the mechanical details of scheduling. . . . The best way to insure a broad distribution is to distribute the questionnaires to the pay

[5] Use has been made throughout this section of the "Educational Services Section," "Administrative History of the Bureau of Naval Personnel" (MS on file in the Office of Naval History, U. S. Navy Department).
[6] U. S. Navy Department, Bureau of Naval Personnel, NavPers 16963 (Washington: Educational Services Section, Bureau of Naval Personnel), pp. 12-25.

lines, chow lines, or prior to movies. . . . If it is impractical to use the questionnaire method, some of the same information may be gathered by tabulating the results of counseling interviews or by taking informal polls in any kind of group meetings. It would also be wise to check the rates of men attached to a particular ship or station and to consider the possibility of offering related courses. . . . A useful procedure followed on some bases has been the establishment of an educational counsel made up of one man from each division, chosen for his educational background, his interest in the educational program, and his ability to secure the confidence of the men in his division. . . .(2) *Develop a curriculum.* Either a survey of interest or the experience of other ES centers should provide the basis for initiating a new program of voluntary classes. . . . Here are a few special considerations in deciding upon class offerings: (*a*) experience shows that classes designed to increase general knowledge and cultural attainments are popular, so don't overload the curriculum with courses designed purely for academic credits or vocational experience. . . ; (*b*) the cultivation of a hobby is a worthy project and is often a popular one. . . ; (*c*) it has often proved popular to adapt a few classes to local conditions and opportunities. . . ; (*d*) there are local educational institutions offering classes to servicemen, so try to avoid duplicating their offerings. (Avoid, too, running classes that cover the same ground as any set up by the training or education officer for training in Navy rates. (3) *Procure instructors.* . . . The success of the voluntary class program will be determined in large measure by the qualifications of the instructors. Unlike a public school situation, students in adult education classes are free to drop out any time they feel their instruction is poor or dull. Men selected as instructors in the ES program ought first of all to be enthusiastic about teaching; they should regard teaching as a pleasant task and they should really want to be of help to their shipmates who attend the classes. Instructors should also have adequate technical qualifications; particularly in vocational type classes it has been found that practical experience in the field being taught is at least as important as educational training in that field. . . . On almost every station of any size competent instructors can be found, even for the wide variety of courses usually offered in the ES program. . . . Here are some ways of uncovering teaching talent: (*a*) Provide in the educational interest questionnaire a place for those interested in teaching volunteers. (*b*) Make use of the bulletin board, plan of the day, screen slides, and general announcements to request volunteers. Permanent posters may be left in BOQ's, clubs, and enlisted barracks; announcements of the need for instructors in particular subjects may be most effective for quick results. (*c*) See the personnel officer and request his permission to go through the files of NavPers 609 (Enlisted Personnel Qualifications Card) and NavPers 305 (Officers Qualifications Record Jackets) to discover former teachers. (*d*) Contact personal friends. (*e*) In some areas it may be possible to secure civilians as instructors if they are interested in the project on a voluntary basis. Natives of the area may be especially helpful for language classes and area study. . . . (4) *Provide necessary gear.* Teaching takes tools, textbooks, manuals, outlines, films, training aids, and so on. Education manuals and reprints of standard texts and others designed to be self-teaching are available from the ES Section. . . . Films adaptable for class use may be available from film libraries. . . . (5) *Set up classrooms.* At overseas bases there is often a shortage of classrooms and the ESO's first step is to make a survey of the base to discover rooms that might be used for classes and then to contact the first lieutenant or other officer charged with assignments of gear and space. (6) *Advertise the classes.* The extent of advertising given a class must be determined by available facilities. Classes should not be over-advertised if classrooms are small, supplies of necessary gear are low or instructors prefer small groups. All profitable media should be used in publicizing the class offerings; stories and announcements in ship or station paper, radio, memos, movie slides, talks, bull horn, local AFRS branch, bulletin boards, etc. . . . any advertising of a class should include: (*a*) name of the course, (*b*) a short and nontechnical description of the course, (*c*) prerequisities and recommended backgrounds, (*d*) probable length of the course, (*e*) scholastic level, (*f*) date and time of first meeting, (*g*) place of meeting with a complete description of the location. (7) *Develop a schedule.* Classes must be scheduled when personnel are free to attend them, whether in on-duty or off-duty time. Check such matters as hours for chow, movies, watches, and special events. . . . Classes lasting from ten to sixty days have proven successful . . . two or three meetings a week, with one- or two-hour periods have been fairly standard. . . . (8) *Enroll the students.* Men may be registered for classes by interviews, by telephone, or at the first class meeting. The best method, when practicable, is by personal interviews. . . . (9) *Supervise the program.* The ESO in the voluntary class program is primarily an administrator. To do his job properly, he must do a certain amount of supervising—not through "snooping," but by making occasional class visits. In addition, he will be wise to hold regular faculty meetings to discuss various problems with the instructors of the whole class program. Regular reports on enrollment, attendance, and achievement in the program should also be required. . . . (10) *Provide testing.* Many men will enroll in voluntary classes primarily to obtain credits for postwar academic work. Others may need to have this possibility explained to them . . . the introductory talks should also make clear that men need *not* take the course for credit of any kind and that the taking of the end-of-course test is voluntary. This will put at ease those who might shy away from the idea of being tested. . . . (11) *Anticipate accreditation.* The ESO should take two steps . . . which will facilitate the application of students for such credit: (*a*) See to it that USAFI tests are given and that results are on permanent file at the USAFI Headquarters at Madison, Wisconsin. . . . and (*b*) provide an outline of the course for the permanent file of the ES Section, so that civilian schools can be referred to the ES Section for that information. . . . (12) *Recognize achievement.* Any officer or enlisted man completing a voluntary class is entitled to an ES Certificate of Completion, and the ESO should include a statement concerning completed class work in a man's permanent service record or an officer's jacket. . . . (13) *Commend instructors.* Those who do a good job of teaching in the class program and devote their own free time to it should receive commendations for their work . . . the best procedure is for the ESO to initiate a letter of commendation for the commanding officer's signature. . . . (14) *Maintain office records* . . . among the records that should be kept by every ESO as a part of standard procedure are these: (*a*) student's enrollment cards . . . (*b*) instructor cards . . . (*c*) class record cards . . . (*d*) course outline . . . (*e*) achievement records . . . (*f*) commendation letters . . . (*g*) class schedule. . . . The ESO should also keep careful records of supplies needed, on order, in stock. . . .

There are no available statistics as to the number of classes in various subjects offered as part of the voluntary off-duty program. The opinion of those who were intimately concerned with the program indicated that classes in mathematics (review of arithmetic, algebra, trigonometry, geometry), languages (Spanish, French, German, and that of the immediate area), history (American, European, Far Eastern, World), business (bookkeeping, accounting, business law), science (physics, radio psychology), vocational subjects (auto-mechanics, drafting, blueprint reading), and avocational subjects (photography, public speaking) were among the most in demand and were probably most widely offered.

According to the Educational Services Section, the completion rate of the voluntary, off-duty classes was high. "A study of some 250 classes, enrolling about 5,000 students, taken from official reports, indicates that between 60 and 65 percent of students who signed up for a class completed it. Taking into account the noncompletion due to transfer and especial duties, the number who finished is remarkably high." [7]

SELF-INSTRUCTION

In addition to the other programs operated by the Educational Services Section, educational materials for self-instruction

[7] U. S. Navy Department, Bureau of Naval Personnel, "The Educational Services Program" (MS on file in the Office of Naval History, U. S. Navy Department), pp. 10-11.

were made available to personnel of the Navy. These materials were *Educational Manuals,* either reprints of standard texts with paper covers and reduced margins or books especially prepared or edited for military personnel. In general, a man who procured texts for self-study did so because he could not attend an off-duty class or program or because correspondence instruction was not practical. It is estimated that, during 1944, well over half a million men availed themselves of these manuals to continue their studies.[8]

A serviceman who completed this type of instruction was privileged to make application to USAFI for an appropriate examination in order to demonstrate mastery of the subject.

The advantage of self-study materials for naval personnel is obvious, for if a man found himself suddenly detached for duty elsewhere, the textbooks could be taken with him and his study continued. Or if he were assigned to duties that prevented attendance at class meetings, the self-instruction texts permitted him to continue to work and resume the class later at the level the class had then attained without an undue loss in continuity. Furthermore, this particular type of text made a valuable and useful addition to a station's or a ship's library.

MARINE CORPS

The emphasis in the off-duty educational program of the Marine Corps was somewhat different than that of the Navy. As has been indicated, the Navy considered voluntary classes as the very heart of its program. The marines, however, considered these as secondary to the correspondence phase.

Special Services officers were advised that their first step in organizing a class program was to determine (1) the needs of the command, and (2) the needs and interests of the men.[9] Initially, the approval of the commanding officer had to be obtained and a check of the policy file made to make certain that the entire educational program was within the bounds of established policy. After estimating the morale, training, and educa-

[8] "The Educational Services Program," p. 23.

[9] U. S. Marine Corps, *A Guide in Organizing an Off-Duty Education Program* (Washington: Education Section, Welfare Division, Special Services Branch, Headquarters, U. S. Marine Corps), p. 1.

EDUCATION SECTION, WELFARE DIVISION

EDUCATIONAL INTEREST SURVEY FORM

Name	Rank	Serial Number
Station	Organization	Date

Principal Military Occupation

1. *School preparation*
   a) Highest grade attained in elementary school..........
   in high school..........
   b) Years in college.......... Degree held..........
   c) Major field of study in college..........
   d) Do you wish to continue your education and obtain a high school diploma? .... A college degree?..........
2. *Civilian experience*
   a) Principal civilian occupation (job)..........
   b) Do you anticipate returning to this (job) occupation?..........
   c) If not this occupation what do you anticipate?..........
3. *Educational opportunities*
   (Consult MCI and USAFI Catalogs)
   a) *Marine Corps Institute* (correspondence courses). List below the courses you would like to take in order of preference:
   b) *U. S. Armed Forces Institute* (correspondence or self-teaching courses). List below the courses you would like in order of preference:
   c) *Class Instruction.* Perhaps you would like to attend a class in your off-duty time. List below the subjects you would like to study in the order of preference:
   d) *Discussion Group.* Would you like to join with a small group of marines for the purpose of discussing interesting questions? Suggest some subjects that interest you:
   e) *Clubs.* Would you like to be in an informal club with men interested in the same work that appeals to you? For example, a Railroaders Club. Name the club that interests you:
   f) *Movies.* What educational subjects or titles would interest you?
4. Could you assist in an educational program by teaching a class, leading a discussion group, or taking charge of a club?..........
   If so, what kind?..........

Note: If you have suggestions as to an off-duty education program, or wish to supply additional information, write on the reverse side of this sheet.

FIG. 7.—Educational Interest Survey Form used by the Marine Corps.

tional needs of the command, the needs and interest of the men were to be determined for off-duty classes as well as other parts of the education program by means of an "interest survey." Figure 7 on page 118 is an example of what was used.

For a text the *Education Manual* previously described was used. In addition, Special Services officers made available self-teaching manuals to men who wished to pursue a subject by themselves. The manuals made available to the Marine Corps by the end of the war are classified in Table 8.

TABLE 8

EDUCATION MANUALS MADE AVAILABLE TO MARINE CORPS PERSONNEL

TYPE OF SUBJECT	ST*	HQ†	CQ‡	C§	TOTAL
Agriculture	4	1	1	....	6
Business	15	10	6	....	31
English	7	1	....	2	10
Mathematics	12	1	5	....	18
Biological science	....	2	....	....	2
Physical science	5	6	....	2	13
Chemistry	....	....	1	....	1
Social studies	13	4	1	....	18
Psychology	....	4	....	....	4
Mechanical and technical	5	13	1	....	19
Spoken languages	15	....	....	....	15
Total	76	42	15	4	137

* ST—High school level, self-teaching textbook
† HQ—High school level, standard textbook
‡ CQ—College level, standard textbooks
§ C—Junior college level, general education

In addition to these manuals the Marine Corps Institute cooperated in the group-study program. The policy of MCI in this direction was stated as follows:

The Marine Corps Institute will require an application for enrollment from every prospective student, whether he is a member of an organized study group or is to study on his own. All student lesson papers must be submitted to MCI for correction. Should a student be transferred while a group-study class is in progress, he may continue study on his own. Group enrollees may be given a final examination as a group when the class schedule is completed.[10]

[10] U. S. Marine Corps, Marine Corps Institute, *MCI Bulletin* (Washington: Marine Corps Institute), pp. 16-17.

COAST GUARD

The voluntary classes of the Navy were utilized by the Coast Guard wherever possible. Since Coast Guard personnel were frequently stationed near naval facilities, such utilization constituted a large part of the Coast Guard's voluntary class program.

Where it was necessary to organize a class especially for Coast Guard personnel, the education officer was instructed to arrange for an instructor and meeting-place and to apply to the Navy Educational Services officer for textbooks. Instructors, the directive pointed out, were to be obtained from whatever military or civilian sources were available. Care was to be exercised in avoiding duplication of classes already organized by the Navy where Coast Guard personnel could conveniently be enrolled in such classes.[11]

The Coast Guard encouraged the use of the self-study technique through the use of the educational manuals prepared and distributed by USAFI. From April 1, 1945, to June 30, 1945, 880 coast guardsmen were newly enrolled with USAFI for self-teaching courses as compared to 1,795 for correspondence courses. Even the start of demobilization did not show a marked drop in interest in self-study, for from July 1, 1945, to September 30, 1945, 761 coast guardsmen enrolled for the first time for self-teaching courses as compared to 1,398 who signed up for correspondence courses.

In May 1945, the Coast Guard announced a special off-duty program for officers. This permitted officers, with the approval of headquarters, to enroll in private institutions for certain courses, the cost to be borne by the Coast Guard. The course selected either had to meet a specific need of the Coast Guard or "improve the officer's general professional knowledge or round out his or her background in such a manner as to increase his or her usefulness to the Coast Guard." [12] Public speaking, business management, accounting, and safety were cited as typical of the latter type of course.

[11] U. S. Coast Guard, *Personnel Bulletin,* Nos. 27-45, 16 March 1945.
[12] *Personnel Bulletin,* Nos. 44-45, *op. cit.,* 9 May 1945.

V. ARMY POST-HOSTILITIES SCHOOLS[1]

MENTION HAS already been made of the Army Education Program which was designed to help civilians in uniform learn how to be civilians again. This program falls within the scope of the present study because it was voluntary and rested upon felt needs and interests of the persons concerned. It does not, however, fit within two of the other limitations outlined earlier: in some cases it was on- rather than off-duty, and its most significant development occurred after the cessation of hostilities. Nonetheless, because of its great interest and its relevance to the problems of civilian adult education, the program will be briefly described here.

NEED FOR POST-HOSTILITIES EDUCATION

The experience of the American Expeditionary Force after World War I provided valuable background for planning a sound Army education program for the post-hostilities period of World War II. Experience demonstrated amply that without an adequate substitute for military duty, administered with vigor and conviction, cases of absence without leave, desertion, insubordination, petty misdemeanors, and even serious crimes mounted week by week. This experience also showed that "busy work" was not an adequate substitute for progressive training. Forced military drill, when the reason for the drill had largely or completely disappeared, was no more than busy work, and amusement and recreation was not likely to restrain natural restlessness.

The only dependable answer was an education program that would prepare military personnel for resumption of life and work as civilians. The Army Education Program for the post-hostilities period was worked out to supply this constructive training.

Early thinking on the AEP envisaged a program which would occupy a major part of each working day for troops

[1]This section, with minor editorial changes and some abridgment, is largely excerpted, with permission, from the manuscript, "History of Military Training: History of the Army Education Branch" (on file in the Historical Division, War Department Special Staff).

whose essential military duties had been reduced to necessary housekeeping and guard duties for their own units. For military personnel serving in an Army of occupation or for units with similar definitely assigned military duties, it was contemplated that the education program would be adjusted to consume only such working time as could be spared from military duties.

While maintenance of morale and discipline were the immediate objectives of this post-hostilities program, its long-range objective was the preparation of military personnel for civilian life. Every individual should be equipped, it was believed, with one or more useful vocational or professional skills or with basic education leading to such skills. In addition, it was believed that AEP should reorient individuals to civilian problems, opportunities, and ways of thinking; and it should keep Army personnel informed on the Army's plans for them during the period of demobilization and about opportunities which service personnel might expect.

AEP courses, it was believed, should be of two types: general courses of value to all individuals on their return to civilian life, and specialized and vocational courses designed to develop individual qualifications and provide specific training for civilian opportunities for employment or further study. General training for preparing all Army personnel for returning to civilian life, it was contemplated, should include (*a*) facts about jobs which Army personnel might expect to find open after their release from the service, requirements of those jobs, and training necessary to qualify for them; (*b*) information about national, state, and local problems likely to confront military personnel when they should return as civilians, with an explanation of the historical, geographical, and economic backgrounds of these problems; and (*c*) knowledge of international problems facing the United States, similarly presented against backgrounds of their historical, geographical, and economic developments. Specialized training designed for individual qualifications and for developing specific skills should, it was believed, cover a wide range of carefully selected courses. These should include literacy training and vocational training, employing on-the-job training as well as more formal classroom instruction.

Special facilities would be required in order to carry out an extensive post-hostilities educational program. One requirement would be a comprehensive system of schools for military personnel in areas where large numbers of troops were likely to be held for considerable periods awaiting demobilization. These institutions would include *unit schools* offering literacy training and general education at elementary and secondary levels. They would also include centralized *technical schools* offering vocational or technical training. *University centers* would likewise be needed, established either as Army universities resembling the University at Beaune in 1919, or in cooperation with established foreign civilian institutions.

AEP planners recognized also that this system of schools would require a large staff of qualified supervisors, with additional training schools necessary for the preparation of this staff. The supervisory staff, it was believed, should be drawn from commissioned personnel already in the service, with steps taken at an early date to procure and train them. It was contemplated that teachers could be selected within divisions and units from commissioned and enlisted personnel qualified through training and experience acquired either as civilians or in the Army. It was expected that teachers would receive the guidance of supervisors selected and specially trained for this purpose.

Formation of an effective AEP required more than schools, supervisors, and teachers. Equally necessary was a coordinated system of classification and guidance for individual Army personel, through adaptation of the Army classification system in such a way as to include a translation of civilian and military aptitudes into prospective civilian skills. Necessary also were accurate and comprehensive records of educational achievements. Still another need already substantially provided for through the work of the USAFI editorial staff was a stock of good teaching materials.

PLANNING THE ARMY EDUCATION PROGRAM

The Morale Services Division was authorized in November 1943 to formulate policies and to supervise the preparation of plans for general education, technical education, and training in civilian vocations. Military personnel affected were those designated for rehabilitation or discharge, those whose military duties had been reduced before actual cessation of hostilities, and those in all organizations after hostilities terminated.

A Special Projects Branch of the Morale Services Division was immediately authorized to coordinate Army Education Program planning with other interested agencies of the War Department and to provide additional personnel and organization for the work. The Special Projects Branch worked under the supervision of the Chief of the Education Branch.

In May 1944, a statement of tentative policies was issued for the guidance of personnel responsible for the AEP. This statement anticipated that, when hostilities ceased, the military training program would be greatly reduced and that the time of military personnel would be largely filled by nonmilitary training including AEP. The plan provided for unit schools, technical schools, and college and university study centers in inactive theaters in accordance with interests and needs of military personnel and with the facilities available. Courses were to cover the range of general and specialized training. The plan also provided for group and individual assistance in choosing courses, and reorientation on problems significant to military personnel being demobilized.

Instructional materials and equipment needed to operate the AEP were listed in this statement. These included textbooks, language guides, and such other materials as movies, filmstrips, radio programs, *G.I. Roundtable* discussion pamphlets, and tests. Materials available for distribution through USAFI were listed and described in a looseleaf *Catalog of Publications* for the Army Education Program begun in June 1944. Provision was made for supplements to this catalog as additional materials became available.

During June 1944, work was under way on translating demobilization training plans into necessary administrative regulations and organization plans for the selection, training, and assignment of supervisory, guidance, and teaching personnel of the AEP. In August 1944, plans for the AEP became part of the official War Department plan for readjustment of military personnel after the defeat of Germany. A more detailed outline of this program was published on September 15. This provided that the Commanding General, Army Service Forces, should arrange for the publication of a catalog of courses for the Army Education Program and a manual for education officers, in order to implement this program further.

The manual for education officers, *Army Education Program for Inactive Theaters,* was published in November. It provided information necessary to staff officers in the planning and supervision of education programs. It also presented a suggested instructor-training course.

A system of educational records and reports for the AEP was prepared late in 1944. Objectives of these records, as later published, were threefold: (1) to provide a summary statement of the participation of each student in the AEP so that his records could be evaluated intelligently by a civilian educational institution which the student might later desire to enter; (2) to furnish prospective employers with documentary evidence of educational achievements, occupational skills, and experience acquired by each student participating in the AEP; and (3) to provide a uniform system of records and reports for all military units participating in the AEP.

Both the European theater of operations and the Mediterranean theater of operations submitted requisitions late in 1944 for classroom supplies for use in AEP schools. Since hundreds of schools were expected to be established in these areas, it was recognized that huge quantities of such supplies would be needed. By the end of 1944 adequate supplies of these materials had been shipped to both European and Mediterranean theaters to start operations of the AEP.

During the fall of 1944, ETO and MTO were particularly concerned with the planning phases of the AEP. Research was under way to help education officers: (1) determine what courses most interested military personnel; (2) find potential instructors for unit schools; (3) form a basis for educational advisement; and (4) inform military personnel about the AEP and interest them in enrolling in the courses that would benefit them most individually.

Considerable attention was given during the last half of 1944 to the matter of providing reliable information through the AEP on postwar employment problems and possibilities, and relating these to the in-service education and experiences of military personnel. By the end of December, various materials were in some stage of development, procurement, or distribution. These included the booklet *Your Postwar Career;* the mimeographed *Educational Advisory Manual;* an education film, *Your Next Job;* the Vocational Information Kit referred to earlier; the *G.I. Roundtable* entitled *Will There Be Work for All?* and an *Occupational Brief* series.

The first half of 1945 witnessed the first actual operation of the post-hostilities Army Education Program in the European and Mediterranean theaters. Plans developed during 1944 were revised to keep pace with changing conditions within the theaters. By April the early end of hostilities in those theaters was apparent. A wide variety of materials and information concerning the opening and conduct of the program had been prepared.

Under theater plans, participation in the duty-time AEP was limited to personnel to be retained for a continued service in their current commands and to those to be demobilized. Units to be transferred to another theater or to the United States and units to be reorganized were not designated for participation in the duty-time program. Participation in the off-duty AEP continued to be available to the personnel of all units.

The selection and training of key personnel for AEP schools was in progress during the entire first half of 1945. AEP staff schools and instructor-training schools were in operation. Qualifications of military personnel were surveyed to locate potential administrative and instructional personnel for use in the program. Early plans were based on utilization of only military personnel, but it was found necessary to recruit civilian specialists from the United States in order to obtain personnel familiar with the most recent developments in the various fields of work to be offered in the university study centers and the centralized technical school.

An attempt was made to spread the procurement among as many colleges and over as wide a geographical area as possible in order that students might have the benefits of different points of view and contacts with representatives of as many different institutions as possible. It was also considered desirable not to place too heavy a burden on any one college. University presidents and deans were consulted as to the availability of candidates and in general cooperated with the Army Education Branch in releasing men. At first a limit of three instructors from any one college was established, but it was later decided to change this ceiling in cases where college authorities found it possible to release a larger number of instructors.

While the war was in progress, the AEP met with resistance on the part of many officers who were wholly concentrated on the prosecution of combat. To them the program had a very low priority and was in fact dangerous in that it might distract attention from the essential business of fighting. It is not surprising, therefore, that most theaters were not well-prepared to put the program into operation after VE and VJ Days. The Mediterranean theater was a notable exception.

THE PROGRAM IN OPERATION

The Army university center [2] in MTO was at Florence, Italy, in connection with the University of Florence. It opened July 9, 1945. In the ETO, two centers were operated—one at Shrivenham, England, opening on July 30, 1945, and the other at Biarritz, France, opening on August 21, 1945. All three universities were operated for about six months. Other education centers were opened in Austria, the Hawaiian Islands, the Philippines, Okinawa, Japan and elsewhere after VJ Day.

Warton American Technical School at Warton, England, which opened September 15, 1945, was the only technical school to be opened in Europe although several were operated in Japan after VJ Day. Additional schools could not be opened because of the difficulties in sending shop equipment and vocational-

[2] For excellent descriptions of Army university centers, see Walter Crosby Eells, "How Mussolini Provided for a GI University," *The Educational Record,* XXVII (April 1946), 178-88; and John Dale Russell, "Biarritz American University," *Higher Education,* II (January 15, 1946).

education equipment to overseas destinations. Warton enrolled four thousand students in twenty-one trade courses, each eight weeks long. Primarily a refresher school for men of the skilled trades, Warton had on its faculty nearly two hundred men from American industry.

While it is known that a number of unit schools were established in ETO shortly after VE Day, no comprehensive data are available concerning their enrollments or the variety of courses offered. In MTO there were sixty-six duty-time and forty-five off-duty unit schools in operation in June 1945. These schools enrolled a total of 20,962 students in 161 different courses and on-the-job training assignments. This work required the services of approximately 1,000 instructors, who were largely selected from military personnel available within the units participating. It is believed that altogether there were more than 2,000 unit schools at one time or another in various places. The descriptions in chapter iv of off-duty classes and schools give the reader a conception of the character of the unit schools.

Immediately following VE Day, an intensive program to acquaint military personnel with the AEP was conducted in ETO and MTO. Considerable publicity concerning the program also appeared in the press in the United States. This publicity naturally came to the attention of some military personnel whose units, for military reasons, were not designated for participation in the program, and resulted in some cases in expressions of disappointment from these soldiers and others interested in their welfare. A somewhat similar situation developed among other individuals who were impatient for the program to get under way.

In the European and Mediterranean theaters by February 1, 1946, 35,000 had attended the university centers in Florence, Biarritz, and Shrivenham, and the Technical School at Warton. These centers were the apex of the program and were unanimously praised. Thirty thousand took part in the Training within Civilian Agencies program which also received wide acclaim. An estimated 500,000 had to some degree been affected by the unit school program.

The AEP did not reach the full stature intended primarily because the war against Japan ended sooner than had been expected. The program was based on early War Department plans for redeployment and demobilization. At that time it was assumed that victory over Japan would not follow victory in Europe for at least a year, that it would be impossible for shipping reasons to return and discharge more than half a million men a month at the maximum, and that the process of replacement of veterans by selective service would be continuous and orderly. None of these assumptions was confirmed by later events. VJ Day followed VE Day by three months, the demobilization figures for December 1945 exceeded one million, and Selective Service was not making necessary replacements in the fall of 1945.

The sudden ending of the war created enormous problems of transfer and demobilization of men. The constant public pressure prevented any breathing spell in which order could be created and maintained. What General Eisenhower called the "near hysteria" of demobilization not only drove the importance of occupation forces out of the heads of the civilians and the soldiers, but also removed a keystone in the structure on which AEP was built. This keystone was that both the public and the Army would be concerned about the adjustment of the returning soldier to civilian life and particularly about his chances for a job. Had this concern been even a fraction as intense as the desire to get the troops home, many of the administrative problems would no doubt have been solved.

VI. ORIENTATION AND INFORMATION

EXPERIENCE in World War II has demonstrated conclusively that one of the major problems in the rapid mobilization and effective maintenance of a citizen army is that of making each man in uniform conscious of the reason he is in service, who his enemies are, who his country's allies are, and of his personal importance as a member of the armed services of the United States. Military leaders became increasingly aware as World War II became a global conflict that morale based on understanding was important.[1] Evidence mounted on every side to show that a well-oriented and well-informed soldier, sailor, marine, or coast guardsman was a more valuable fighter than one who was not. It became apparent, too, that initial orientation provided in basic and recruit training was more effective when followed up with orientation and information activities in overseas camps and bases, close to the battlefronts of the world.

To meet the broad needs for orientation materials, the motion picture industry, professional organizations of scholars, artists and illustrators, radio script writers and actors, and many other technicians devoted an increasing amount of time and talent. As a result of these efforts and despite weaknesses in the orientation programs due primarily to the more insistent demands of military necessity, American armed forces in World War II were vastly better informed than their predecessors in World War I or most of their allies in World War II.

ARMY[2]

Throughout World War II, orientation efforts worked toward the mental conditioning of military personnel. As time went on, six objectives were stressed. The soldier should (1) know why he fights, (2) know his enemies, (3) know his allies, (4) know

[1]For further discussion of the problem of morale and orientation which faced the armed services and the efforts being made to solve it, see "Army Orientation: To Make Men Think about Why They Fight," *Fortune,* XXIX (March 1944), 150-55.

[2]This section, with minor editorial changes and some abridgment, is excerpted, with permission, from the manuscript, "History of Military Training: Army Orientation" (on file in the Historical Division, War Department Special Staff).

the news and its significance, (5) know and have pride in his outfit and personal mission, and (6) know and have faith in the United States and its future.

EARLY ORIENTATION EFFORTS

In June 1942, the orientation course given in basic training, which was instrumental in orienting troops in Army Ground Forces, Army Service Forces, and Army Air Forces, became an Army Service Forces function under the direction of Special Service. Following this transfer the work done by the Army orientation course was divided between two sub-branches, Education and Information. Education was responsible for administering the introductory lectures and for arranging the lectures by civilians. Information was responsible for the publication of *Newsmap* and for the production of the orientation films. This lasted until October of 1942, when the Chief of the Orientation Section of the Education Branch moved over to the Orientation Section of the Information Branch. The Army Orientation Course remained a section of the Information Branch until September of 1943 when Orientation became a separate branch.

The high importance of orientation was not immediately recognized by the General Staff. Thus, to do a continually better job, the Special Service Division availed itself of the facilities of its Research Branch to keep a constant check on the effectiveness of its programs and materials. During the summer of 1942, for example, the Research Branch completed a report on the effectiveness of orientation lectures and films. This report, typical of many prepared by the Branch, covered "the experimental comparison of the usual lecture-method presentation and of presentation of comparable material by means of motion picture film with accompanying commentary." Effectiveness was defined in the light of one or both of two educational functions: (1) to increase the enlisted man's store of knowledge of factual information on a subject itself; and (2) to change the men's attitudes and opinions in a desired direction—for instance, to improve their regard for one of our allies.

For the purposes of the study, a film with both sufficient factual material and sufficient emotional impact to effect both kinds of changes was assembled from news films and compared with the results of four different lectures given in such a way that they paralleled the film. A pre-test and post-test were prepared for three groups of men—a group which saw the film, a group which heard the lecture, and a control group which saw or heard neither. The results of the study showed that "both factual information and emotional attitudes are influenced to a greater degree by a brief film presentation than by the usual form of presentation by lecture, and that it requires an outstanding lecturer to equal the film in effectiveness." The report suggested that a combination of film and lecture or film supplemented by questions and discussions would prove more effective than either medium used alone. The fact that films were a superior medium had long been known, but the study revealed that an *excellent* lecturer could still match and at times outstrip a film. The combination of the two was finally settled upon by Orientation, with the result that orientation officers were supplied with brief introductory materials for films, and the post-showing discussion was encouraged as the best method of getting full benefit from a film.

In this careful manner Orientation documented the use of its materials and program. It continued to use the Research Branch studies to check the effectiveness of media and discover attitudinal areas in which specific orientation was needed. One basic state of affairs revealed by Research Branch studies was the relatively low level of the informational background of inductees in the area of international affairs. It was necessary for Orientation to prepare to remedy this basic lack even before and while trying to improve attitudes toward the job facing our Army in 1942. The need to instruct troops in the causes of the war was present, and surveys by the Research Branch on over 15,000 men (representative of 500,000 in the Army Ground Forces) showed that lack of understanding of the war and lack of conviction about the national objectives were still fairly widespread and were sufficient to constitute a serious handicap in training.

Orientation in 1942 consisted of five features: a course of fifteen lectures of background information called Introductory Phase, a nebulous program of current information called Current Phase, a film program still largely in the planning and production stage, *Newsmap,* and intermittent lectures by civilians. It was then planned (1) that the background lectures of Introductory Phase be replaced by seven films to be shown on training time; (2) that Current Phase orientation be continued because "the weekly or more frequent discussion of current events and related military problems by company officers has become an accepted and popular feature of training in many commands, tending to strengthen the bonds of confidence and understanding between officers and men;" (3) that the film program proceed; (4) that *Newsmap* be continued and expanded because it was keenly stimulating to military discussion; and (5) that the policy of employing civilian lecturers be discontinued.

By the summer of 1942 the orientation program had received considerable public attention, most of it favorable. Yet the initial suspicions that the Army intended to remold American youth into undesirable patterns were still present to a certain extent despite the objectivity of the orientation efforts.

In August 1942, the decision was made to call the main series of orientation films *Why We Fight.* It was planned that this series would include seven films, tracing the course of the war. In addition, there would be a series of strategic films, chiefly military but also economic and social, showing the campaigns of war, and a series on the countries of the world entitled *Know Your Enemies* and *Know Your Allies.* Of the projected films, only the *Why We Fight* series was completed in full. Even so the last film did not appear until the spring of 1945.

Although the *Strategic Battles* series was never completed, the subject-matter areas contemplated for this series were fairly well covered in releases through *G.I. Movies* and the *Screen Magazine,* which made such films as *Report from the Aleutians, War on the Seas, Tunisian Victory, Attack, The Memphis Belle,* and *The Liberation of Rome* available for orientation purposes. Similarly, only one of the *Know Your Allies* series (Britain) and two of the *Know Your Enemies* series (Japan and Germany) were released, but *Peoples of Canada, The Dutch Tradition, Fighting French, Twenty-seven Soldiers, Hitler Youth,* and other similar short films appeared through *G.I. Movies* and *Screen*

Magazine. Of *Special Films, The Negro Soldier, Your Job in Germany,* and several others were released.

Before the films became available, the Current Phase limped along in most units and camps, handled by first one officer and then another. Sufficient materials and guidance were lacking and there was no strong and clear direction. To fill in the gaps training films were often used as part of the program. Ingenuity was displayed in certain posts where the theatrical air of the program was emphasized in regular quiz programs, in truck-mounted displays, in orientation newsreel theaters where available films were shown at stated hours, in "rumor clinics", and in orientation workshops. This type of development was quite effective at many posts; however, the main objectives of orientation were often lost and a quiz program or a living newsreel show often tended to swamp the program itself.

As time went on a *Guide to the Use of Information Materials* was produced, revised, and became the Bible of orientation work. The purpose of the *Guide* was to set a standard to which the orientation officer could turn concerning various issues. It was a yardstick by which he could measure his own views and to which he could compare the ideas of others. For example, should the question of the abilities of Negro troops arise, the orientation officer would find:

> Problems of race are a proper concern of the Army only so far as they affect the efficiency of the Army, no more, no less.

But another paragraph contains the following statement:

> To contribute by act or word toward the increase of misunderstanding, suspicion, and tension between peoples of different racial or national origin in this country or among our Allies is to help the enemy.

Again, if the orientation officer were to discuss the war in Europe, he would have an unequivocal statement that the United States is committed to unconditional surrender. "Thus, in shaping the attitude of the armed forces, there is no room for discussion of anything short of total military victory over the enemy." If the question of British India should come up at a discussion meeting, what should the orientation officer do? Certainly not whitewash, yet certainly not abuse the British. "Opinion-forming elements in the armed forces discuss the internal problems of the British Empire; they are entitled to considered information about them."

And so the *Guide* went on, outlining the approach to the handling of information materials. The *Guide* became an important text in training orientation officers at the School for Personnel Services at Lexington, Virginia; it figured prominently in the short schools conducted in the field, and it was used as a basic guide to activities in the field.

Possibly the most significant over-all advance made in the *Guide* was the frank recognition that truth alone without interpretation and understanding was not sufficient in training men for war, especially in a period when truth had for some years been obscured and full information neglected. The *Guide* opened with a section on truth and falsehood:

> To speak the truth is not enough; there must be a steadying judgment as to when it should be spoken, and to whom it should be addressed. A truth need not only be well-rounded, but the utterance of it should take account of the stresses and objectives of the moment. Truth becomes falsehood unless it has the strength of perspective. The presentation of facts is self-justifying only when the facts are developed in their true proportion.
>
> Information which does not inform, counsel, warn, stimulate, remind, instruct, or reiterate for the purpose of training the mind for war, is innocuous and therefore of no value to the military service.

A main line in the development of orientation, therefore, was in the change from emphasis on the presentation of facts *per se* to the emphasis on facts as a basis for the understanding of ideas. For instance, information alone on the individuals composing the Junkers, the industrialists, and the Nazi party was considered insufficient for a real understanding of fascism and its threat to America and all peace-loving nations. It became Orientation's job to give meaning to that factual information so that the soldier would fully understand the basic life and death struggle which the war represented.

At first, thought of making better citizens on the soldier's return to civilian life was not considered. But this effort assumed a more important position as the war drew to a close. By 1945, programs included material on the return to civilian life. This concern with the wider implications of orientation gradually became an official War Department policy.

WORK OF THE ORIENTATION BRANCH

When Orientation became a separate branch in 1943, the Information Branch retained its supervision of the *Special Service Digest* (later called *The Digest*), Army News Service, camp newspapers, radio services, and orientation films, including the *Army-Navy Screen Magazine*. *Newsmap* was transferred to the new branch but within a short time was returned to the Information Branch for production and distribution. On matters of policy concerning orientation, the two branches operated closely, with especially frequent consultations on such matters as the content of films and *Newsmap*.

With training in orientation made mandatory and the assignment of full-time, trained orientation officers, the need for additional materials and guidance, especially for the Current Phase, became even more pressing. Several types of new materials supplementing those already in use were devised in the fall of 1943. The first was the institution of periodically issued collections of materials, designated as Orientation Kits and designed to improve the quality of Current Phase teaching by providing supplementary materials of immediate but permanent interest.

The content of the first kit was typical of those that were to follow. A large wall map of the world and Europe, a booklet on how to understand maps, a sheet of map symbols, and a check list of the maps that had previously appeared in *Newsmap* were included. The prologues to the films and the substitute lectures which had appeared earlier in the *Training Guide* were included along with *The War in Outline* and a booklet, *Defeat of the German Army—1918*.

Most important of the new material, however, was the inclusion of the first five *Fact Sheets*. These *Fact Sheets* were to give information which could be used in Current Phase orientation in addition to the news. They were basic to the development of materials for guided discussions and, in later kits, were developed into short discussions of the vital problems of the day, providing factual background material to the discussion leader. Later

Orientation Kits contained increasing amounts of materials, especially reprints of articles and pocket-sized books. Altogether nine kits were issued with at least one issue reaching a total number of 65,000.

While training for orientation officers began in 1943 at the school at Lexington, the need for in-service training inspired the development of an orientation team to be sent into the field after early 1944 to demonstrate orientation techniques on the spot. Techniques for conducting discussions, construction and use of an orientation center, the use of the camp newspaper as a medium of orientation, daily or weekly news services, and the procurement and use of reference materials received special attention in these meetings. Following the meetings, members of the team conducted meetings with troops as demonstrations of "how to do it." Following the demonstrations, critiques concluding with a clinic in which individual problems could be discussed were held. Model orientation centers were actually constructed by the team in seven of the service commands. The work of the team was so successful and so well-received that soon it became a permanent part of the Field Operations Section of the Orientation Branch.

By 1943 the series of weekly *Army Talks* began to be published. These were to contain prepared material for use in the discussion hour. Such leaflets had already been popular in the European theater and were an advance on the *Fact Sheets*. That *Army Talk* filled a big gap in field materials was apparent almost from the beginning. The initial print order was for 52,000 copies. Although its use was not mandatory, *Army Talk* increased its print order to 110,000 in its first four weeks. Overseas requests increased rapidly. The publication was planned primarily for domestic use but by the end of the first month the North African theater was receiving 12,000 copies. The European theater which continued to produce its own *Army Talks* was taking 500 copies. By November 1944, the domestic *Talk* was being reproduced from page proofs supplied by air in the Middle East, South Atlantic, Mediterranean (formerly North African), India-Burma, China, Far East, and South Pacific theaters.

The reason for the popularity of *Army Talk* lay primarily in its design for ready use. Originally a four-page publication, it was later enlarged to eight pages and equipped with outlines, supplementary materials, discussion questions and aids, and practical hints on special approaches suitable to troops of each major command. Over eighty titles were published, on such topics as *Mental Fitness for Combat, The Interdependence of People, How Strong Is the Japanese War Machine?* and *How Do We Look to Other People?*

Other activities of Orientation included the development of programs for troops and hospital ships, and for other special situations. A redistribution station program was worked out which was intended to orient personnel returned from overseas and awaiting reassignment. This program included provision for a "sound-off session" where returnees might air their grievances, doubts, or commendations and six hours' discussion of timely topics, such as the GI Bill and the postwar period.

The "Educational Reconditioning Program, Hospitals" was begun in the summer of 1944. All sixteen of its discussion topics, which were so arranged that they could be given either in one- or two-hour sessions as desired, were distributed by January 1945. The theory behind this program was that, through discussion groups and other orientation techniques, patients were more quickly aided in returning to their normal outlook. The program was integrated with the physical reconditioning of patients. Convalescent officers and enlisted personnel were utilized to supplement the work of the regularly assigned personnel in carrying out this program.

A specialized program for Army Ground Forces Replacement Training Centers was prepared to help make the ground soldier ready for combat. This seventeen-week program, in addition to the use of films and such discussion topics as fascism, enemy propaganda, Russia and China, American citizenship and democracy, and interdependence of peoples included talks to be given by regimental commanders on combat leadership and fear in battle.

Orientation apparently was quite successful in reaching the majority of soldiers. An I and E research report states that studies made in April and May 1945 showed that 52 percent of men returning from overseas had regularly scheduled discussions, 25 percent had attended a regular weekly hour, and 69 percent said orientation was "very important," with an additional 19 percent saying it was "important."

INFORMATION ACTIVITIES

When the Information Branch and the Orientation Branch were separated in 1943, Information became responsible for the *Why We Fight* films and the other information films used in orientation work and described in Section 30. The other main efforts of Information were *Yank,* Armed Forces Radio Service, Army News Service, *Newsmap,* and *Pocket Guides.*

Yank was first issued in June 1942 with a printing of 175,000 copies. By August 1945 its circulation had risen to 2,400,000 copies. It was published simultaneously in New York, London, Paris, Naples, Manila, Strasbourg, Cairo, Calcutta, Panama, Sydney, Okinawa, Honolulu, Saipan, and Tokyo. Previously it had been published also in Brisbane, Puerto Rico, and Trinidad. Nearly a thousand men submitted stories, poems, or cartoons and fifteen hundred men wrote to the editor each week.

In the summer of 1945 the Research Branch made a study of *Yank* readership. The survey showed that GI taste was similar the world over. The six regular features of *Yank* which were most popular, in order of popularity, were as follows: "The Sad Sack," "Male Call," a letters-to-the-editor feature, combat stories, home-front news, pin-up girls, and sports news.

The Armed Forces Radio Service became world-wide and the largest broadcasting system the world had ever seen. There were 177 Army broadcasting stations, plus over 50 foreign government stations in use. Produced programs and transcriptions included special Army programs such as "Command Performance," and "G. I. Journal," and rebroadcasts of popular domestic programs in great number. While most of the programs of this great radio network were of an entertainment nature, some educational programs were carried, the ratio being roughly the same as in regular domestic broadcasting.

Early in the war the Education Branch became concerned with the use of radio for its purposes. In November 1943, it was proposed that radio lend valuable assistance by supplementing instruction in such topics as educational guidance; vocational information; civic responsibilities of veterans; health education; current political, economic, and social problems; American institutions; appreciation of music; peoples, customs, and geography of countries in which American troops were stationed; family adjustments of the returning soldier; subjects of general education, such as foreign languages, English, history; and subjects in vocational education. It was recommended also that radio facilities available to the Army be more fully utilized for educational purposes. This program represented the joint efforts of the Army Education Branch, the Army Information Branch, and the latter's Armed Forces Radio Service.

A subsequent survey indicated specific material which was being incorporated in Army radio programs. This material included postwar job opportunities; health education; appreciation of music; and peoples, customs, geography, and geology of foreign countries. In addition, announcements promoting the United States Armed Forces Institute were being used. It was stated, however, that "the present effort cannot be represented as an extensive use of radio for educational purposes."

By late 1945 Information and Education were cooperating on four half-hour programs per week of an educational nature. These programs, which attempted to present material suggested by the American Council's *A Design for General Education,* were "This Is the Story," "Science Magazine of the Air," "Heard at Home," and "Our Foreign Policy." A study of station schedules by the AFRS, requested by the Army Education Branch, revealed that somewhat over half of all AFR stations reported regular scheduling of the four educational periods being supplied each week.

The Army News Service transmitted news overseas—80,000 words a day by cable, radio, teletype, Signal Corps facilities, and air mail. It thus serviced Army radio stations and newspapers.

Stars and Stripes was published in three editions. The European theater edition of eight pages had by 1945 a daily circulation of 1,200,000. The Mediterranean edition was eight pages daily, sixteen Sunday, and had a circulation of 200,000. The Hawaiian edition had a circulation of 70,000. Many weekly papers were published in various parts of the world. Information sponsored a newspaper service to supply clip sheets and mats to 3,000 of them.

Newsmap was one of the great successes of the Orientation and Information Branches. Nearly 200,000 copies weekly were being printed and distributed by 1945. One side consisted of a map or maps of significant military operations. On the reverse side was material skilfully presented to add to the soldier's general information, including such topics as service ribbons, *Mein Kampf,* teamwork, and rumor.

Pocket Guides to Foreign Countries, mentioned earlier, included booklets on twenty-two countries in which GI's found themselves. *Pocket Guides to Foreign Cities* included guides to Paris and cities of northern France, cities of southern France, Italian cities, and cities of Norway, Denmark, Belgium, Luxembourg, and the Netherlands.

THE FILM PROGRAM

The film program included the *GI Movie Weekly,* first sponsored by the Education Branch and later taken over by Information and *Army-Navy Screen Magazine,* originally an Information function. In both of these efforts films were assembled into packaged collections of shorts gathered from various sources, official and commercial, and distributed as a program of thirty to forty-five minutes in length to military units for off-duty showings, in locations such as day rooms, recreation halls, or outdoors at night.

These services supplemented entertainment films shown by Army Motion Picture Service through a chain of theaters designed especially for this purpose. No admission fee was charged. Attendance was limited to personnel of the armed forces.

GI Movie Weekly was shown overseas as an "extra attraction" with latest Hollywood entertainment films, reaching men behind the lines and on battle fronts in all theaters of war. Overseas, *GI Movie Weekly* was distributed by the Signal Corps to some three thousand installations. Overseas installations were served by twenty film exchanges located throughout the world.

NAVY[3]

WAR ORIENTATION

The War Orientation Program as administered by Educational Services had a varied career. At one time it was given great emphasis by the Educational Services Section but later was relegated to a secondary position. As this is the one aspect of the Educational Services Program which eventually was made obligatory in certain instances, its inclusion in this study might be questioned. Since there remained a large element of the voluntary in this program, a brief description of it seems warranted.

As early as the autumn of 1942, an officer was assigned in the Bureau of Naval Personnel to distribute to naval stations certain informational material, such as the Army *Newsmaps*. When the Educational Services Section was finally established, a war-orientation unit was included and more funds became available for the distribution of publications designed to provide a background of knowledge about the war.

Activities of the war orientation program

There was not much doubt that a war orientation program was needed. Those who first started trying to impart some knowledge about the nature of the war to the personnel of the Navy were astonished to find that many men were serving their country at the time of its greatest need without any understanding of either the meaning or responsibility of citizenship or democracy. Many men in uniform were unacquainted with even the simplest facts of geography and sociology, and their knowledge about American history in World War I was sketchy, to

[3] Use has been made throughout this section of the "Educational Services Section," "Administrative History of the Bureau of Naval Personnel" (MS on file in the U. S. Office of Naval History, U. S. Navy Department).

say the least. They were also ignorant of the functioning of representative governments and the responsibilities of their citizenry.

In addition to the weekly *Newsmaps,* the Navy began to seek other material that could be used in the War Orientation Program. From the Army they secured pocket guides, informational pamphlets, maps, reference books, and such discussion guides as *Army Talk* and the *G.I. Roundtable* series. They developed a series of *NavWar Maps* providing background information concerning the physical, political, economic, and historical characteristics of the major theaters of war. Also, considerable use was made of the *Why We Fight* film series. Other materials were obtained from civilian sources, such as *The New York Times* and *Time Magazine* in their overseas editions, and appropriate *March of Time* films.

In the spring of 1943, an event took place which led the War Orientation Program eventually to be introduced as compulsory material during the recruit training period. It did not, however, give to the program the additional impetus on a part-time basis that might have been expected. At this time the training center at Bainbridge, Maryland, reported that it was having some trouble with men seeking discharge from the service by pretending to be psychoneurotics. Many felt that improper attitudes toward the war were responsible for this phenomenon. After some delay the Educational Services Section was given permission to put a war orientation officer into one of the wards. Informal talks were given for an hour daily. At the end of the trial period, a great many men in the ward asked to be returned to active duty. Immediately the inclusion of war orientation as an integral item of recruit training at all boot camps was ordered. It is difficult to understand why the success of this experiment did not lead to the general prospering of the War Orientation Program. Lack of personnel to perform this work was certainly a factor, but it might also be said that many Navy officers could not see the value of this program and did not encourage its use.

Furthermore, it was understood at least tentatively that controversial issues were not to be the concern of the orientation classes or forums. Thus, the problems of labor, racial issues, and political ideologies, and like topics were tacitly ruled out of the discussions.

There were some instances in which the War Orientation Program functioned more effectively than was the general rule. Good results were sometimes obtained at the stations where chief petty officers taught on an informal basis in the men's quarters. These ranking enlisted men were adept at leading "bull sessions" and the men felt freer to express themselves.

There were other stations where the War Orientation Program was carried on with considerable effectiveness. At Manus, for example, thirteen weekly radio programs were conducted in February, March, and April of 1945. Subjects of general interest such as the GI Bill of Rights were discussed. In May, June, and July, a second twelve-week series, developed to provide information and promote interest in educational facilities, was offered under the title *I Want to Know.* Arrangements were made for a forum service to assist discussion groups by providing speakers and discussion leaders as well as materials. The center at Pearl Harbor carried on a highly successful weekly illustrated program of war orientation entitled "On Target". Each week a specific topic was selected, and slides and scripts were prepared; then the completed program was made available to all activities in the 14th Naval District. It was estimated that during July and August of 1945, this program reached 290,000 naval personnel.

According to the *Educational Services Manual,* the orientation program rested on six basic concepts.[4] These were:

(1) We need to recognize that neither nations nor individuals can shut themselves out from what is happening in the world around them, that we need intelligent understanding of the interests and purpose of other great powers no less than our own.

(2) We need to recognize that our own peace and security in the future depends upon world peace and security, that what happens in Whangpoo will affect the farmers of Iowa unless we sincerely and permanently play our part in international cooperation.

(3) We need to recognize that the Navy has a peacetime role within the limits of our national policies and international commitments, that its effectiveness in war depends upon its maintenance in peace.

[4] U. S. Navy Department, Bureau of Naval Personnel, NavPers 16963 (Washington: Educational Services Section, Bureau of Naval Personnel), p. 3.

(4) We need to recognize that just as every citizen has rights and privileges, so he has duties and obligations, that he endangers his democracy when he fails to fulfill them.

(5) We need to recognize the lesson of World War II that we cannot escape history any more than we can do business with Hitler, that we came desperately close to losing our way of life because we ignored the lives of others.

(6) We need to recognize that public affairs are our affairs, that our awareness of current home front developments must be followed by intelligent action.

The manner in which the War Orientation Program was carried on varied from station to station. In general, however, the following devices were commonly used: lectures, broadcasts, forums, quiz programs, pamphlets, film showings, and map displays. A few months before the war ended the Educational Services Section described its War Orientation Program as follows:

The program has continued to develop along these four lines: (1) *Newsmaps* are now distributed for regular posting in quantities of 27,500 each week, according to the standard Navy distribution lists. Special bulletin boards have been built at hundreds of naval activities to accommodate map and photographic displays both indoors and outdoors. Talented enlisted personnel enthusiastically participate in the creation of the displays. . . [there were also developed] in the Bureau, a series of six *NavWar Maps*. These full-color poster maps tell the Navy's story in vivid, terse, graphic terms, covering all the areas of the world where the ships of the Navy have sailed. With the same emphasis on the Navy's participation in the war, the publication of a series of Navy posters was begun for the back of the weekly *Newsmap*. The titles are self-explanatory: "Your Battleship," "The Amphibs," "Your Submarine—Versatile Warship." The first issues of the group of photographic posters dealing with the submarine service have also appeared. . . . Complementing the Navy-wide distribution of maps and posters, the Section provides its officers with the weekly map issued by the Office of Strategic Services and provides activities with large sectional wall maps and other special maps on request. . . . (2) The display idea and the plan to distribute printed material to all hands has merged in the "war room." The war room idea takes many forms; it may appear in the corner of the lounge, at one end of the library, or in a room set aside for the purpose. The purpose is simple—to provide a place where men may gather in off-duty time to learn about the progress of the war on all fronts and to increase their knowledge of the political, economic, and social forces at work in the world. . . . Since the *Pocket Guide to Foreign Lands* was first distributed, other pamphlets numbering over 70 titles have been procured and put into the hands of the men; carefully selected for freedom from political bias, for convenient size and readability, the subjects covered have ranged through the entire field of war orientation. . . . The one million *Pocket Guides* and pamphlets distributed during 1944, read and re-read by naval personnel all over the world, are but a beginning toward satisfying the desire for facts and toward building up a confidence that comes from the knowledge of the facts. . . . (3) Films of the war and its background have been a staple of the program afloat and ashore. . . . (4) Springing from the early talks given by Educational Services officers to enlisted men comes the most significant current development of orientation—a program of discussions and forums in which enlisted personnel exercised the democratic privilege of pooling their experiences and judgment in the consideration of vital topics. . . .[5]

In spite of this description, however, the same publication indicates that all was not well with the War Information or War Orientation phase of the Educational Services Program, pointing out that a lack of appreciation of the importance of keeping personnel informed about the war, about their responsibilities during the war, and in the post-hostilities period had in many instances hindered the development of this part of the program. It is also pointed out that there was difficulty on the part of the Navy in comprehending the place of this type of program. Furthermore, the separation within the Navy of the various informational programs did not assist the War Orientation venture, for whereas Educational Services built up a strong field staff to carry on informational and orientation work, the program had no control over the major informational media in the Navy, namely, the ship and station papers and the radio.[6]

INFORMATIONAL SERVICES

While a large part of the contents of *All Hands* was at all times devoted to information about the Navy, a considerable section was devoted to other news and this general information function loomed large in the minds of the editors. The analysis of the contents of certain issues of *All Hands* in Table 9 is indicative of its contents.

[5] U. S. Navy Department, Bureau of Naval Personnel, "The Educational Services Program" (MS on file in the Office of Naval History, U. S. Navy Department), pp. 21-22.
[6] *Ibid.*, p. 33.

TABLE 9

ANALYSIS OF THE CONTENTS OF CERTAIN ISSUES OF "ALL HANDS" BY NUMBER OF PAGES DEVOTED TO EACH CATEGORY

Issue	Action Stories	Navy News	Navy Information	Legislation*	Home Front†	Decorations and Promotions	WAVES	Special Features‡
October 1942...	2½	13	15½	1	3	15½	4½	6
January 1943..	10	9	20½	....	....	9	1	13
August 1945...	13	15	19	3	4	10	2	11

* Includes discussion of all legislation with which naval personnel might be concerned, as the GI Bill of Rights.

† Includes stories on the role of the Merchant Marine, labor, American youth, etc.

‡ Cartoons, pictures, etc., as well as the monthly news, "Fantail Forum" (an inquiring reporter feature), maps, and periodic reports on the war.

In April 1945 it was announced that the Ships Editorial Association (SEA) was being formed, giving service to the various editors of ships' and stations' newspapers. All such editors were eligible to become members of this association, subject to the approval of their commanding officers. The association which was operated in the Bureau of Naval Personnel primarily by the same people who published *All Hands,* had as one of its services the distribution of a weekly clip sheet which was called the *Clipper.* Also offered was a monthly magazine called *Watch,* which was to be published for ship and station newspaper editors. At the end of 1945, SEA had nearly 1,000 members.

In June 1945 the plans for Navy's Informational Services Program were considerably expanded. There was to be a weekly magazine produced by a field office in New York; daily newspapers called *Navy News* were to be published in key spots in the Pacific Ocean area; a recreation journal was to be established for the guidance and information of all welfare and recreation officers; a radio news service was to be operated from San Francisco; and a conventional news service was to be operated from Washington. Since the end of the war came soon thereafter, this ambitious program was not realized in its entirety before Japan surrendered.

MARINE CORPS

The Information program of the Marine Corps (an integral part of the Education program) had three stated purposes: (1)

to maintain the high standard of morale of Marine Corps personnel by informing them of the origin, progress, and objectives of the war; (2) to explain the individual's part in the conflict; and (3) to increase the general knowledge of Marine Corps personnel.[7] To attain these purposes Special Services officers were advised to concern themselves with several types of information: current news background and the historical development of the war, strategy, tactics and weapons, war aims of allied nations and enemy nations, geography, economy and peoples in various theaters of operations, and the individual, his outfit and base, and the relationship of this part with the total war.[8] The following means of disseminating information were outlined for the use of the Special Services officer.[9]

1. Radio
   a) News broadcasts
   b) Special features
2. Current news sheets
3. *Newsmaps*
   a) Headquarters bulletin boards
   b) Unit bulletin boards
4. News review
   a) Summary of news for past week
   b) Special features—reviews of books, magazine articles, news interpretation, background information
   c) New films available
   d) Training and education—announcement and description of courses, classes, books and pamphlets available
   e) Base facilities and activities
5. Films
   a) Brief introductory talk, questions and discussion topics based on films
6. Display boards (outdoors and indoors)
   a) At headquarters and base units
   b) Maps, news summaries, posters, special announcements
7. Information Kits
   a) Books, pamphlets, maps, mimeographed materials—distributed by Education Section

[7] U. S. Marine Corps, *A Guide in Organizing an Information Program* (Washington: Education Section, Welfare Division, Special Services Board, Headquarters, U. S. Marine Corps), p. 1.
[8] *Ibid.*, p. 1.
[9] *Ibid.*, pp. 1-2.

8. Library
   a) Special shelf for Information materials
   b) Library books publicized through Information
9. Weekly meeting of unit Information officers
   a) Training in purposes and methods of Information and the conduct of discussion groups
   b) Review of material for discussion groups
   c) Showing of new films
   d) Special announcements
10. Discussion groups
    a) Material: films, *Newsmaps,* Information releases
    b) Special lectures chosen from units or provided by Education Section
    c) Brief talks followed by discussion
11. Miscellaneous
    a) Information display contests
    b) Poster contests
    c) Essay contests
    d) Quiz programs for radio and discussion groups

It should not be assumed that all of these means of disseminating information were used by or even available to all Special Services officers. The Navy and Marine Corps had no extensive means of educating by radio and were limited to the time they could get from local civilian stations and the Armed Forces Radio Service. This time was devoted largely to such subjects as the GI Bill of Rights, National Service Life Insurance, and information about the Marine Corps.

One of the questions most frequently asked about the Information program was the extent to which it omitted important but controversial topics. Evidence on this point is not available in official form. Unofficially a Marine Corps officer concerned with the program said, "Naturally, military subjects of a restricted nature that might be harmful to the war effort could not be used in the Information program." For the most part the decision was left to the individual commanding officer and it seems safe to assume that in most instances the dissemination of information about, and subsequent discussion of, a number of basic social and economic issues were carefully avoided.

COAST GUARD

In the fall of 1945 war orientation was made a compulsory part of the Coast Guard recruit-training program. However, it did continue on a voluntary basis throughout the rest of the Coast Guard service. Rather than initiating materials of its own, the Coast Guard again utilized those prepared by the Army and Navy. These were shipped to Coast Guard activities, there to be utilized as the local educational officer saw fit.

VII. LIBRARY SERVICES

During World War II, books, magazines, and entire libraries went to war along with America's armed services. Some 500,000 books were purchased by the Army Library Service for the convoy ships which carried the North African invasion forces. WAC's in New Guinea kept up with the latest fashions at home through reading current American magazines in their day rooms and barracks libraries. Sailors aboard ship had libraries stocked with a minimum selection of a book per man. Marines in inactive theaters had available a wide range of books on technical subjects provided by the Navy Library Section. Supplies of new books were augmented with large numbers of readable volumes contributed by American citizens in Victory Book campaigns.

Libraries established by the armed services in camps in the states and in the overseas areas were informal, comfortable, smoke-filled clubrooms conducive to reading for recreation and for educational advancement. Where these libraries were established, and in fact wherever Army and Navy library facilities were available, the men and women of our armed forces read books and magazines, many of them more extensively than ever before. Without these Army and Navy library facilities, the off-duty education programs would have been seriously limited in their effectiveness in providing educational programs for service personnel.

ARMY[1]

The aim of the Army Library Service was to provide soldiers with the books and magazines they wanted and, wherever possible, also give them library service comparable to that furnished by the best civilian libraries. In active overseas theaters and in small, isolated stations, emphasis was placed on the first objective; the foremost consideration was simply to get books and magazines to the men in such quantities and variety that there

[1]This section, with minor editorial changes and some abridgment, is excerpted, with permission, from the manuscript, "The Army Library Services, 1940-1945" (on file in the Historical Division, War Department Special Staff).

would be enough for everyone and something for every taste. In the continental United States, in inactive theaters, and in large communications-zone posts, the objective was to provide genuine library service with professional direction and reference service, full and balanced collections of books, comfortable club-like rooms for reading and study, branch libraries or bookmobile service for men in outposts, and both reading rooms and ward service for men in hospitals.

EXPANSION OF CONTINENTAL LIBRARY SERVICE

At the beginning of the expansion program prior to World War II, there were 147 permanent Army libraries in the continental United States, containing 569,648 volumes; and there were 8,046 additional volumes in traveling libraries. Most of the books were worn and obsolete, and the only magazines available to soldiers in libraries were usually donated copies and discards. Post libraries were operated by enlisted men, usually untrained, under the general supervision of post chaplains.

The expansion of library service in the continental United States began with the adoption in the fall of 1940, for posts with strengths of 5,000 men or more, of the new SC-3 type service clubs, which included space for housing 5,000 volumes plus 2,000 square feet of floor space for use as a reading and writing room. The authorization for each new SC-3 service club carried with it a grant of funds for the purchase of 5,000 volumes and for the hiring of a professional civilian librarian. This arrangement insured the establishment of libraries at all posts large enough to be entitled to a service club of this size. The placing of libraries in the service clubs was otherwise undesirable, since it deprived them of any semblance of quietness during the later afternoon and evening hours when they were most in use.

The smaller SC-4 service club, for posts serving 3,000 to 5,000 men, contained 700 square feet of library floor space and shelf space for about 2,500 books. A librarian was authorized for this type of club.

Libraries at posts with fewer than 2,500 enlisted men were usually operated by enlisted personnel or sub-professional civilians under the supervision of the post Special Services officer. Regulations provided that service command librarians should visit such posts and assist in rendering their services more efficient. Books were provided for them in traveling libraries, and periodical distributions of free or inexpensive publications were made.

The construction of specially designed separate library buildings was not authorized until 1943. While the construction of service clubs housing libraries was still pending, action was taken to establish standards for the qualifications and pay of professional civilian librarians. Professional librarians with administrative experience were made eligible for employment as corps area (later called service command) librarians; and the requirements for post librarians included graduation from college and from an accredited library school, plus a year's experience in library work.

From 1940 through 1942, librarians were generally assisted by enlisted men (and later enlisted women) assigned to that duty. Some help was also received from enlisted personnel who were paid from local funds for working in the library after duty hours. From 1943 on, as military manpower became increasingly critical, civilian assistants had to be employed.

Between September 1940 and November 1941, 238 post librarians were hired and peak employment of 600 was reached early in 1944. Owing to the inactivation of many posts and to the transfer of librarians to the European theater of operations and to the Central Pacific base command, the number of post librarians on duty in the United States had fallen to less than four hundred in May 1945.

In 1940 and 1941, books for post libraries and traveling libraries for which procurement was initiated by the Library Branch were secured centrally by the Office of the Quartermaster General in accordance with standard quartermaster procedures. For every procurement it was necessary to submit lists of books to all dealers who had ever expressed an interest in furnishing books to the Army, and then examine bids from the comparatively few dealers who actually desired to undertake that particular order. Every order list had to be reproduced in hundreds of copies, and the whole procedure was ill adapted to the book business in which it is customary to place orders with either publishers or jobbers at fairly standardized discounts.

To remedy this situation the Library Branch in cooperation with the Office of the Quartermaster General developed the contract bulletin method of purchasing books. According to this method individual publishers or jobbers designated to act for them in dealing with the Army contracted to sell books in quantities of from one to five hundred to Army agencies at a fixed discount. In the case of larger purchases, the purchasing agency was authorized to negotiate for a more favorable discount.

After corps area librarians had been appointed, the procurement of books for newly activated posts was decentralized to the corps area. The purchase of new books to refresh existing collections was generally delegated by corps areas to the individual posts.

At the beginning of November 1941, it was estimated that there were approximately one million books in Army libraries. This quantity was entirely inadequate to the needs of the Army, and Victory Book campaigns were inaugurated to supply the deficiencies. The 1942 and 1943 Victory Book campaigns netted more than four million books for continental United States posts.

Through purchases made from appropriated and nonappropriated funds in the fiscal years following 1941, in addition to the Victory Book campaigns, book stocks in continental United States installations were increased to a peak of approximately eight million books at the beginning of 1944. During the period 1941 to 1945, the total number of volumes placed in libraries, hospitals, and day rooms was approximately twelve million.

In the fiscal years 1940, 1941, and 1942, no distinction was made in the annual congressional appropriation between funds for continental and for overseas library service, but most of the library expenditures in those years were for continental United States service. The appropriations for reading materials were as follows:

1940	$ 12,655
1941	1,160,686
1942	622,668

Later appropriations were broken down into United States and overseas funds. The United States funds were as follows:

1943	$3,984,595
1944	2,656,491
1945	2,842,000

Appropriations for overseas library service for the fiscal years 1943–45 were as follows:

1943	$5,482,120
1944	5,622,942
1945	8,417,000

The basis of the 1943, 1944, and 1945 appropriations was $1.00 per man per year for reading materials.

The Post Library System of the Eastern Signal Corps Training Center, Fort Monmouth, New Jersey, may serve as an illustration of the type of library service that could be provided by a post library system which received adequate support from post and service-command officers. The figures given are for 1944.

The total inventory was 50,056 volumes and the total circulation, 153,400. A total of $18,959.77 was spent on books, magazines, newspapers, binding supplies, equipment, furniture, and printing. All of this money was drawn from nonappropriated funds. New books totalling 7,403 were purchased at a cost of $12,558.04.

Library facilities included one central library, four branches (including a hospital branch), and forty-three deposit stations (in day rooms, recreation halls, guest houses, and so on). The staff consisted of twelve professional librarians, four subprofessional assistants, and four clerks; there were eleven Gray Lady volunteer workers in the hospital branch; and each of the forty-three deposit stations had the part-time service of an enlisted man. Attendance at the central library and the three branches in which records were kept numbered 202,488.

Many other posts had well-organized library service comparable to the Fort Monmouth system, but they were rarely able to spend more than a fraction of the amount spent by Fort Monmouth on reading materials, supplies, and personnel. At the beginning of the expansion program, when many service clubs were being built, certain amounts were earmarked for the establishment of service-club libraries with a specific allocation for each club. Throughout the course of the war, specific amounts were also earmarked for the establishment of libraries in general hospitals. After the fiscal year 1941, these allotments absorbed only a small percentage of the total library appropriation. The remaining funds in the appropriation were included in the general allotment of Welfare of Enlisted Men funds made to commanding generals of service commands, who in turn made sub-allotments to posts, camps, and stations on the basis of their strength and requirements.

The Ninth Service Command provided an excellent example of centralized operation at the service command level. The service command library depot in San Francisco employed a staff of nine professional librarians, assisted by a small number of clerks and enlisted men, all under the supervision of the service command librarian. The depot processed all purchases of books from appropriated funds for posts within the command; made periodical shipments of book kits to isolated posts; provided bookmobile service for small posts within a three-hundred-mile radius of the depot; gave a ten-day training course to all newly employed post librarians in the command; and sorted, stored, and redistributed donated books and books from inactivated posts.

The redistribution work increased in importance as the war progressed. Donated books and those from inactivated posts were examined on arrival and those fit for further use were placed upon stack shelves according to subject. Books were then drawn from the stacks as required in preparing balanced library units of 300, 750, and 1,500 volumes. Many of these units were sent to posts in Alaska, the Aleutians, and the South Pacific, as well as to posts within the Ninth Service Command. Beginning in 1945, however, they were used almost exclusively for troop transports sailing from West Coast ports of embarkation. At the same time, the Special Services Division agreed to make a quarterly allotment of $17,500 to the Ninth Service Command to be used in purchasing new books for those transport collections. Under this arrangement 80 to 90 percent of each collection was composed of used books a year or more old and 10 to 20 percent of books published within the last six months.

One serious problem pertaining to continental United States library service was that the Quartermaster General required the accountability of library books. A lost book could only be removed from a Special Services officer's property records by means of a report of survey showing in detail the precautions taken to prevent loss and the action taken to recover the book. Post librarians in 1941 and later sent thousands of letters to soldiers who had failed to return books before being transferred. Often these letters went through eight or ten headquarters in the United States and overseas before reaching the man addressed. Librarians had to spend much time on paper work of this sort, simply in order to have sufficient evidence to support a report of survey. Because of the problems involved in accounting for the loss of a single book, many Special Services officers discouraged librarians from pursuing an active circulation policy. Accountability procedures inevitably caused them to place a strong emphasis on the preservation of books.

HOSPITAL LIBRARY SERVICE

At the beginning of the war, the majority of Army hospitals in the continental United States had no real library service; there were only small collections of donated books and magazines which were circulated to patients by the untrained volunteer Gray Ladies of the American Red Cross. The situation as regards general hospitals was partially remedied when the Adjutant General authorized the granting of $7,000 to each general hospital for the purchase of reading materials. Station hospitals continued to be entirely dependent on local funds for reading materials. Some hospital commanders made such funds available in adequate quantities, but the majority depended on gift books and such service as volunteer workers without professional supervision could render.

A study of station-hospital library service made by the Research Branch, Morale Services Division, at the beginning of 1944, revealed that library service in most station hospitals in the continental United States was still entirely inadequate, and that thousands of sick and wounded men in those hospitals rarely, if ever, saw a new book. Supporting its case with this study and with letters from the Surgeon General, the Air Surgeon Service Command Special Services officers and librarians, and from members of the Council on Books in Wartime, the Library Branch requested the Deputy Director, Special Services Division, to earmark $180,000 in the continental United States library budget for the purchase of armed services editions for hospitals. This action was taken, and as a result armed services editions were made available to United States hospitals in September 1944.

In December 1942, the employment of civilian camp librarians at all general hospitals and at station hospitals having 1,000 or more beds was authorized. By May 1945, the employment of one librarian and one assistant librarian for each 1,000-bed unit in general, convalescent, and regional hospitals, and the employment of one additional assistant librarian for each additional 750 beds was authorized. This change was made to meet the needs of the many large hospitals built in 1944 and 1945.

In November 1944, a special training program for hospital library personnel was inaugurated. Service commands were requested to send all hospital librarians to a hospital in the command for a short in-service training course in the special techniques of hospital library service. Emphasis was placed on book-truck service to ward patients. After taking the course, librarians were encouraged to conduct similar courses for volunteer workers in their own hospitals.

OVERSEAS LIBRARY SERVICE

At the beginning of the war, library service in the Hawaiian, Panama Canal, and Antilles Departments was already organized along the same lines as library service in the Zone of the Interior. There were permanent librarians at a few of the larger posts, but little was done to provide reading material to soldiers at small posts and in outlying areas.

In the Hawaiian Department, library service expanded rapidly and a well-integrated system was developed. It included twenty complete post libraries; nineteen hospital libraries; three large district libraries in Hawaii, Maui, and Kauai; a fully equipped bindery; a shipping section which distributed portable libraries, consisting of fifty clothbound books and selected magazines, to units on outlying islands and to task forces prior to their moving into combat areas; the construction or remodeling of post and hospital libraries; and a staff of eighteen professional civilian librarians, fourteen civilian clerks, and seventy trained enlisted personnel.

Library service in the Panama Canal Department and the Antilles Department was developed along similar lines, although on a considerably smaller scale. Library service in each of these departments was directed by a professional civilian librarian and the individual libraries were generally operated by civilians.

In other overseas theaters it was rarely possible to employ civilians, much less professionally trained civilians. Fixed libraries were comparatively few, and they were nearly always operated by enlisted personnel. A brief manual for the guidance of enlisted librarians was issued by the Library Branch in 1941. A somewhat longer manual, entitled *Small Army Libraries,* was published in November 1944. In these theaters, library service was limited for the most part to the distribution of books and magazines to unit recreational buildings or tents by the Special Services officer.

Books and book sets

In the first years of the war, the requisitioning and procurement of books for overseas theaters was not standardized in any way. In some instances, the Library Branch made emergency purchases of books for units ordered overseas and the units carried the books with them when they departed. Generally, however, requisitions originated by overseas units were consolidated by theater headquarters and channeled through the ports of embarkation to the Library Branch in the War Department.

One of the largest book purchases during this period was made in the summer of 1943 when 400,000 paperbound and 100,000 clothbound books were purchased for delivery to the convoy of ships which took part in the invasion of North Africa. Although it turned out that no space was available in the convoy and the books remained behind for later shipment, the planning that went into this purchase is worth noting. It was considered desirable, obviously, to include a large number of works on Africa in this collection of books. Yet to order books on Africa alone might lead publishers to surmise that an invasion was being planned. Hence, many books on the Arctic and on the Pacific regions were also included. Thus had the books been sent, the men who went to Africa would have received a great many books on such remote parts of the world as Iceland and New Guinea and perhaps attributed these incongruous selections to War Department stupidity. But they also would have received the books on Africa.

In 1943 the first steps were taken toward furnishing standardized sets of reading materials to overseas troops. Four sets of books (not including Armed Services Editions) were developed: the RB (reference book) Kit, consisting of 100 clothbound reference books packed in a shelved crate designed for use as a bookcase when the lid was removed; the RB Library, consisting of the 100 reference books of the RB Kit, plus 400 fiction and nonfiction books of general interest, the whole packed in 5 shelved crates; the PB (paperbound book) Kit, consisting of 500 miscellaneous paperbound books and pamphlets with a large proportion of thrillers and other light fiction; the C Kit, consisting of 1,900 paperbound and 100 clothbound books, also packed in shelved crates.

It was originally intended that the RB Kits, RB Libraries, and PB Kits would be stocked in ports of embarkation and issued to units passing through the port to overseas theaters. Because of shortages of shipping space on troop transports, this generally proved impracticable, and the majority of the kits were sent overseas in response to requisitions from theater headquarters.

Theaters which did not have professional librarians to do the work of assembling balanced libraries for the use of units found this method of shipping books much more satisfactory than the old method of bulk shipments. After 1944 no more RB Kits were purchased, as the demand for RB Libraries was much greater. At the same time the quantity of books included in the PB Kit was reduced from 500 to 300 because of the limited number of desirable titles available in paperbound books.

Occupational information materials, described more fully in chapter ix were gathered and distributed in increased numbers between 1944 and 1946.

Unit magazine sets

From 1940 until the spring of 1943, magazines were sent to task forces, divisions, air force groups, and similar overseas units on a bulk subscription basis, in response to requisitions sent directly from the unit to the War Department. On receipt of each requisition, the Library Branch would place as many subscriptions as were called for (from twenty to one hundred as a rule) to five, ten, or more magazines through the American News Company, furnishing it with the mailing addresses.

The bulk subscription method proved unsatisfactory both because of the lack of adequate means of distribution within the theaters and because of the complications involved in keeping thousands of subscriptions up to date, including increases and decreases of quantities, frequent renewals of subscriptions, and changes of address.

It was decided that a more feasible plan would be to send a weekly package of magazines to all overseas units of company size and also to small detached units and hospitals overseas. This method of distribution was begun in May 1943. Fourteen magazines per week were included in the original unit set of magazines: *Life, Time, Newsweek, Sporting News, Popular Mechanics, Reader's Digest, Collier's, Look, Western Trails,* and other popular publications. By July the number of weekly packages had risen to 16,000 and the number of individual magazines dispatched per month was 1,000,000. The number of magazines included in each set was steadily increased by adding more publications and more copies of the most popular publications. The total number of magazines per set per month rose to 70 in October 1943, later to 80 and, finally, with the addition of multiple copies of specially manufactured comic magazines, to 123. The number of sets dispatched likewise gained week by week. Finally, 8,000,000 magazines were sent overseas in 1943, and 62,000,000 in 1944; and, by May 1945, they were being dispatched at the rate of 12,000,000 per month.

As soon as the unit-set method of distribution was placed in operation, the Library Branch began to encourage magazine publishers to produce special overseas editions without advertising, printed on lightweight paper and where possible on a small-size page. After publishers had had time to experiment with printing special lightweight editions, it was determined that only such editions of magazines would be eligible for inclusion in the unit set. This requirement became effective in January 1944. The War Production Board cooperated in encouraging publishers to produce such editions for the use of servicemen overseas by allowing them to use paper in addition to their normal quotas.

In several overseas theaters, the contents of the unit magazine set were supplemented by locally printed copies of *Time, Newsweek,* and *Reader's Digest.* Local printing was undertaken in Hawaii, Australia, the Persian Gulf, India, Rome, Manila, and Paris.

In the fall of 1944, a special unit magazine set consisting of magazines of feminine interest was developed for the use of overseas WAC units. The WAC unit set consisted of one copy each of ten women's magazines and was dispatched monthly.

POST-HOSTILITIES LIBRARY PROGRAM

The Library Branch began planning for post-hostilities activities in overseas theaters in the summer of 1944. At that time a tentative program was prepared, calling for the establishment of libraries containing 1,000 to 5,000 volumes in assembly areas and other large troop concentrations, of unit libraries for smaller separate installations, and of depots for the assembly and distribution of reading materials. Recommendations were also made regarding methods of distribution and publicity and personnel requirements.

The final program for the European theater of operations provided for unit libraries of from 500 to 1,000 volumes in all installations with a strength of 1,000 men; libraries of 2,000 or more volumes in larger troop concentrations; special libraries with a preponderance of technical and educational material at Army school centers; and unit libraries in all general and large station hospitals.

As regards personnel, it was recommended that a library officer and two enlisted librarians be designated in each Army Air Force and Base Section, one library officer in each division, and two enlisted librarians in each unit of regimental size. Each assembly area was to have two library officers, a professional woman librarian, and two enlisted librarians. Detailed plans were made for facilities, including the operation of 50 mobile libraries or bookmobiles to service small isolated units in the theater.

A manual for the guidance of enlisted librarians was prepared by the theater library staff in collaboration with the Chief of the Library Branch, and in April 1945 the officer in charge of the Overseas Library Service Section was sent to the European theater of operations to conduct a training course for enlisted librarians and library officers. At the same time action was taken to select and process 120 professional women librarians for transfer to the theater. Only librarians with previous experience in Army library work in the continental United States were selected for transfer.

NAVY[2]

Libraries for newly commissioned ships and extra-continental shore stations were in general established on the basis of one and one-half books per man. Shore stations within the United States were allotted two books for each man. Every effort was made to keep libraries fresh and vital. Afloat, a division of ships was considered the basic unit. With the exception of the necessary

[2] Use has been made throughout this section of the "Library Section," "Administrative History of the Bureau of Naval Personnel" (MS on file in the Office of Naval History, U. S. Navy Department).

technical and professional material, there was no duplicating of books within the libraries of ships of the same division. This permitted the ready interchange of books. Any Navy or Marine Corps library, afloat or ashore, could request books at any time—new books, special books, or replacements. When possible the Library Service complied.

The Library Section made every effort to have the libraries both as informal and as inviting as possible. Considering the role of the librarian as that of a stimulator of reading, record-keeping was kept at a minimum. While this made analysis of circulation impossible, it did promote reading. The head of the Library Section described the simplification of records in this manner:

> As for the records required, they are the simplest. Our instructions for the organization of ships' libraries recommend that for larger ships non-fiction be classified by the Dewey classification and the fiction arranged alphabetically by author; also that a catalog be maintained with the least possible information on the card (simply the author, title, date of publication, and, of course, the classification number), with the source from which the book was obtained. Instead of a dictionary catalog, we recommend a class catalog which is then used for a shelf list and for inventory purposes. No reports are required. This drastic step was taken several years ago in order to eliminate paper work. As for small ships, such as destroyers, we recommend no such elaborate system. Books are divided only into fiction and non-fiction and except that a record must be kept of all non-fiction on board, there is no other. Throughout the service, no one is accountable for fiction, so that it may be exchanged freely between ships or between a shore library and a ship. Also it can be disposed of when worn out without paper work.[3]

A visit to a Navy library located at an extra-continental naval shore station in an inactive area revealed a colorful room and comfortable chairs. Men, a good number of them, were lounging around, legs draped over chair arms, and a good many of them were smoking. All in all, they presented a distressing sight in terms of conventional library behavior. They were also reading.

This attempt to bring color, charm, and informality into the library was a concerted one, and it may have implications for civilian libraries which serve the veteran. One Navy librarian describes her room in these words:

[3]Isabel DuBois, "Navy Libraries," *The Library Journal*, LXVII (May 15, 1942), 445.

We have seating space for 250, not including the 35 chairs in the writing room. . . . We have 30 sofas and many comfortable chairs, arranged in groups accommodating, at most, ten readers. Great care was taken in planning these groupings, with a colorful sofa or pair of bright chairs in each and convenient low tables for books and ashtrays. . . . Not a row of tables and chairs anywhere! . . . Our success in avoiding the stereotyped was due, perhaps, to the fact that after the minimum essentials for the operation of a library were definitely decided, we forgot that it was a library and planned a beautiful room, with the books only a part of the decorations. . . .[4]

The logistics problem involved in getting large supplies of books distributed was one of considerable magnitude. Books were stocked at the naval supply depots in Norfolk, Virginia, and Oakland, California. For some years there had been a supplementary stock pile of books at Pearl Harbor which serviced ships operating from that part. There was a similar service in the Canal Zone. The two continental depots provided libraries for all activities both afloat and ashore at the time of commissioning and outfitting, and made monthly, automatic distributions of books to all units. The numbers varied with the titles available and the personnel at a ship or station. Two new overseas stock piles for supplementary and emergency use were established as the war progressed—one at Espiritu Santo and the other at Guam. A third was in the process of establishment at Subic Bay when Japan surrendered.

Material selected for Navy libraries was chosen primarily with an eye to what naval personnel wanted to read and the use to which books might be put. As a rule of thumb, new libraries were furnished with two-thirds fiction and one-third nonfiction, the latter being selected in relation to the type and duty of the ship or station at which the library was being installed. Lack of circulation records made studies of the reader interest difficult. All libraries reported that Western stories were the most popular of fiction. However, there was also considerable demand for poetry, particularly in the forward combat areas. While this interest in poetry may have been due to the prevailing tension level, it is also possible that some veterans will retain this reading interest.

[4] Melissa M. Speer, "Instead of a Blueprint," *Wilson Library Bulletin,* XIX (January 1945), 334.

Particularly impressive was the diversity of requests which were received by the Library Section. Cartoon books, legal tomes, books on house-planning, philosophy—all were in demand. One request from an inactive area for a surprisingly large number of volumes on child care caused some concern in Washington. Investigation revealed that through this medium fathers who had been away from their children for several years were vicariously enjoying parenthood. With the addition of the Women's Reserve to the naval service, it was found necessary to add books of feminine interest. As the mental age of the Navy declined, with the coming of Selective Service, it became necessary to procure books of low reading level for the slow readers.

As to what Navy men read, the evidence is far from conclusive. Most people in the Navy library program who were consulted agreed in general with the study of Army reading habits which indicated that the taste of service personnel did not differ in any important way from that of civilians.[5] The Navy librarians, however, were somewhat dubious about the statement made in a popularly written article that "there is an intriguing, and perhaps pregnant difference . . . between the tastes of the serviceman and . . . of the civilian in that the former shows more interest in books . . . which explain the human mind. . . .[6] This, it was felt, was probably wishful thinking.

One Navy librarian reported that Western stories and mysteries accounted for almost 40 percent of the fiction or slightly more than a quarter of the total circulation.[7] The non-fiction demands at this library indicated a great diversity of interests. During one week requests were received for the following: mineralogy, poultry farming, orchids, Latin, air conditioning, architectural drawing, steam operation, bee-breeding, palmistry, hypnotism, librettos of Italian operas, admiralty law, Hawaiian antiquities and folklore, Mormonism, credits and collections, model trains, camouflage, photography, diet, the training of bird dogs, Beethoven's Seventh Symphony score, the sexual side of

[5] Capt. John Jamieson, "Books and the Soldier," *Public Opinion Quarterly* (Fall issue 1945), 331.

[6] David G. Wittels, "What the G.I. Reads," *The Saturday Evening Post,* CCXVII (June 23, 1945), 91.

[7] Rose McClennon, "The Military Library Illumines Postwar Planning," *Wilson Library Bulletin,* XX (September 1945), 45.

marriage, a graded speller, and the economical use of meat in the home. There was an increasing demand for books in useful arts. Also read were contemporary biographies, social science, music, and art. Philosophy and religion had few readers, and philology and general works were least popular.[8]

Until the fall of 1943, publishers provided the Library Section with review copies of new books on the basis of which orders would be placed. Later, books were reviewed in galley-proof form. Some 50 current books were selected each month and approximately 2,500 copies of each were purchased. In addition, the Navy received between 1,000,000 and 2,000,000 each year from the Victory Book campaigns.

The Navy Library Service staff feels that its centralized review and purchase of books was most advantageous. Not only did it permit the securing of greater discounts, but books were read before they were ordered. Thus the waste which accompanies purchase on the basis of publishers' statements and the reviews of others was avoided. Nor did this centralization seem to stifle individual libraries. Local welfare funds were still available to meet particular demands, and requests for special books were granted whenever possible.

ARMED SERVICES EDITIONS

Shortly following the entrance of the United States into World War II it became apparent that a way would have to be found to supply men overseas with books which were both economical and compact. The problem was neatly summarized in a memorandum written to the members of the Council on Books in Wartime by the late Warder Norton of W. W. Norton and Company.

> It has long been felt that a major contribution of the industry could properly be along a new and completely different line, that of making freely available to our Armed Forces the entertainment, information, the morale, and even the inspiration which is in books. Older books have long been available in paper-bound form and because they are expendable, require little shipping space; and can be acquired cheaply in great quantities, have answered a real need. But new books, which must be supplied in a hard-bound and bulky form, not expendable nor easily shipped,

[8] *Ibid,* p. 46.

not sufficiently low in price nor economical in materials to be available in adequate quantities for forces of millions of men, have remained, through no fault of anyone, a kind of luxury.[9]

The original idea for the Armed Services Editions must be credited to the Army and Navy Library Services. The armed forces took the idea to the Council on Books in Wartime, the logical organization to undertake such a project. The suggestion was received enthusiastically by the Council, which established Editions for the Armed Services, Inc., a separate, non-profit corporation with its own staff to accomplish this purpose.

The first of the Armed Services Editions were delivered to the Army and Navy in September 1943. Initial delivery consisted of 30,000 copies of 32 titles a month or a total of 1,600,000. This figure grew until it included a peak of over 150,000 copies each of 40 titles for a monthly total of 6,200,000 copies.[10] The cost per copy to the services averaged less than six cents.[11]

The books were made small enough to be carried in men's pockets and so designed that they would not be damaged by being so carried. They also had to be in a format that could be printed on presses available for very large press runs. It was finally decided to make the books in two sizes (5½″ x 3⅝″ and 6½″ x 4½″), to bind the books on the short instead of the long side, and to print two columns of type on each page. An important reason for choosing sidebinding instead of lengthwise binding was that a sidebound book could be slipped into a hip pocket and sat upon without damaging the spine of the book or of the user. A two-column format was chosen for these reasons: (1) it allows the use of a smaller type face without detracting from readability; (2) 12 percent more words can be printed in the same size of type on a two-column page than on a one-column page; and (3) in poor light it is less fatiguing to read a short line than one of the conventional four- or five-inch length.

The method of printing the Armed Services Editions had peculiar implications for selection. These books were printed two at

[9] Quoted in material furnished by Editions for the Armed Services, Inc.

[10] S. Spencer Scott, "A Thumbnail Résumé of the Council's Activities," *Publishers Weekly*, CXLIX (February 9, 1946), 1022.

[11] "Council on Books Holds Fourth and Last Annual Meeting," *Publishers Weekly*, CXLIX (February 9, 1946), 1018.

a time or four at a time and then separated. Each of a group of books thus had to have an identical number of pages; for example, two books of 512 or four books of 256 pages. This made necessary the creation of an elaborate system of character counting. The problem was further complicated by the requirement that the titles represent a good sampling of all types of books.[12]

Practically all books were made available for use in this series, current best sellers as well as older publications. This permitted the inclusion of all types of books as is indicated by the following analysis of the first 774 titles issued.[13]

Category	Number
Adventure	17
Aviation	6
Biographies	57
Classics	21
Contemporary fiction	127
Travel	31
Current affairs	12
Drama	4
Fantasy	19
Historical novels	89
History	17
Humor	91
Miscellaneous	10
Music and arts	6
Mysteries	50
Nature	8
Poetry	17
Science	16
Sea stories	23
Self-help	6
Short-story collections	48
Sports	11
Westerns	88
Total	774

This was a publishing venture almost without precedent and necessitated experimentation both in selection and distribution. The selection process started with the publishers who nominated titles from their own lists, both forthcoming and in print. These

[12] Material furnished by Editions for the Armed Services, Inc.

[13] *A List of the First 774 Books Published for American Armed Forces Overseas.* (New York: Editions for the Armed Services, Inc.), p. 1.

suggestions were screened by a committee of distinguished publishers, book critics, authors, and librarians. Final selection from this list was made by the advisory committee and the editorial board of Editions for the Armed Services with the approval of the librarians of both the Army and the Navy.[14]

After being printed, books were delivered to a consolidated warehouse of the Army and Navy for distribution. The Army mailed individual cartons to almost every Army unit that existed rather than shipping in bulk to each theater of war. This not only speeded up delivery but made certain that all units received the complete series of books.[15]

Each book, after it reached the men and women of the armed services was considered expendable, being expressly designed to be carried in pockets and to be passed freely from reader to reader until worn out.

At the end of the war it was planned that Armed Services Editions would continue to operate only until October 1946, by which time it was estimated that 1,180 titles would have been printed.[16] However, at the request of the Army and Navy the contract was extended for a year and a new series of 25,000 copies, each of 12 titles a month, was planned.[17]

The most significant estimates of the success of the ASE have come from both word-of-mouth reports from the front and from the many letters which had been received from both enlisted men and officers. Mr. Ray L. Trautman, formerly Lt. Colonel, who headed the Army Library Service during the war told of men in France with monthly salaries of $55 offering to pay 500 francs, the equivalent of $10.00 at that time, for the privilege of being next in line to read an ASE, of how men gathered around while one read by flashlight and after the batteries were exhausted, by the light of stubby German candles, of the books being dropped by parachute on Vis Island off the coast of Jugoslavia where they were read aloud in translation by English-speaking inhabitants, of men lightening their packs in England before D-Day and throwing away into a huge head all manner of articles—but leaving behind not a single ASE, of a car being ransacked one night on the continent while standing next to an MP station for safekeeping and of nothing being taken from it but a carton containing 32 ASE.

[14] Material furnished by Editions for the Armed Services, Inc.
[15] *Ibid.*
[16] "Council on Books Holds Fourth and Last Annual Meeting," *Publishers Weekly*, CXLIX (Feb. 9, 1946), 1018.
[17] Letter from H. Stahley Thompson, Manager, Editions for the Armed Services, Inc., June 13, 1946.

An Army officer in a hospital in England wrote: "From the Airborne Infantry of the front lines to the chair-borne Finance Corps of the rear, you can find boys reading as they have never read before. Some in my company have admitted without shame that they were reading their first book since they were in grammar school."

There have been many reports, some eloquent, some halting, many tragic, but all of which are more than rewarding for the time and effort which went into publishing ASE.[18]

The fact that these books were so cheaply produced made it possible to classify them as expendable and thus eliminate record-keeping. While the situation in the services will not be duplicated in civilian life, the large-scale use of inexpensive books may be an important avenue of development for civilian libraries.

[18] Material furnished by Editions for the Armed Services, Inc.

VIII. LITERACY TRAINING

THE TASK of learning to read and write one's native tongue is traditionally and logically a responsibility of childhood. In modern times, the great majority of American children have had the opportunity to acquire these basic skills, at least adequately enough to meet their simple, immediate needs. But even today there are some children who are denied this privilege. As one examines the successively higher age brackets of the population, one discovers an increasing number of men and women who, for convenient reference, are called illiterates.

In the strictest sense, literacy training is not a proper function of adult education. But the skills of reading, writing, and elementary arithmetical computation are so basic a part of learning that other education cannot take place until they have been mastered. Where there are adult illiterates, therefore, an enlightened social policy will insist that they be given the opportunity to learn. They cannot start any earlier.

Both major branches of the service, drawing as they did to so large a scale on the masses of American people, had to face the problem of literacy training.

ARMY [1]

Early in the vast mobilization program undertaken by the government, it was recognized that a manpower problem would exist in the country. Accordingly, taking into account the experiences gained in World War I, provision was made in the autumn of 1940 for the organization of special training battalions at reception centers. These battalions were to be organized only when directed by the War Department and were to handle illiterates, non-English-speaking men, individuals suffering from temporary physical defects at the time of induction, and men with extremely low intelligence rating or other indications of marked

[1] This description of the Army literacy training activities was condensed from an unpublished document prepared for the Commission by Dr. Samuel Goldberg. Extensive use was made of Selective Service and War Department sources in this description. The authors of the study are grateful for this assistance.

lack of competence. Authority was also granted to give selectees assigned to special training battalions "such specialized treatment and training" as were required to develop them for full field service or limited service. Schools for non-English-speaking men and illiterates were to be established as required.

Although the groundwork was laid early in the mobilization program for the reception and training of large numbers of handicapped men, no special training organizations were established in 1940. Such directives were not issued for several reasons. First of all, the Selective Training and Service Act of 1940, approved by the President on September 16, 1940, was a peacetime conscription law, and real dangers did not yet beset the country. Consequently, the size of the manpower problem was not fully appreciated. Second, there was little realization of the extent of such special problems as illiteracy in the population. And, third, the prime job of the Army was to expand its facilities so that at least 800,000 men per year could be trained and assigned to the reserve at the end of each year. It did not appear feasible to burden the Army, already overtaxed, with the additional responsibility of training illiterate, non-English-speaking, and otherwise handicapped men.

Registrants called in the early days of the draft, November 1940, were, therefore, inducted into the military service if they were able to meet physical standards and "to understand simple orders given in the English language." A surprisingly high number of illiterate men found their way into the Army, however, in the early months of mobilization. Between October 1940 and May 1941, there were 6,374 persons inducted into the Army who could neither read nor write. In addition, there were approximately 60,000 near-illiterates. This situation soon brought about a modification of policy, made on May 15, 1941:

> "No registrant in continental United States will be inducted into the military service who *does not have the capacity of reading and writing the English language as commonly prescribed for the fourth grade in grammar school. All registrants who have not completed the fourth grade in grammar school will be examined at induction stations prior to induction by means of tests to be prescribed by the War Department.*" [2]

[2] Mobilization Regulation 1-7, *Reception of Selective Service Men,* Change No. 9 (April 18, 1941).

The establishment of a fourth-grade standard was not considered a prohibitive requirement. It was believed that a fourth-grade level was the minimum necessary to comprehend written instructions, orders, sign boards, and regulations. Further, it was assumed that few persons would be unable to attain a fourth-grade standard since education was so general throughout America.[3]

The deferment of illiterates at this time enabled the Army to explore various approaches to the problem. A War Department letter dated July 28, 1941, directed that a special training unit be established at each replacement training center. These units were organized to train those illiterate, non-English-speaking, and slow-learning men who were already in the Army, and to determine by experience both their training ability and their usefulness in the service. At the same time, a number of cooperative efforts were initiated with civilian school systems, through the United States Office of Education, and with Selective Service to determine the practicability of raising the literacy level of illiterate selective registrants prior to their induction.

The deferment of illiterates continued until August 1, 1942. By that time, manpower needs were so great that it was no longer possible to overlook the 200,000 men in the nation, physically able and available for military service, who thus far had been deferred for illiteracy alone. Effective August 1, 1942, therefore, induction stations were authorized to accept for induction, on any day, illiterates in numbers not to exceed 10 percent of the white and 10 percent of the colored registrants. Only those illiterates could be inducted who possessed "sufficient intelligence to absorb military training rapidly. . . ."[4] Appropriate screening procedures were developed for application in the induction stations. The policy of accepting illiterates to the extent of 10 percent of the white and colored registrants at each induction station on any day soon overtaxed the housing facilities available at replacement training centers. It became necessary, therefore, in November 1942, to direct army, corps, service command, division, or other unit commanders to establish special

[3] First Report of the Director of Selective Service, *Selective Service in Peacetime* (1940-1941).

[4] War Department Circular No. 169, Section IV (June 1, 1942).

training units within their commands. In February 1943, when induction stations began the processing of selectees for both Army and Navy, and the Navy began to accept Negroes for service, the Army reduced from 10 to 5 percent the number of illiterate and non-English-speaking men who could be inducted on a given day.

Several major changes in policy took place, effective June 1, 1943. The great need for additional manpower resulted in the removal of all limitations governing the percentage of illiterates to be inducted. At the same time, to insure the induction of only better qualified illiterates, new screening and testing procedures were introduced at the induction stations and reception centers.[5] To accommodate the greatly increased numbers of illiterate, non-English-speaking, and slow-learning men entering the Army, commanding generals of the service commands were directed to organize special training units at or near reception centers.[6] The organization of special training units at the reception-center level served two purposes: (1) replacement training centers and organizations were relieved of the extra burden of training illiterates and could concentrate their energies and facilities on training the regular troops; and (2) the illiterates were provided with an opportunity to achieve literacy and other pre-basic military skills before they entered the regular training cycle. Finally, it was stipulated and later explicitly emphasized by directive that special training units would train only illiterate, near-illiterate and non-English-speaking men, and would not serve as training stations for all low grade personnel in the Army.

During the year 1944, new and improved test procedures were introduced in the induction stations, effective June 1, but no new basic policies with regard to the selection of illiterate registrants were formulated. As the Army reached its peak strength and the emphasis was placed more and more on quality of personnel, policy changes were made within the Army affecting the training and assignment of illiterate personnel. For example, in August 1944, it was specified that only personnel who could suc-

[5] War Department Letter, AG 201.6 (4-28-43) OC-o, Subject: *Mental Induction Standards and Procedures* (May 11, 1943).

[6] War Department Letter, SPX 353 (5-14-43) OB-D-SPGAE, Subject: *Establishment of Special Training Units* (May 28, 1943).

cessfully complete basic training would be forwarded from the special training units, and that the emphasis should not be placed on accomplishment of academic standards alone.

Shortly after VJ Day, when the emphasis in the Army turned to demobilization procedures and to the utilization of only maximally effective personnel, a War Department letter dated September 21, 1945, directed that the induction of illiterates be discontinued. Provision was made for the transferring and training of illiterates who were already inducted, providing that such men would be forwarded to a special training unit prior to October 15, 1945. By January 1946, the last of the special training units was closed.

EXAMINATION PROCEDURES

As indicated in the previous section, policy changes at different stages of the war made it necessary to vary examination procedures in induction stations and reception centers. In the earlier months of Selective Service, a Minimum Literacy Test was developed for use in induction stations to aid in determining whether the selectee possessed the capacity for "reading and writing the English language as commonly prescribed for the fourth grade in grammar school."

In August 1942, a much more comprehensive type of screening procedure was introduced. In June 1943, when literacy ceased to be a bar to induction, further revisions were made. Variations in examining procedures were made necessary not only by policy changes but also by experience and experimentation with the testing instruments themselves which led to their refinement and improvement.

With more experience, careful screening procedures with proper checks and balances were developed in the induction stations and reception centers. Their purpose was to select only those illiterate, non-English-speaking, and slow-learning men who demonstrated sufficient intellectual capacity to make satisfactory soldiers. Those selectees who demonstrated that their lack of learning accomplishment was in effect a consequence of a feeble intellect and not of environmental deprivations were rejected at the induction stations.

NUMBER AND CHARACTERISTICS OF ILLITERATE AND GRADE V MEN [7]

No complete reliable figures are available on the number of men who received special literacy training prior to June 1, 1943, nor are the data on the number of illiterate and Grade V men who were inducted into the Army during this period entirely clear. The data for the period subsequent to June 1, 1943, during which all inducted illiterate, non-English-speaking, and Grade V men received literacy training, are entirely valid.

The data which are available for the period prior to June 1, 1943, indicates that there were approximately 107,075 illiterates (inclusive of non-English-speaking men) inducted between August 1, 1942 and May 31, 1943. Figures for August, September, and October 1942, which are included in the total, represent the best available estimates which have been officially accepted by the records division of the Adjutant General's Office. Of the total number of illiterates inducted in this period, 64 percent were white and the remainder Negro. There were 685,362 Grade V men inducted between March 1, 1941, and June 1, 1943. Because of the established processing and recording procedures in induction stations and reception centers, during this period, it is likely that the figure representing Grade V personnel includes many of the illiterates contained in the previous figure showing illiterates inducted. Of the total number of Grade V men inducted, approximately 60 percent were white and the remainder Negro.

Between June 1, 1943, and October 1, 1945, there were 217,053 illiterates and 82,006 Grade V men accepted in the Army.[8] These 299,059 men represented 10.8 percent of the total number of men inducted into the Army during the same period. The white illiterates and Grade V men represented 6.6 percent of the total number of white men inducted. The comparable figure for the Negroes was 43.3 percent. Although all sections of the country contributed illiterate and Grade V men to the special training units, the data show clearly that the Fourth

[7] Men classified as slow learners by the Army General Classification Test.

[8] Based on official data on file in the Personnel and Procedures Branch, Operations and Training Division, The Adjutant General's Office, War Department, Washington, D. C.

and Eighth Service commands [9] contributed a disproportionately greater number of white and Negro illiterate and Grade V men for literacy training. This is not surprising, considering the per capita cost of education in these sections of the country.

The greater majority of the men in special training were native-born illiterates—men who could speak and understand English but who were unable to read it. Among the non-English-speaking personnel in special training units were the Spanish-speaking men of the Southwest; the French-speaking Acadians of Louisiana; and the Italian-, Chinese-, Portuguese-, and Spanish-speaking individuals who came from the urban communities, industrial centers, and seacoast towns of the country. Notwithstanding the marked progress which has been made in American education in the past twenty-five years, there were a considerable number of illiterates in the younger draft group.

As a rule, the men in special training units had notably poor social and emotional adaptations. Great numbers of them had never emancipated themselves from the immediate family unit and were unprepared to function as members of larger social units. The AWOL rate among special training unit personnel was greater than for personnel of other units. It was more difficult for them to understand their presence in the Army, and it was not easy to get them to show initiative or to assume responsibilities.

THE DEVELOPMENT OF ACADEMIC TRAINING MATERIALS FOR SPECIAL TRAINING UNITS

When the Army was confronted with the problem of training the vast numbers of illiterates coming into the Army, it found a dearth of available instructional materials. While there were some publications for teaching adult illiterates, none seemed especially appropriate as basic texts, though all had some value and were used in the early days by some of the units as collateral reading materials.

The earliest text to be used extensively in special training units was *Army Life*. This privately published text was tentatively

[9] The Fourth Service Command consisted of the following states: North Carolina, South Carolina, Georgia, Florida, Alabama, Tennessee, and Mississippi. The Eighth, of the following: Texas, Oklahoma, Louisiana, New Mexico, and Arkansas.

adopted by the Army about June 21, 1941. By August 1942, this was replaced by the *Soldier's Reader,* also a privately printed text. This reader was built around basic military activities and was divided into four parts which corresponded in reading level to elementary grades one to four. Additional materials were prepared by the War Department to supplement the basic text. Among them were the following: *Manual for Teachers of Adult Elementary Students,* which contained valuable suggestions for instructors in special training units: *Our War,* a monthly news periodical which contained stories, feature articles, news accounts, a cartoon strip, and other interesting material written mainly at a third- and fourth-grade level; a filmstrip, *Special Training in Reading, Writing, and Arithmetic,* which provided drill on commonly used military words, and simple arithmetic exercises in the fundamental processes.

Later that year, in November 1942, two supplementary publications were prepared for use in special training units: *Your Job in the Army,* a pamphlet which contained descriptions of suitable Army jobs for graduates of special training units; and *Newsmap Supplement,* a single sheet sent out weekly to give trainees a simplified version of the material appearing in the regular *Newsmap.*

The foregoing materials helped to standardize the special training program in replacement training centers and organizations during 1942 and through the spring of 1943. The basic reader and accompanying instructional materials, however, did not quite reach desired standards, and the writing of a new text and preparation of new supplementary materials were begun. In May 1943, two new texts—a reader and an arithmetic book, prepared by the War Department as technical manuals—were ready for distribution. These and other materials soon were applied in the special training program which was organized at the reception-center level in June 1943. Along with the additional publications which were prepared in 1944 and 1945, these materials served as the major instructional materials with which the bulk of the illiterates in the Army were trained.

All literacy-training materials developed by the War Department were highly functional in character. They were intimately related to the man's Army experiences and thus were close to his interests and needs. The content of all publications was checked against standard word lists and was analyzed by statistical and other techniques to insure that it was properly graded in level of difficulty. And, wherever possible, the material in reading, writing, and arithmetic was correlated to make it easier for the instructor to integrate his instruction in the different areas.

Practically all of the special training units developed local materials to meet their own needs. Among the types of instructional materials prepared were the following: work books, drill exercises, flash cards, visual aids of various sorts, supplementary reading materials in academic and military subject matter, and instructor's guides.

ORGANIZATION AND OPERATION OF SPECIAL TRAINING UNITS

From July 1941 to June 1943, special training units were organized at replacement training centers and in such other commands as armies, corps, service commands, divisions, and smaller organizations. At one time during this period, a count of the number of units in existence revealed 239 separate organizations.[10] Some of these special training units numbered fewer than 5 men, others more than 1,000.

During this period, special training units were authorized to receive five types of men: illiterates, non-English-speaking men, slow-learners, men emotionally unstable to a degree prohibiting their immediate success in regular training units, and men who were physically limited. The training consisted of two parts: basic military training and educational instruction. The latter included three hours daily in reading, expression (writing and conversation), and arithmetic. An eight-week schedule was recommended and the maximum time limit was three months in which to qualify a trainee as literate and capable of assimilating regular training.

Two different reports on the operation of the program during this period give an indication of the size and character of the training job. One report, received in October 1942, revealed

[10] "The Army Teaches the Three R's," War Department *Special Service Digest*, May 1943.

that at the time there were 26,766 men in special training units. A second report, which covered the period from January 16 to February 15, 1943, was based on 118 reporting installations and showed a total number of 30,592 men in training. The latter report contained the following breakdown for the different categories of personnel in training:[11]

Categories	Percent
Illiterate	61.7
Non-English	12.5
Grade V	16.7
Physically handicapped	6.8
Personality disorders	2.3

Apart from isolated attempts in some of the units to provide special programs for physically handicapped men and for those who were emotionally and socially unadjusted, no special programs to meet the special needs of these men were prescribed. They profited from the specially adapted program of military training in special training units which was conducted at a modified rate, and from the sympathetic type of handling given them by the specially selected instructor personnel in the units. Accordingly, they were aided in their adjustment to the Army and were prepared for regular training. The bulk of the men in the specal training units were those requiring literacy training, and the major effort of the War Department was concerned with the development of a program to salvage them.

After June 1, 1943, special training units were organized at the reception-center level, and shortly afterward the other special training units were inactivated. The organization of special training units at the reception-center level permitted men requiring literacy and preliminary basic military instruction to receive it soon after they were processed at the reception centers. The typical length of stay at the reception centers for these men was about three to five days, during which time they were clothed, inoculated, and given preliminary military orientation. By receiving their special training so early in their military careers,

[11] Memorandum for the Director of Military Training, ASF, AG353 (4-3-43) OT-C, Subject: *Summary of Reports of Special Training Units and Literacy Schools in the Army* (April 3, 1943).

illiterate, non-English-speaking, and slow-learning men did not find it necessary initially to compete with men more adept than they were. Furthermore, their original specific limitations in academic skills were considerably minimized in degree by the time they were forwarded for regular training. And, with their pre-basic military instruction, also acquired in the special training program, they did not constitute an outstanding impediment to the progress of the regular training organization when assigned to it.

Twenty-four units were organized at the reception-center level soon after June 1, 1943. Each service command had at least one unit, and two service commands had at least six each. By December 1943, the number of units had been reduced to nineteen, through the consolidation of smaller units within service commands. Further reductions in the number of units continued to take place when definite trends indicated a reduction in the number of personnel requiring special training. However, each service command continued to operate at least one unit until July 1945.

The new program continued to call for eighteen hours weekly of academic instruction and thirty hours weekly of preliminary basic military training. In May 1944, a revision of the basic mobilization training program was made. The revision increased the number of hours allocated weekly to academic subject matter and correspondingly reduced the number assigned to military instruction. Under this program, approximately 60 percent of the time was given to academic subjects which, in addition to reading, language expression, and arithmetic, now included orientation and current events. Although authority had been granted in the previous mobilization training programs to modify the recommended program to suit local and individual needs, the current revision specified modified programs for non-English-speaking personnel and for the Grade V men as differentiated from that recommended for the illiterates.

The typical illiterate followed the prescribed eight-week schedule, in which the time allocation was 60 percent for academic material and 40 percent for military subjects. If he required the full twelve weeks of special training, authority was contained in the training program to plan the remaining four weeks to suit his special needs. Any division of time between the academic and military could be made. For those Grade V men who could approximate fourth-grade standards in reading and arithmetic soon after entrance into the unit, authority was granted for an abbreviated special training program (three to four weeks), in which one hour per day was given to reading, one to arithmetic, and six to military training. For the non-English-speaking men, it was permissible to modify the program so that for the first three or four weeks, six hours daily were given to language instruction and two were given to military.

The special training program was highly individualized. Men were forwarded for regular training as soon as they were able to pass the prescribed academic "graduation tests" and were able to show by their accomplishments in military subjects that they were capable of becoming soldiers. Illiterate, non-English-speaking, and Grade V men were honorably discharged from the Army as soon as it became apparent by their performance in special training units that they were incapable of attaining the prescribed standards of proficiency in the allotted amount of time.

ADDITIONAL LITERACY TRAINING ACTIVITIES

Additional literacy training activities were also conducted by the Army. In the main, they served those illiterates who had been inducted into the Army prior to June 1, 1943, and consequently had never received the regular program of special training. Also included within some of these programs were men who had at one time acquired literacy training early in their military careers, but who had regressed to a lower level of skill because of forgetting and because of an insufficient opportunity to apply and retain their newly acquired skills.

A considerable part of the additional literacy training activities was conducted in off-duty hours and was organized by Special Service officers, education officers, and chaplains. Provisions for the conduct of literacy training during duty hours for those men requiring it were contained in the special training programs prescribed for rehabilitation centers, disciplinary barracks where general prisoners of the Army were confined and trained, and convalescent hospitals.

There are no official figures available on the total number of men who participated in the literacy training programs outside of the special training units.

EDUCATIONAL CHARACTERISTICS OF THE PROGRAM IN SPECIAL TRAINING UNITS

The program of instruction in special training units was broad and constructive. Its objectives have been summarized as follows: [12]

1. To teach the men to read at a fourth-grade level to enable them to comprehend bulletins, written orders and directions, and basic Army publications.
2. To give the men sufficient language skill to enable them to use and understand such everyday language as is necessary to get along with officers and men in the Army.
3. To teach the men to do number work at a fourth-grade level to enable them to understand their pay accounts and deductions from it, their laundry bills, and conduct their business in the PX; etc.
4. To facilitate the adjustment of the men to military training and Army life.
5. To have the men understand in a general way the reasons which made it necessary for this country to fight Germany, Japan, and Italy.

In general, the methods of instruction were those which have been used extensively with the slow learner in civilian life. Instructional groups were small in order to modify and adapt the program to suit individual capabilities, needs, and interests. Extensive use was made of illustration and demonstration. Through the use of the many teaching aids and devices, the men were able to secure meaningful drill and applicatory exercises. Instruction in academic subject matter was integrated with military training.

No single method was recommended for the teaching of reading. Instead, several different approaches were suggested and

[12] Samuel Goldberg, "Psychological Procedures Employed in the Army Special Training Units," *Journal of Clinical Psychology,* I (April 1945), 118-25.

it was left to the discretion of the instructor to select those techniques most suitable to his needs. Fundamentally, it was recommended that the men be given a basic stock vocabulary through sight-recognition techniques and a multiple sensory approach; that no new words be taught, the meaning of which the men did not know; and that rich associated meanings be developed in connection with words and phrases. Exercises and flash cards containing first words, then phrases, and then sentences were recommended to increase the recognition span of the beginning reader. Word-blending techniques and phonics in general were recommended more for third- and fourth-grade men than for beginners. Men were taught to read for detail, to follow directions, to derive meaning from paragraph material, to predict outcomes and for ordinary enjoyment through extensive and varied reading instruction and exercises. Although the development of a fair rate of reading was one of the objectives of the reading program, the achievement of a fairly high degree of accuracy of comprehension was the major aim.

Men were taught to use and understand oral and written language. Improved language abilities facilitated progress in reading and vice versa. Written language exercises were preceded by periods of oral expression. In this way, adequate opportunity was provided for the development of rich ideas and associations, unencumbered by limited spelling and handwriting skills. Written exercises were concerned fundamentally with clarity of expression and not with accuracy of spelling and quality of handwriting. Men were taught to spell only those words which they used in writing. At times, because it was necessary to spend the major time available to teach reading, inaccurate spelling was tolerated if the word was recognizable. And, while legibility of handwriting was sought, no extended efforts were made to obtain perfect alignment, letter formation, spacing, or great speed.

Arithmetic was taught in a variety of ways. The emphasis was on whole numbers and the fundamental processes. Section three of the *Army Reader* was concerned almost entirely with number relationships and operations as they are found in the life of the soldier. Both arithmetic computation and reasoning were involved in the solution of many of the situations provided. Consequently, the soldier was able to derive a better understanding of the meaning of numbers and group relationships.

In the academic phase of the program, the men were classified on the basis of objective tests in reading. Inadequate reading ability represented their greatest single limitation and accounted for their initial assignment to a special training unit. Major efforts in the program were, therefore, directed toward the eradication of this deficiency.

The accomplishments of the men in special training were evaluated on the basis of formal and informal tests and procedures. In the academic phase of the program, objective tests were used. The men progressed from one grade level to the next only after demonstrating, on unit reading tests, sufficient ability to obtain the prescribed critical score. Similarly, they were ready to be graduated from the academic department only after they were able to achieve the required scores on objective tests of reading and arithmetic. In the military subjects, written and performance tests were used to determine the trainee's status. In subjects like organization of the Army, military courtesy and discipline, and interior guard, simple true-false and completion types of tests were employed. For men in levels three and four, the tests were often written in very simple language. When men of the first two levels were tested, true-false questions were generally presented orally, and the trainee indicated the truth or falsity of the statement by punching an answer card appropriately. In subjects like first aid, infantry drill, and manual of arms, the test was of a behavioral type in which the officer personnel rated the efficiency of the soldier's performance.

Emphasis on academic and military skills alone, with the socially and emotionally immature personnel typically found in special training units, might readily have permitted the development of many feelings and attitudes which could serve only to inhibit effort and interfere with accomplishment. Thus, the program of training made provision for subject matter which was designed to facilitate the man's social and emotional adjustment.

Through the orientation and current-events instruction, each man acquired a better understanding of the reasons which put this country into the war, of his own role and responsibilities in the struggle, of the progress of the armed forces, and of the problems concerned with occupation and the making of a peace. Through required mental-hygiene instruction, usually given by the post psychiatrist or unit of personnel consultant, each trainee was given an insight into his adjustment problems.[13]

In addition, counseling programs were organized in each of the special training units. Noncommissioned officers were trained and assigned as counselors, working under the supervision and direction of the psychiatrist or unit personnel consultant. Through this type of program, men with simple problems were quickly helped to solve them.

Those men who experienced more serious difficulty in adjusting were referred for fuller clinical study. Use was made of appropriate test, interview, and treatment techniques by professionally qualified personnel in order to understand and improve the situation. When indicated, remedial programs were developed. When it became apparent on the basis of clinical study that the trainee was inapt, lacked the required degree of adaptability, or possessed undesirable habits or traits of character, he was recommended for separation from the service.

TEACHER SELECTION, TRAINING, AND SUPERVISION IN SPECIAL TRAINING UNITS

Instructors for the special training units were selected from those men in uniform who had either prior experience as teachers or an aptitude for teaching. Only those men were sought as instructors who had a sympathetic appreciation of the needs of illiterates, non-English-speaking and Grade V men and could provide the type of encouragement and motivation which were necessary to make the program successful. In March 1944, a drive was made to recruit civilian teachers for the academic phase

[13] TB Med 21, *Lecture Outlines for Enlisted Men on Personal Adjustment Problems* (March 15, 1944), served as the official guide for this instruction.

of the program in order to replace physically fit instructors who could be prepared for overseas shipment.[14] Despite the teacher shortage during the war, many units were successful in obtaining needed civilian instructors who were qualified to do the job.

Each of the special training units was required to conduct a troop school for the indoctrination and in-service training of instructors. Training was provided for all instructors to prepare them to conduct the military and/or academic training prescribed by the program and to insure that a high level of instruction was maintained. Three national training conferences were conducted for selected instructors and supervisors of special training units.

ACCOMPLISHMENTS OF THE SPECIAL TRAINING PROGRAM

Of the 302,838 men who were received in special training units after June 1, 1943, there were 254,272 men who successfully completed the program and were assigned for regular training, 44,499 men who were discharged from the Army, and 4,067 men who were transferred to a non-duty status. The number of men assigned represented 84 percent of those who entered the special training units which were operated at the reception-center level. Of those men who successfully completed the program, 79 percent required sixty days or less to achieve the standards.

There were 135,470 white men who successfully completed the program. They represented 83 percent of the total number of white entrants into special training. There were 119,296 Negroes who were graduated from the units, representing 85 percent of the Negro entrants. Analysis of the data on the rate of accomplishment reveals that 81 percent of the successful whites required less than sixty days to graduate and the comparable percentage for the Negroes was 76.

No extensive follow-up data are extant on the accomplishment of the illiterate non-English-speaking and Grade V men after they left special training. Although some of them failed to make the grade, the great majority were able to complete regular basic training and serve in some useful capacity.

[14] Army Service Forces Letter, SPTRR 231-28, Subject: *Civilian Instructors for Special Training Units* (March 11, 1944).

NAVY

The Navy, like the Army, found many men in its ranks who were not sufficiently literate to undertake the training necessary for modern warfare. Inability to follow written instructions, read simple charts, comprehend a written order—all of these were weaknesses which had to be remedied before such illiterates could be trusted amidst the complexities of a modern Navy.

The problem of the illiterate did not press upon the Navy as early as was the case with the Army. Until June 1, 1943, the illiterate was kept out of the Navy. On that date, however, the literacy standards for induction into the Navy became the same as those of the Army, and illiteracy alone was no longer considered valid grounds for rejection.[15] Early in 1944 a special training program for illiterates was established at the Naval Training Station, Great Lakes, Illinois. The next month this instruction, for all but Negro illiterates, was transferred to Camp Peary, Williamsburg, Virginia.

Instruction at these centers was only for men entering the Navy. During 1943, however, illiterates had been accepted and assigned to duty without being taught to read and write. As a result there were many requests from commanding officers for permission to transfer these illiterates to Camp Peary for instruction. These requests were denied and the responsibility for finding suitable duties for the illiterates placed with the commanding officer.

In the summer of 1944, a Navy-wide literacy training program was undertaken for both recruits and men on active duty. The materials for this work were prepared by the Standards and Curriculum Division of Training, the Bureau of Naval Personnel.[16]

In many ways, the kind of material prepared for this program was its most interesting facet. The *Navy Life* series consisted of workbooks, basic readers, supplementary readers, tests, and teachers' manuals. The first book used by the student was not a reader but a workbook. Thus the instructor was

[15] Samuel A. Lynde and Edgar A. Schuler, "The Undereducated Serviceman and the G.I. Bill of Rights," *Adult Education Bulletin,* IX (December 1944), 35.

[16] Charles S. Ross, "Literacy Training in the Navy," *School and Society,* LXIII (March 23, 1946), 203-4.

forced down from the platform to work among the students. The first of the readers was not introduced until considerable reading ability had been developed through chart, blackboard, and workbook reading experiences.[17]

The Navy also utilized the already existing appeal of the comic book. These comic books were written so that their characters used naval terminology. As rapid, supervised, classroom supplementary reading material, these comic books were most successful.

The source of the Navy's illiterates will surprise no educator. A study of 7,000 literacy trainees at Camp Peary revealed that 95 percent came from twenty-four states, chiefly rural and southern. A third had attended one- or two-room schools. About half of the schools attended by these illiterates had stove heat and outside toilets. One-fourth had no artificial light and nearly one-fifth of the schools made drinking water available only in a bucket.

The Camp Peary literacy trainees averaged twenty-three years of age. Three-fifths were married and had an average of two children. The families of these trainees averaged seven children, about half of whom had completed the sixth grade. Only one in thirteen of such children had completed high school.

About 5 percent of the trainees had not completed one grade in school and only 16 percent one or two grades. Slightly less than 50 percent had finished the sixth, seventh, or eighth grade. Seven individuals confessed to having attended school through the twelfth grade.

The Navy established again the fact that illiteracy is not necessarily a function of low intelligence. By comparing the performance of 3,200 illiterates with those of general service recruits on the Navy Non-Verbal Test, the conclusion was reached that there was "but slight difference between regular services and special recruits in regard to intelligence." [18]

A study of 460 of these trainees was undertaken to determine the improvement observable. These recruits were given the

[17] *Ibid.*, 204.
[18] U. S. Navy Department, Bureau of Naval Personnel, "Report on the Educational Status of Special Recruit Trainees" (MS on file in Office of Naval History, U. S. Navy Department).

Sangren-Woody Reading Test before and after eight weeks of training. For all recruits the median improvement was from 28.1 to 38.5, for Q_1 from 14.1 to 22.5, and for Q_3 from 41.7 to 53.9.[19]

Invaluable as the literacy training of recruits was, it suffered from certain limitations. The time available was limited to about twelve weeks. Seldom was it possible to develop more than fourth-grade skills in that time. Nor was this period devoted exclusively to such instruction, for military training with all its distractions and physical fatigue proceeded along with it. And, finally, the purpose of this training was to develop only a minimum command of literacy skills for the purposes of military service. The development of the responsible, adult citizen of a democracy could not in the nature of the case be included as an objective.[20]

However, the Navy's experience in this field should encourage civilian educators. One man who participated in the planning and execution of this program wrote:

> Those actively interested in adult-education will hardly be surprised to learn that experience with these men in the Navy Special Recruit Training program has been most encouraging. Our experience, based on a total of over 20,000 trainees, shows the older men, while unable to learn as rapidly as their younger mates, to be characterized by a stronger drive to learn the fundamental skills. This compensating factor of motivation apparently more than makes up for whatever increased learning difficulties may accompany increasing age. . . . If sound planning and effective execution can eliminate illiteracy from the entire military service age-bracket of the population, *our nation has an excellent chance of breaking the vicious circle of low educational standards that make illiteracy self-perpetuating.*[21]

[19] *Ibid.*
[20] Lynde and Schuler, *op. cit.,* 35.
[21] *Ibid.,* 37-38, 40.

IX. GUIDANCE ACTIVITIES

ALL OF THE BRANCHES of the armed services established programs of guidance and counseling connected with the procedures of induction, selection, assignment, and separation.[1] The Army's Adjutant General's Office and the Navy's Bureau of Naval Personnel developed such programs for all recruits. These programs were not adequate, however, to serve the continuing need for assistance. Early in the organization and establishment of both Army and Navy off-duty educational programs, individual education officers became aware of the need for counseling and guidance among the personnel of the armed services. Some servicemen and women wanted advice in the selection of USAFI courses and in the planning of an educational program for their leisure-time study. Others wanted to know more about opportunities for postwar education and vocational training. Still others recognized the need for counseling in preparation for picking up the scattered threads of civilian life after separation. A few felt the need to discuss personal problems with some individual who was neither a chaplain nor a military superior. Hospital patients needed effective counseling as a first step in vocational rehabilitation.

The educational officers and librarians in both the Army and Navy did all that they could to be of assistance in meeting these needs. At the start their resources were meager or nonexistent but, as time went on, organized efforts were made to provide them with the materials and skills which they required.

ARMY

The story of guidance activities in the Army's off-duty educational programs is again the familiar story of individual initiative. Many Information and Education officers, as well as instructors, chaplains, and others, performed excellent guidance services to the men with whom they came in contact. There were, however, few formal guidance services organized by the

[1] These programs, being concerned with direct military training, are not included in this study of off-duty educational activities.

Information and Education Division or by the Library Branch. Personnel services were always considered a part of the Adjutant General's Office which was in charge of the classification system for the Army.[2]

ACTIVITIES OF THE I AND E DIVISION

The branches of I and E were concerned with supplying educational and occupational information to servicemen and produced many materials with a guidance slant. Much of the material produced by the Information Branch consisted of filmstrips and films designed for use at the time of separation. Filmstrips produced for this purpose include: *So You're Going To Be Discharged, You Can Take It With You,* and *Your Counselor and Your G. I. Bill of Rights.*

The Education Branch produced films dealing with the discharge point system and the Army Education Program. It also prepared a *Vocational Advisory Manual* showing how military skills could be translated into civilian job skills. It sponsored the Vocational Information Kit already referred to and prepared *Your Postwar Career,* a guidance textbook for the GI.

The Vocational Information Kit was widely used by Information and Education officers and frequently served as a library unit. The kit contained a large number of pamphlets and leaflets covering a wide range of vocational and educational information. These materials were filed according to a uniform system which helped keep the kit in order but made it difficult for direct use by persons unfamiliar with the system. In the AEP it was used as a reference library for courses in vocational information and postwar career planning. Each kit was accompanied by a poster designed to attract the attention of as many soldiers as possible.

Materials included in the kit were found useful in describing the relationships existing between individual vocational interests and the various off-duty, correspondence, and AEP courses

[2] An excellent brief résumé of the personnel work of the Adjutant General's Office may be found in the statement by Major Howard E. Page in *Swords into Plowshares.* Sponsored jointly by the University of Michigan and the State Department of Public Instruction (Lansing, Mich.: Superintendent of Public Instruction, 1946).

available to soldiers. The discussion groups established by I and E officers used these materials for information about postwar vocational opportunities. Soldiers in hospitals were especially interested in the contents of the kit and for those who required vocational rehabilitation the materials frequently suggested new types of jobs for which they might qualify. Counselors in these hospitals, especially the counselors in general hospitals in the United States, made particularly effective use of these materials.

Interest developing from reading materials in the kit frequently led to enrollment in the off-duty class program. Courses elected by the GI in off-duty classes or in the USAFI program were often those which had been suggested by kit materials. I and E officers found greater opportunities for informal discussion of vocational opportunities and training as a result of the use of the kit. For many, this new interest in postwar vocational opportunities led to a broader interest in the postwar world and in participation in group discussions concerning these problems.

For others, interest in vocational plans pointed up personal problems which the GI was anticipating in the postwar world. Problems of civilian jobs overseas, the prospects of re-enlistment, family problems, personal finances, tax arrears, marital relationships, and a variety of others were brought to the attention of individuals or discussed in small groups. Some counselors made an extensive effort to have available some reading materials for soldiers who were concerned with these problems. An initial interest in postwar occupations frequently led to conscious planning for life after the war.

Your Postwar Career was a 150-page textbook primarily intended for AEP courses. It discussed fields of work with emphasis on those which might offer the best prospects for postwar jobs. Chapters in the text were devoted to making one's own living, taking a government job, and the opportunities for returning to school. The book's main purpose was to get the GI to watch his interests, abilities, and training in his choice of educational or vocational opportunities after discharge.

Probably the most nearly complete group of guidance services offered by the Army was in connection with the AEP program for the post-hostilities period. This program, as developed at Shrivenham, consisted of providing information for the soldier-students to aid them in the selection of activities appropriate to educational achievement, occupational skills, interests and aptitudes. Conferences were held with students at the time of their arrival to orient them to the university atmosphere and to aid them in the wise choice of their programs. These conferences were followed by such group activities as the "How to Study" classes. General Educational Development Tests (high-school level) were administered to all who wished test results. Often these requests for test administration were a part of a soldier-student's plan to enter college upon his return to civilian life or to seek credit for educational experience in the Army. Assistance was given in the completion of Accreditation Form 47 distributed by USAFI.

In the AEP, registrations for self-teaching and correspondence courses through USAFI were encouraged. Students with advanced college standing were urged to schedule additional course work through correspondence study. Others used the opportunity to select additional educational materials under the guidance of trained counselors for further study after leaving the AEP program.

At some camps I and E officers were able to collect college catalogs. These were widely used by soldiers eager to know the entrance requirements of universities back home. It was also essential that information concerning the general provisions of the GI Bill of Rights be readily available. As the war drew to a close, interest developed tremendously in the postwar educational opportunities for veterans and created an increasing need for trained counselors.

To the list of guidance materials made available by the Army should be added: (1) a number of pamphlets included in the *GI Roundtable* series; (2) a special supplement to the *Directory of American Colleges and Universities* prepared by the American Council on Education at the request of the Army Education Branch; and (3) a set of occupational briefs prepared by the United States Employment Service covering 110 occupations of particular interest to men and women in service. Also during the fall and winter of 1945 and the spring of 1946, the Army Education Branch prepared and dispatched to overseas theaters a series of information memoranda on vocational and educational developments in the United States of particular interest to GI's looking forward to their return to civilian life.

GUIDANCE MATERIALS PROVIDED BY THE LIBRARY BRANCH

The Adjutant General's Office was responsible for the selection, procurement, and distribution of necessary materials for the counseling of military personnel at the time of separation or in anticipation of separation from service. It was desirable that comprehensive occupational and vocational library materials be made available for the information of soldiers in separation centers and hospitals. In view of the fact that the Library Branch in the Special Services Division had the over-all responsibility for post, camp, and station libraries, the Director of the Special Services Division was requested by the Adjutant General in October 1944 to undertake the additional function of securing, evaluating, and distributing occupational library materials to separation centers and hospitals.

Occupational materials to be distributed to separation centers and hospitals were of two general types: (1) occupational material for reading by soldiers while awaiting separation; and (2) job pamphlets, related to soldiers' occupational interests, which might be given to them for personal use later.

It early became apparent to all concerned with this activity that it would be necessary to distribute readable occupational materials not only to separation centers but also to all the post, camp, and station libraries in the continental United States and overseas. Inasmuch as Army libraries were centers for information and reference as well as for recreational reading, soldiers would naturally go to them for occupational information.

The first task was to obtain copies of as much published occupational material as possible. This necessitated the sending of approximately 2,000 requests for samples of material to industries, associations, periodicals, government agencies, and educational institutions. By June 1945, about 1,500 publications had been received, catalogued, and filed. This number included about 175 books. It was found that much occupational material had been written for the counseling of high school students and was not usable by mature soldiers and veterans. To aid in the evaluation of occupational materials, a contract was made with the Occupational Index, Incorporated, of New York University to evaluate and annotate material received by that organization. Contacts were made with associations, industries, and publishers in an effort to stimulate the production of occupational material which would be of value to military personnel anticipating discharge from the Army. Much material was purchased or obtained from other government agencies and sent out from time to time in kits to the libraries served.

NAVY[3]

Shortly after the first Educational Services centers were established, the needs for counseling sketched at the beginning of this chapter became apparent. To provide a solution to these problems ". . . the Navy took . . . steps to develop an educational and vocational counseling program having three foundation stones: trained counselors, adequate occupational and related information, and a testing program."[4]

GUIDANCE

In order to assist the ESO's to perform the counseling function, special training was given them in the use of the following relatively elaborate Navy counseling aids which were available at Educational Services centers or could be requisitioned from the Bureau of Naval Personnel.

(1) *The Enlisted Personnel Qualification Card.* This is a Navy form which gives data on language fluency, leisure-time activities, sports, educational level, specialized training, civilian

[3] Use has been made throughout this section of the "Administrative History of the Bureau of Naval Personnel" (MS on file in the Office of Naval History, U. S. Navy Department).

[4] George T. Donahue, "Counseling in the Navy's Off-Duty Educational Program," *Occupations, the Vocational Guidance Magazine,* January 1945, p. 210.

employment, and information on the scores which the man makes on the Navy's basic test battery. This battery, given to enlisted men starting in July 1943, included: (*a*) the general classification test (GCT) which measures ability to learn and solve problems and is designed to indicate probable success in academic work and abstract learning ability; (*b*) the reading test which measures the ability to read manuals and instructions on the use of Navy equipment; (*c*) the arithmetical reasoning test, which measures the ability to calculate and apply calculations to practical problems; (*d*) the mechanical aptitude test which measures potential ability for work of a mechanical nature; (*e*) the spelling test which measures the ability to identify misspelled words; (*f*) the clerical aptitude test which measures speed and accuracy in alphabetizing, checking paired numbers, and checking paired names for differences; (*g*) the mechanical knowledge test—mechanical items by which knowledge of mechanical tools, principles, and operations are measured; (*h*) mechanical knowledge test—electrical items—measures the knowledge of electrical tools, principles, and operation. ESO's were given instructions on how to interpret the scores on these various tests.

(2) *The General Educational Development Tests.* These are a part of the testing program of USAFI. They provide a measure of educational maturity as based on a comparison of scores made by a large number of high school seniors or college freshmen and sophomores. These tests, the ESO's were told, were useful to diagnose the weaknesses of the individual's educational background and to provide a basis for the selection of appropriate study materials or courses to overcome these deficiencies.

(3) *The Dictionary of Occupational Titles.* ESO's were advised to use this publication of the Department of Labor for the following purposes: (*a*) to learn to which industrial field a job belongs; (*b*) to learn the assortment of jobs to which the same job title is applied in other industries; (*c*) to learn what work is performed in any given job; and (*d*) to broaden the knowledge of ways by which people earn their livings.

(4) *The Occupational and Related Information File.* This was a collection of informational materials about jobs, job fields, and educational information of various kinds. The ESO's were instructed that the material found in this file was to be loaned to the counselee with the understanding that it would be returned.

(5) *Occupational Information films.* About twenty-six films presenting such fields of work as farming, bricklaying, carpentry, and machine trades were obtained for counseling use. Due to the great demand, however, they were primarily confined to the Rehabilitation Program.

(6) *Vocational forums.* ESO's were advised that groups of interested personnel might well be organized for discussion of the common problem of formulating educational and vocational plans.

(7) *Exploratory work experience.* Wherever possible, advantage was taken of the variety of work activities in garages, greenhouses, and machine, carpentry, and electrical shops where counselors on a try-out basis might gain some firsthand experience in a job field that interested them.

(8) *General informational materials.* These included: (*a*) *A Guide to the Evaluation of Educational Experiences in the Armed Forces,* a compilation of recommendations for scholastic credit which resulted from the joint action of the American Council on Education and the various regional accrediting associations; (*b*) *A Guide to Colleges, Universities and Professional Schools of the United States;* (*c*) *Occupational Briefs,* leaflets which covered seventy-two specific jobs in the professional and agricultural fields; (*d*) *Apprentice Training for Returning Servicemen,* a twelve-page leaflet published by the War Manpower Commission, describing the apprentice training program and the opportunities for such training under Public Laws 346 and 16, which was also furnished to Educational Services officers; (*e*) *America's Vocational Schools,* a booklet published by the American Vocational Association, Incorporated, summarizing the opportunities available to the returning servicemen in vocational schools; and (*f*) *What about a Job?*—a sixty-page booklet intended as a guide to the thinking of the serviceman faced with

the selection of a vocation. Style and presentation of this last booklet were developed with a view to appealing to the average serviceman, and its aim was to satisfy his general need in choosing an occupation.[5]

It is also of interest to note the instructions for counseling procedures which were given to the Educational Services officers and which shaped the ESO's counseling programs in the field. First, the officers were advised to go through a reasonably elaborate pre-interview procedure where possible. The counselor's time was saved during the interview period and the counselee was pleased to discover that someone had taken an interest in him. The ESO was advised to check the man's Enlisted Qualifications Card to see whether or not scores were available on the Navy Basic Test Battery. The second step of the interview procedure was to be conducted on as informal a basis as possible. The ESO was advised to have a brief period of general conversation, and to try to put the interviewee at ease. The general attitude was to be one of friendly helpfulness, with the counselee doing the talking. Where possible, the counselee was to leave the interview with something specific to do as a result of his visit. These instructions also outlined the post-interview procedure, directing that, immediately following the interview, impressions should be recorded and data gained during the process entered in the counseling record form. As soon as possible, a variety of possible solutions to the man's problems should be listed from which the man could select those most in keeping with his interests and needs. After the man formulated a plan of action and decided to undertake some specific activity, the Educational Services officer was advised to make a follow-up, in order to determine what he was doing and how well he was succeeding.[6]

The advisory functions of the Educational Services officers were strictly limited in certain particulars. Officers could not advocate one educational institution in preference to another, nor could they guarantee that specific credits would be received for any course undertaken.

[5] U. S. Navy Department, Bureau of Naval Personnel, NavPers 16963 (Washington: Educational Services Section, Bureau of Naval Personnel), pp. 44-50.
[6] *Ibid.*, pp. 50-53.

EDUCATIONAL SERVICES AND THE REHABILITATION PROGRAM OF THE BUREAU OF MEDICINE AND SURGERY

In the summer of 1943, an experiment was inaugurated in assigning Educational Services officers to naval hospitals. This experiment was so successful that, by the spring of 1944, the Educational Services function was incorporated as a regular feature of the Rehabilitation Program of the Bureau of Medicine and Surgery.

The Rehabilitation program, in general, has been described as follows:

> "Rehabilitation includes all activities and procedures that contribute to the recovery of a patient from his ailment and prepare him to resume a normal life. The Rehabilitation Program has cognizance of procedures which supplement ordinary or usual professional treatment to expedite recovery and prepare the patient for the course he will follow after discharge from the hospital, and includes physical therapy, occupational therapy, physical training, educational services and civil readjustment." [7]

The Bureau of Medicine and Surgery indicated that the Educational Services officer should direct his activities along two lines: (1) educational and vocational counseling; and (2) education and training. Vocational counseling was to be provided to those patients who were to be discharged from the service, while educational counseling and education and training were to be available to all patients.[8]

The Rehabilitation program in each naval hospital was headed by a rehabilitation medical officer who coordinated all aspects of the program. The ESO customarily served under him on a basis of equality with the officers charged with supervision of physical fitness, welfare and recreation, occupational therapy and physiotherapy. Patients in naval hospitals are classified into groups depending on the seriousness of their illness and the restrictions on activity thus imposed. Educational Services officers, as well as the other members of the rehabilitation team, limited their efforts with the patient accordingly.

[7] U. S. Navy Department, Bureau of Medicine and Surgery, *The Rehabilitation Program of the Medical Department,* NavMed 71716 (Washington: Bureau of Medicine and Surgery, Navy Department), p. 1.

[8] *Ibid.,* p. 12.

By a memorandum of September 1944, the Chief of Naval Personnel outlined the two types of patients with which ESO's would have to deal. There were, in the first place, the men who would be able to return to active duty. In such cases, it was the role of Educational Services to assist the Bureau of Medicine and Surgery to return as many men as possible to active duty, with skills maintained or improved during hospitalization or new skills acquired where desirable. The other category included men who would be discharged from service upon release from the hospital. With these it was the function of the Educational Services to provide adequately for procedures which would facilitate their postwar adjustment.

As far as was feasible, all of the activities of the Educational Services programs were made available to hospital patients, including individual counseling in wards, group counseling when desirable, classroom procedure, correspondence courses, films for educational training, war orientation, lectures, and discussions. In addition, the ESO had a secondary responsibility in that he was to offer this program for members of the hospital staff.

The ESO's principal function at hospitals turned out to be counseling and the developing of opportunities for prevocational training. Work-experience kits were obtained in large numbers for use with convalescents. By this means, patients were enabled to perform almost complete operations or experiments related to radio, electricity, auto-mechanics, blueprint-reading, and cartooning. At Pensacola, men were sent to the Hospital Maintenance Corps, learning such occupations as gardening, laundering, electricity, plumbing, carpentry, and transportation. The Marine supply depot at Philadelphia conducted training courses for Marine patients in motor repair, traffic control, photography, storekeeping, laundry, and other subjects. These hospitals, located adjacent to industrial communities were apt to have training offered in cooperation with private industries.

Almost without exception prevocational shops were established in the areas of radio repairing, diesel auto-mechanics, machine shop, and wood shop. In several instances, facilities which already existed in the area were used rather than creating new establishments within the hospitals.

In addition to using the various written tests, the ESO in the Rehabilitation program made great use of manipulative tests in counseling. Some of these were the Minnesota Rate of Manipulation Test, O'Connor Tweezer Dexterity Test, Purdue Peg Board, Nut and Bolt Test, Penn Bi-Manual Work Sample, Western Electric Test, and the Kuder Interest Inventory.[9]

At some hospitals the problem of rehabilitating patients was more elementary than the provision of vocational training, involving the very will of the men to readjust themselves to civilian life. In the case of psychoneurotics, for instance, it was found necessary to develop special types of orientational training. Discussion groups were formed, designed to inculcate in those suffering from some form of war neurosis a renewed sense of responsibility. Particularly successful results were obtained through building up a sense of the meaning of community life and the individual's place in it.

Perhaps the work of the Educational Services officers can best be illustrated by the presentation of an actual case.[10]

Counseling Case Number 3

Sam Jones, S1c, had his left leg so badly crushed by a gun explosion that it had to be amputated. He is now a patient at a continental Naval Hospital and is anxious to know what he can do to become self-supporting. Less than a week after his arrival at the hospital the Educational Services Officer visited him. Prior to this visit the Educational Services Officer had the following information on Jones from his Qualification Card: Age, 19; home, Wheeling, W. Va.; marital status, single; enlisted 7-10-44, shortly after finishing a general high school course. The scores of his Navy Basic Battery of Tests are shown on the following page.

In the Navy, he was a S1c and had a citation for "devotion to duty beyond the call of service." His Navy training consisted of only ten weeks of boot training after which he was shipped out on an LST. Work experience: Helped in local hardware store on Saturdays and during summer holidays while in high school. Waited on customers and did some repair work.

The Medical Officer's report shows that Sam had sustained his injury two months prior to his admission to this hospital and had been hospitalized at Pearl Harbor before being sent east. He is regarded as a long-term

[9] U. S. Navy Department, Bureau of Naval Personnel, *Manual of Educational and Vocational Counseling for Use in Rehabilitation Program of the Medical Department, US Navy,* NavMed 888 (Washington: Bureau of Medicine and Surgery and Bureau of Naval Personnel, U. S. Navy Department), p. 9.

[10] *Ibid.,* pp. 22-23.

NAVY BASIC BATTERY SCORES

GCT	58
R. COMP.	55
M. APT.	59
M. KN.	55
E. KN.	59
A. REAS.	54
CL. APT.	46
SPELLING	49

convalescent case for he must be fitted with a prosthetic appliance and taught its use before discharge.

Sam was eager to talk to the Educational Services Officer but quickly admitted that he had no idea what he could do. He was shown the Civil Service *Manual for Placement of the Physically Handicapped* and was surprised to see the variety of jobs being done by people with disability of a leg. During the talk the Educational Services officer learned that Sam didn't do too well in high school, barely passing English and mathematics and flunking French; but he did do well in shop and loved to tinker with things. He remarked that he especially enjoyed working with small things and "liked to take things apart to see what makes them go."

Material describing various jobs in which mechanical aptitude and experience are essential was left with Sam by the Educational Services Officer who told him that he would be back the next day to discuss them with him. Among the literature left with Sam were the following job analyses: an instrument assembler, instrument inspector, watch repairman, instrument repairman, radio repairman, optical-instrument assembler, etc. When the Educational Services Officer returned the following day, Sam was watching for him. He had read all the material and thought he would like the field of watchmaker. He volunteered that he thought this would be a good field also because there was a shortage of good watchmakers in Wheeling. Because of his interest in watchmaking and the indications of his Basic Screening Battery, the Educational Services Officer advised Sam to take a series of manipulative tests. These were: (1) Minnesota Rate of Manipulation Test for finger dexterity, (2) Nut and Bolt Test (tool-dexterity test), (3) O'Connor Tweezer Dexterity Test, and (4) Purdue Peg Board for Small Muscle Coordination. By consultation with the ophthalmologist it was determined that there was no eye condition that would impede his success. These tests together with the others indicated that Sam stood a strong chance of succeeding at watch-repair work. The Educational Services Officer agreed that this was a good choice because of Sam's scores on the Basic Battery and manipulative tests, as well as because of his own interest and its future job possibility in his home town. A check with the Veterans Employment Service Representative revealed a need for watchmakers in Wheeling. Sam was eager to get started while still a patient at the hospital. Because of his enthusiasm, contact was made with a local watchmaker who was willing to teach Sam and arrangements were made with his Ward Medical Officer to grant him liberty three afternoons a week. In addition to this, arrangements were made with the Red Cross for the Motor Corps to transport Sam back and forth from the hospital.

A follow-up at the end of a month showed Sam still enthusiastic and a report from the watchmaker stated that he was proving a very apt and industrious pupil. Sam was then told by the Educational Services Officer about the apprenticeship training program for watchmakers being conducted by a nationally known watch manufacturer.

At the time of his discharge, the Civil Readjustment Officer referred him to the Veterans Employment Representative and the apprenticeship representative who arranged the details for his indenture.

MARINE CORPS

The Commandant of the Marine Corps issued in June 1945 the following instructions concerning educational and vocational guidance:

> Information and guidance concerning academic and vocational study will be made available by commanding officers to all personnel who desire it. Before guidance is undertaken, and in order that a logical course of action may be recommended, the service-record book and qualification card will be examined to determine the background of the individual. Guidance may include recommending enrollment in a particular subject indicating whether by correspondence, attendance of an off-duty class, or by the self-teaching method. In some instances only testing or accreditation procedures will be necessary to meet the needs of an individual. Guidance will be construed as involving recommendations and suggestions, not promises or directives.[11]

In general the Marine Corps guidance program closely resembled that of the Navy. The Navy Counseling Kits were used by the Marine Corps. In the case of counseling in the hospitals, Marine Corps personnel were trained in the same way as naval officers engaged in this activity. Inasmuch as Special Services officers were charged with so many responsibilities, it is probable that the Marine Corps guidance program was

[11] Letter from the Commandant of the Marine Corps to all commanding officers, June 29, 1945.

more modest than that of the Army and Navy. However, even this generalization was not true in certain instances where the Special Services officer was particularly active and motivated by an interest in this field.

COAST GUARD

The Coast Guard counseling program was less ambitious than that of the other branches of the armed services although it must be remembered that, in a large number of instances, the counseling services of Navy Educational Services officers were available to members of the Coast Guard. To the extent that Coast Guard educational officers did counsel, they were directed to concern themselves primarily with guiding students to the appropriate USAFI courses. The Coast Guard used either Navy or Public Health Service hospitals and thus developed no hospital program.

X. MOTIVATION AND RECRUITMENT EFFORT

IN THE OFF-DUTY education programs the problem of recruitment was basically that of adequately informing military personnel of the availability of the educational services provided. This was a continuing process. The almost daily changes in personnel characteristic of any large Army camp or Navy base meant that there were always new people to interest in available educational services. Also, among those men and women who remained for some time, there was a constant necessity to reinforce the stimulus to participate.

The voluntary nature of the off-duty programs resulted in motivation which was almost entirely the result of an individual need. Successful completion of a particular activity depended entirely upon individual perseverance and the continuation of interest in the activity until objectives had been achieved.

ARMY

There is little new or startling to say about recruitment efforts undertaken by the I and E Division or the Library Branch, except to comment on the resourcefulness of individuals working under the chaotic conditions of war. Plugs in newspapers, spot announcements, and programs on the radio, posters, films, and other usual media were employed to interest the GI in educational work, much as such media would be used in civilian life. Especially effective posters were developed to publicize educational programs. The use of humor, sex appeal, and cartoons added to the intrinsic interest of these media. Always there was an effort to unbend, to meet the soldier at his own level. The wide distribution of USAFI catalogs and other booklets, together with frequent mention of education and reading materials in discussions, made soldiers aware of the educational opportunities available.

Toward the end of the war, a series of Occupational Briefs, sponsored jointly by the armed services and the United States

Employment Service, brought to the attention of the serviceman those USAFI courses which would help prepare him for the job of his choice. Such briefs were distributed as give-aways not only to answer soldier questions but to show them that answers could be found in educational offerings.

NAVY

In May and June of 1945, the Navy made two attempts to discover what motivated naval personnel to participate in off-duty programs. One of these concerned participation in USAFI and the other in off-duty classes. Both of these studies[1] indicate that the main reasons for participation in both the class and correspondence courses were about the same. Table 10 summarizes these motivations.

TABLE 10

REASONS FOR PARTICIPATION IN OFF-DUTY CLASSES AND USAFI

Reasons	Off-Duty Classes		USAFI	
	Percentage	Rank	Percentage	Rank
Because I wanted to learn something which interested me personally	26	1	18	3
Because the subject was related to my Navy job	25	2	12	4
Because the subject was related to work I hope to do when the war is over	16	3	28	1
To get high school or college credit	10	4	25	2
All other reasons	23	....	17	....

The above studies substantiate in essence the following estimates made by a former officer in charge of Educational Services.

What are the purposes which impel these men to spend a large part of their limited leisure time in study? . . . The purposes of those who pursue off-duty studies can be classified in three categories. One group has either an immediate or a post-war vocational objective. . . . Another group of naval men are enrolled in educational services classes for the purpose of continuing or completing their formal schooling. . . . A third group of leisure-time students has no purpose other than that of filling hours not

[1] The data in chap. x and xi on Bureau of Naval Personnel studies and surveys were taken from the reports of Information Survey 2, Research Project No. 432, NavPers 16962 (Bureau of Naval Personnel, Training, Standards and Curriculum Division, Test and Research Section, September 1945).

occupied by military duties with some form of constructive and wholesome activity.[2]

The Navy's Educational Services officers actively recruited students for the various phases of the off-duty program. The form of this recruitment varied from station to station with the facilities at hand, the policy of the station, and the ingenuity of the individual ESO. In general, all means of communication with the men were used including announcements over public address systems, space in station paper, and displays.

Probably never before has an educational program made such concerted use of posters. Many of these were prepared in Washington for use in the field, but others were prepared locally. In general, these posters emphasized the benefits of education which would accrue to the individual. A few pointed out the fact that here was a use for leisure time. Frequently it was found that these posters were more effective if they were clustered around an "attention getter." The weekly *Newsmaps* served this purpose as did more elaborate map displays which showed the progress of the war in the several theaters. Also used were special displays which called attention to the educational program.

There is no record of the specific effect on enrollment of the use of any of these devices. Their value in increasing the interest of naval personnel has been emphasized by many ESO's.

MARINE CORPS

In the description of the several phases of the Marine Corps program, the decentralization of authority and responsibility has been noted. This is in line with traditional Marine Corps policy in all matters. For this reason there were no efforts on the part of the headquarters organization to prepare recruiting material for the field. No posters, announcements, or slides were furnished to commanding officers. The education program was considered a function of command and the extent of recruiting techniques used was governed by the commanding officer and his consideration of the relative importance of the program.

[2] Earl J. McGrath, "Navy Off-Duty Education and Post-War Educational Re-Adjustment," *Harvard Educational Review*, XIV (March 1944), 92-94.

COAST GUARD

The Coast Guard's principal effort to recruit students for the off-duty program was incorporated in a pamphlet concerned with all types of training. This pamphlet entitled *My Training, Rating, and Duties while in the United States Coast Guard* devotes some five of its fifty-one pages to describing the types of programs here under consideration. The Coast Guard also distributed posters from time to time for local educational officers to use as they saw fit.

XI. INVESTIGATION AND EVALUATION

UNDERLYING the off-duty educational programs was detailed and essential information provided by research on attitudes, motivations, needs, and desires. Both Army and Navy had available information concerning the age, schooling, marital status, civilian experience, and avocational interests of their personnel. Neither of the major branches of the armed services was content to use this information alone, however. Each made extensive studies of interests and opinions on a carefully controlled basis and each used the results of such studies to improve its off-duty educational program.

ARMY

Frequent mention has been made in earlier chapters of the contributions of the Research Branch of the I and E Division. An extensive history of this branch and its work, sponsored by the Social Science Research Council, will tell the complete story of what was probably the largest opinion-sampling program ever undertaken in the United States. Therefore, only a very brief description will be included here.

The following quotation [1] gives the Army's own viewpoint on the purposes of the research effort:

> If any program of information and education is to be effective, it must be based on the interests and needs of troops; it must recognize soldier attitudes and assist the soldier in resolving his anxieties and doubts. These matters cannot be left to guesswork. Research techniques, developed by social scientists for use in industry and by students of public opinion, are used extensively throughout the Army for this purpose. Teams of research experts are made available to commanders of high echelons for the purpose of determining the attitudes of troops on various matters which affect their well-being. The findings of these research teams are frequently used in the formulation of War Department and theater policy. Research techniques are used not only to determine initially attitudes which may result in formulation of policy, but also to measure the extent to which the new or changed policy has proved successful.

[1] *The Information-Education Officer,* War Department Technical Manual TM 28-210 (Washington: Government Printing Office, 1945).

Army research is a highly technical job which can be performed satisfactorily only by personnel trained in the vigorous method of science. The complexity of research procedures, furthermore, makes it necessary to centralize research activities at the highest echelon. All Army research studies are planned and controlled in the War Department or in the headquarters of the appropriate theater or department; and personnel trained and experienced in research techniques are made available to commanders at the theater level. The commanding general of a theater or other high command is authorized to conduct research studies within the command when technical supervision is performed by personnel designated by the War Department, who are assigned or on temporary duty with the command. Except under these conditions, no attitude surveys or research studies are authorized, and local commanders are not authorized to initiate or conduct such studies.

For the information-education officer in the field, the substitution of scientific measurement for guesswork has many implications. It is a guarantee that materials supplied by the War Department are adapted to the needs and interests of troops. The information-education officer should understand, however, that the interests and needs of troops as determined by studies of cross-sections of the Army may not truly represent the interests and needs of troops in his particular unit. In the tradition of experienced staff and line officers, he will accept the research findings and the materials which are based on them as a general guide line, to be corrected and interpreted in the light of his own day-to-day observation of the men who are serving with him.

In addition to the use of research as a basis for preparation of information and education programs and materials, the reports of actual research studies are made currently available to all echelons through *What the Soldier Thinks,* a War Department monthly which is distributed down to the company level, and through War Department pamphlets published from time to time. These publications may prove especially useful to the information-education officer by increasing his understanding of the forces which shape men's attitudes, and the impact made upon their thinking by changes in the war situation.

Research, as used by the War Department, is not a tool for "investigating" the problems of any unit, or for comparing one unit with another; nor does it encroach on the traditional and clearly defined responsibilities of the Inspector General. It is, rather, an exact technique for knowing and understanding the attitudes of a citizen Army.

The Military Training Division of ASF in the later years of the war showed marked interest in experimental studies on the relative effectiveness of various training methods conducted by the research staff. The 1944 and 1945 studies of attitudes toward allies and enemies were used by the State Department, and the soldiers' attitudes about jobs, housing, and education were sought by many Government agencies and private groups in planning for demobilization.

Research findings were made available through special reports distributed at the staff level, through a monthly progress report, and particularly through *What the Soldier Thinks,* the publication distributed in quantities of over 100,000 each month.

Studies reported in *What the Soldier Thinks* were conducted according to the following plan:

1. Questionnaires were prepared in consultation with appropriate branches of the War Department and questions were carefully chosen to provide the exact type of information required.
2. Questionnaires were pretested on small groups.
3. The research project was cleared for action with appropriate War Department agencies.
4. The number of men to be surveyed was sufficiently large to insure statistically reliable findings.
5. The men surveyed were selected to insure a true cross-section.
6. The men completed the questionnaires under conditions of absolute anonymity.
7. The data were analyzed by the specialists in attitude research analysis.

Many of the implications to be found in chapter xii of this study were obtained from studies carried on by the Research Branch.

NAVY

Not until the war was almost over did the Navy make a formal attempt to evaluate its off-duty Educational Services program. In the summer of 1945, the responsibility for conducting such studies was given to the Test and Research Section of the Standards and Curriculum Division of the Training Activity, Bureau of Naval Personnel. For this purpose, a sample was selected which was designed to represent a cross-section of both officer and enlisted naval personnel all over the world. Of the men asked to reply to these questionnaires 1,279 were stationed at eight advanced bases in the Pacific, 1,107 were distributed among nearly all types of ships—combatant, amphibious, and auxiliary—chiefly in the Pacific, and 399 were part of the ship's company of a training center in the United States. The Navy affirms that the statistical analyses and reports of this project were prepared by personnel experienced in educational and attitude research. The conclusions as they relate to the off-duty education programs in the Navy are discussed below.

CIRCULATION OF *All Hands*

A survey conducted in the autumn of 1945 showed that the number of naval personnel reporting that they got *All Hands* every month—or nearly every month—was greater than the number receiving any other publication. In addition, 50 percent of those interviewed indicated a willingness to buy *All Hands* at fifteen cents per copy in order to get a personal copy every month, and better than one-third of the respondents said they would buy it nearly every month or once in a while.[2]

PARTICIPATION IN OFF-DUTY CLASSES

This study indicated that, in the first place, most men ashore had off-duty classes at their location. Among the men stationed at the eight different bases in the Pacific, 72 percent said there were off-duty classes conducted at their stations. Of the men stationed at a training center in the United States 82 percent said there were off-duty classes. Most men afloat, however, did not have off-duty classes; only 22 percent of the men aboard ship indicated that there were off-duty classes conducted there, and such classes were most frequently encountered aboard larger ships. For example, among men aboard battleships, carriers, or cruisers, 31 percent said there were off-duty classes; in the cases of amphibious ships and craft, this percentage was only 25; and in the cases of auxiliaries and other types, the percentage was only 17. Among the men stationed at advanced bases, 19 percent said they had attended off-duty classes. At the training center within the United States, 21 percent reported attendance

[2] U. S. Navy Department, Bureau of Naval Personnel, "Report of a Poll Conducted among Certain Enlisted Personnel on the Subject of *All Hands*," *BuPers Information Bulletin* (Prepared for the Director of Welfare by the Field Research Section of the Research Division, Bureau of Naval Personnel, Washington, November 1945), pp. 3-4.

at off-duty classes; and among men afloat, 10 percent said they had attended such classes.

This survey found no significant differences between participants in the off-duty programs and the total sample on such factors as age, length of service, or rank. There was, however, a significantly higher percent of high-school graduates among participants in off-duty classes than there was among the total group of men in the survey—60 percent in contrast to 51 percent.

The study further showed that the men's evaluation of off-duty classes depended largely on their evaluation of the instructors. There was a marked relationship between the value of classes and the quality of instructors. Among men who rated their off-duty classes as very valuable, 74 percent said their instructors were very good; 21 percent, pretty good; 5 percent, poor. Among men who rated their off-duty classes as of some value, 38 percent said their instructors were very good; 55 percent said they were pretty good; and 7 percent said they were poor. Among men who rated their off-duty classes as a waste of time, only 15 percent said their instructors were very good, 40 percent said their instructors were pretty good, and 45 percent said their instructors were poor.

USAFI PARTICIPATION

A similar study revealed the following about patrons of USAFI:

> Only 2 percent of the men who have taken work with USAFI or read textbooks said that it was a "waste of time." In contrast, 47 percent rated their study as "very valuable."
>
> Men who regarded their USAFI study as "very valuable" were compared with men who said the work was "of some value" or "a waste of time." No differences were found between those two groups in such factors as age, length of service, rank, postwar plans, or time elapsed between leaving full-time school and entering the Navy. The inference is that men's judgment of the value of USAFI participation is based not on any of the factors noted above but rather on the inherent value of the material itself.

This same study reveals the following characteristics of USAFI participants in comparison with the total sample:

Characteristics	Percent in Total Sample	Percent among USAFI Participants
Age:		
Under 25	57	64
25 and over	43	36
Education:		
Did not graduate from high school	49	40
High school graduates and higher	51	60
Time available for off-duty study:		
3 hours or more a week	50	64
Less than 3 hours a week	50	36
Postwar plans:		
Go to school	5	11
All other plans	95	89
Time since leaving full-time school:		
Left school to enter Navy	14	21
1 year or less	16	17
Over 1 year	70	62

ORIENTATION AND INFORMATION

These studies also indicated that the interest of the men in war orientation was very high. Most men felt that they were conscientiously keeping up with the news more closely in the Navy than they had before they entered it.

Another survey indicated that most men in the Navy were interested in talks and discussions about the war. In response to the question, "How important is it to you personally to have a clearer understanding of why we are fighting this war?" 87 percent answered that it was absolutely necessary; only 8 percent declared it to be of medium importance, and 5 percent, of little or no importance.

Furthermore, the men surveyed in this report indicated that they wanted to hear talks on the war, although there were some very interesting deviations based on the location of the men. Of those located at a training center in the United States, 65 percent said they would like to hear such talks one day a week or oftener; 22 percent about once a month, and 13 percent, never. Of those men located on overseas bases, 60 percent fell into the once-a-week or oftener category; 25 percent, about once a month, and 15 percent, never. Of those afloat, 58 percent would like to have heard lectures once a week, or oftener; 23 percent, about once a month; and 19 percent never. Furthermore, and this seems important, there was great interest in having discussions, particularly after the men had heard a lecture. They wanted to be able to ask questions of the speaker. Again, there was some variation based upon location. Sixty-one percent of those at the training center in the United States wanted discussion; 16 percent didn't care, 23 percent preferred no discussion. At overseas bases, the three categories were respectively 59, 14, and 27 percent; while afloat, they were 57, 9, and 34 percent. Interestingly enough, this survey also showed that most men never heard any regular talks on the war. In response to the question, "How often do you attend regular meetings (talks and discussions) on the background and progress of the war?" those located at the training center in the United States said, "once a week, or oftener," 21 percent; "about once a month," 20 percent; "never," 59 percent; at overseas bases the replies were 17 percent, once a week, or oftener; 20 percent, about once a month; 63 percent, never; afloat, 20 percent, once a week or oftener; 15 percent, about once a month; and 6 percent, never. This report concluded, "The inference from these figures is clear; the men want more talks and discussion on the background and progress of the war. Only one man in five attends regular meetings on the background and progress of the war, but six men in ten would like to hear talks about the war at least once a week; and after they hear talks, six men in ten want a chance to discuss it with the speaker himself, informally. The fact is that the interests of only a few men in regular talks about the war are now being satisfied. Among men who would like to hear talks at least once a week, only 28 percent actually do hear talks that frequently, and 54 percent of these men never hear any talks."

Another survey on the use of *Newsmaps* indicated that most men were aware of this war-orientation device. In answer to the question, "Are there *Newsmaps* available in your location (or ships) so that you can look at them if you want to?" 92 percent located at a training center in the United States answered "Yes," and only 8 percent, "No" or "Don't know." At overseas bases, 83 percent were aware of *Newsmaps,* and afloat 71 percent.

Again, in an attempt to measure the interest in war-orientation readings, a survey discovered it to be high. A ranking of the type of reading the men would like to do is of some interest. In response to the question, "Would you like to read about this subject?" replies were as follows:

Subjects	Percent
The Main Causes of the Present War	82
How the United Nations Are Working Together	73
The Story of Some of the Great Pacific Naval Battles	73
What the Russian People and Country Are Like	68
What China Has Done in the War	68
What the Japanese People Are Like	67
What the Russians Have Done in the War	67
The Jap Soldier and His Equipment	65
What the Chinese People Are Like	64
The Geography of the Pacific Area	59
What People in Australia and New Zealand Are Like	55
What Sort of People Live on the Pacific Islands	55

In an attempt to get at the men's appraisal of the job the Navy was doing in keeping them up to date on the news, the survey staff came to the following conclusion: "Of the total sample, 45 percent think the Navy does a 'very good' job in keeping men up to date on the news of the day. And an additional 39 percent think the Navy does a 'fairly good' job. The better educated men, perhaps because of their greater interest in news, tend to be more critical of the Navy. The relationship among men's appraisal of the Navy's job, their attendance at regular talks on the war, and their knowledge of the *Newsmaps* suggest that the men's ratings are based on experience. The implication of these facts is that the Navy can gain a higher rating for itself by expanding its program of talks and discussions and by assuring that *Newsmaps* are available for all hands to look at."

EDUCATIONAL COUNSELING

Finally, a study was conducted to determine where the greatest demand for educational counseling rested. As the tabulation below indicates, such demand was greatest among men under twenty-one years of age, men who had left full-time school to enter the Navy, and men who planned to return to full-time school after the war.

Navy Men Who Have the Following Characteristics of	Percent Who Have Asked for Advice
Age:	
Under 21	33
21 and over	22
Time since leaving full-time school:	
Left school to enter Navy	41
Out of school over a year before entering Navy	31
Previous education:	
Had some high school but did not finish	29
Finished high school	26
Had some college but did not finish	31
Finished college	19
Postwar plans:	
Plan to enter full-time school	48
Plan to get a job	23

MARINE CORPS

The Marine Corps did not launch any extensive attempt at investigation and evaluation. As has been observed above, Special Services officers were instructed to conduct an educational interest survey before starting a program at their station. These surveys were used locally and have never been collected and tabulated. It is unfortunate from the standpoint of civilian adult education that this is true, for such a tabulation might have provided considerable insight into the educational needs and desires of returning servicemen.

During the last months of the war the inspection staff of the Inspector General of the Marine Corps started to evaluate Special Services activities. A summary of these evaluations is not available.

COAST GUARD

While educational officers were directed to set up classes only where an interest was indicated, there is no record of how this was done. Nor was any evaluation of the program undertaken, for the end of the war caused the demobilization of the personnel competent to do this and the personnel with whom to work.

XII. IMPLICATIONS

THE FOREGOING panoramic description has reported a great variety of activities carried out on an enormous scale. All of these activities, whatever their specific reference, were concerned broadly with the provision of learning opportunities for mature men and women. Civilian adult educators who have read this description will, therefore, have had occasion to become aware of resemblances between their own work and that of the armed services and to speculate whether such resemblances may help them to solve their own problems.

The director of public school adult education who needs to discover an adequate teaching staff may have noted the method the Army used, and may try to find people with subject-matter competence in his community, giving them some training in teaching techniques. The librarian who is concerned because she reaches such a limited segment of the people of her city may have been encouraged by the report of the Navy's experience in making libraries much more informal and including a wider choice of easy-to-read materials in their book-stocks. The director of training for a nation-wide industry may have been impressed by the parallelism between the structure of authority in the armed services and that of his own company and may have discovered techniques he can use to introduce educational activities into that structure. A director of program for a voluntary association—such as Rotary, the Parent-Teachers Association, the Young Men's Christian Association, the Settlement House, or the American Association of University Women—may have been impressed by the desire of men in the armed services to follow a lecture with a discussion and be led to experiment to see whether this preference might not also be true in the activities of his own association.

The final part of this study is designed to reinforce the immediate suggestions which may already have occurred to adult educators by providing a more systematic appraisal of possible comparisons. What are the implications of all of the off-duty educational programs of the armed services for all of civilian adult education?

A question of this sort is more natural in adult education than it is in any of the other customary levels of education, precisely because adult education has no single agency of operation. Elementary education has the elementary school, secondary education has the high school, higher education has the college and the university—but adult education is undertaken by a wide variety of agencies, no one of which dominates the field. Accordingly, adult educators are customarily engaged—or at least they should be—with reading about one another's programs in order to find implications for their own. Workers in community centers and social settlements are interested in agricultural extension. Educational directors of labor unions are interested in the study programs of consumer cooperatives. And private correspondence schools are interested in the home-study courses offered by universities.

WHAT IS AN IMPLICATION?

It might appear, therefore, that the task of drawing implications would be an easy one. And indeed it is in ordinary situations when relatively simple programs are compared with one another. But when programs of the magnitude of those of the armed services are to be related to the extremely diverse enterprises of modern civilian adult education, it is necessary to make careful distinctions lest one fall into a morass of confusion and uncertainty.

By its very definition, an implication denotes a meaningful relationship. There are two ways in which one adult educational program may be said to have implications for another: (1) when the first is similar in character to the second, and (2) when the existence of the first materially changes the character or scope of the second.

The first kind of implication has already been illustrated by several examples. It assumes the existence of somewhat parallel agencies of the same general sort: public libraries and Navy libraries, evening schools and off-duty class programs, industrial training programs and military training programs. Before one such adult educational program can be said to have implications for the other, certain basic factors must exist. The first program must develop a conception or an activity which proves to be successful when it is tried out. The second program must be sufficiently similar in purpose, scope, or service so that this conception or activity has meaning for it. And, finally, the second program must incorporate such conception or activity successfully into its own work. If, for example, one agency develops a new theory of adult needs as the basis for its program or a successful instrument for measuring such needs, its thought and work will have significance for every other agency which can build its program on a similar basis.

Ordinarily this kind of implication rests basically on practice rather than on principle. This point may be made clear by extending the foregoing illustration. If a settlement house or a community center develops a new method for discovering the educational needs of the people in its urban community, it usually does so by working out, in that situation and through that method, certain general principles. If there are implications in this procedure for agricultural extension, they will obviously be in terms not of the particular method or instrument—for that was developed to serve an urban and not a rural environment—but in terms of the underlying principles concerned.

The second situation in which an implication may occur comes when one program is influenced by the existence of another. This relationship is usually a fairly simple and direct one. If one agency is serving a particular need in a community adequately, the other agencies should not try to duplicate its efforts. Or if one agency is providing an elementary knowledge of a certain subject but cannot offer an advanced one, another agency may wish to build part of its program to meet this broader need.

ARE THERE ANY IMPLICATIONS?

With the foregoing distinctions in mind, the authors of this study set about their task of discovering significant relationships between the armed forces programs of off-duty education that developed during the war and civilian adult education programs. During the course of their study, the authors talked or had correspondence with a large number of men and women who had been more or less closely related to some aspect of the military programs as participants, consultants, or observers. All of these people took a very real interest in the study, and it was apparent that their contact with the military programs had led them to do some thinking about the lessons to be learned. Their opinions concerning the value of the Army and Navy activities to peacetime programs, however, varied widely.

It is not difficult to understand this variation. The persons concerned had had a wide variety of civilian backgrounds which tempered their viewpoints markedly. A business man, an engineer, a college professor, a lawyer, and an elementary school teacher would naturally look at educational problems in different ways; yet all of these professions, and many more in addition, were represented in the group in question. Furthermore, the scope of the military activities was so great that no one man could have an over-all view. In most cases, the person concerned had had experiences with only a single program, usually at only one level of command.

Despite this extreme variance of particular opinions, the majority of the persons interviewed had come to one of two final conclusions. Some believed that civilian adult education had much to learn from the military programs; others felt that it had little or nothing to learn. Those who took the former viewpoint did so for a variety of reasons.

Some had had little direct experience with the Army programs but had read a great deal—usually in popular magazines and newspapers—about the wonderful things that the Army and Navy were doing. These accounts usually announced that a whole new order of educational principles was being evolved in the armed services.

Some men and women who shared this view do so because their own military experiences had been satisfying. Such persons had been assigned to duties which fitted their background and training, had been given ample opportunities and resources, encouraged by broad-visioned commanding officers, and were able to develop and see others develop activities of a most significant sort.

Occasionally some of the people who valued the military programs highly did so because they knew relatively little about civilian adult education. A middle-aged college professor who had gone through the war with no feeling of participation in the most cataclysmic experience of his generation—except perhaps his air-raid warden duties—and who then was asked to go to a European post-hostilities university, might well have felt highly satisfied and encouraged by what he found. The motivation of the students, the broad range of their interests, and the relative freedom of the administrative structure would be very different, perhaps, from such a professor's college-teaching routine and, in the absence of any experience with equivalent peacetime programs, would lead him to conclude that the Army had discovered a new kind of educational experience which should be transplanted to civilian life.

Finally, some who think well of the military programs do so because these programs were developed by "practical" men as distinguished from educators. A close analysis would reveal that this contention is largely untrue, but, nonetheless, it is widely held. Those who do not like professors and pedagogues in civilian life are only too eager to point out the superiority of the Army and Navy as educational theorists and practitioners. Astonishingly enough, many who have this viewpoint are themselves professors, presumably with a professional inferiority complex.

The majority of those who maintain that civilian adult education has nothing to learn from the armed services programs do so because they have had unsatisfactory personal experiences in the Army or Navy. Other persons with this view are educators who are well aware of civilian programs and who are irritated by what they feel to be the exaggerated claims made for Army and Navy programs. The members of these two groups have usually adopted one of the following viewpoints.

Most of them have simply concluded that the Army and Navy programs were no good and the quicker they are forgotten, the better. A former educational officer, in either Army or Navy, who has attempted conscientiously to develop a good program despite the opposition of a commanding officer, the absence of facilities and supplies, the ever-present red tape, and the apparently senseless transfer and reassignment of personnel will not feel that his military experience has been particularly rewarding to him or to civilian adult education. Similarly, a Washington staff officer who has carefully drafted plans and sent them out through channels only to have them ignored or incorrectly executed will not feel that the Army or the Navy is the best kind of vehicle for an educational program.

Others are willing to grant that the Army and Navy programs were good, at least in part, but can point out that they involved the expenditure of far more money and the existence of far higher motivation than civilian institutions can ever command. If this is true, they argue, it is pointless to draw implications.

Still others believe that when the armed services programs were any good they used already recognized educational principles. One eminent educator delivered a speech to a large audience proving to his own satisfaction that when the principles of progressive education were used, the Army and Navy succeeded and when they were ignored, the result was failure. (Incidentally, he included all training activities, in addition to off-duty programs in his analysis.) Doubtless, other educators with different views might make different analyses. All of them would agree, however, that the Army and the Navy had learned nothing new.

Some contend that, while the armed services programs may have been extraordinary and while some implications might have been drawn from them, it is now too late to do so. Only very careful, factual, and objective analysis of particular programs—presumably with control groups and elaborate statistical paraphernalia—could, in their view, justify the drawing of any conclusions at all. Since the Army and Navy, unaccountably enough, were interested in winning a war rather than in educational research, the chance of discovering implications is forever lost.

A similar point of view is that while some implications might be drawn from each single military activity in terms of a parallel civilian activity, there can be no general implication. The study of Army and Navy libraries may have meaning for civilian librarians, but the general study of Army and Navy adult education and the attempt to derive principles from it can have little or no relevance for civilian adult educators of all sorts.

And, finally, some people point out reasonably enough that

the Army and Navy are monolithic systems of authority and that any program carried on in such a system is necessarily and basically different from that which exists in the free air of peacetime civilian life.

The foregoing analysis, while perhaps an oversimplification of a wide variety of viewpoints, does represent the majority of the opinions found by the authors of this study. It will be noted, however, that all of the opinions represent an analysis based on an appraisal of Army and Navy experience but with no comparable survey of the present scope or future development of civilian adult education. This is scarcely the place for such a survey, but the statement of a few broad generalizations may give a background against which it will be possible to develop a rationale for the statement of implications.

One major point has already been made. There is no one agency which dominates the field of adult education and, as a logical corollary, there are relatively few people who refer to themselves simply as "adult educators." The field includes at least four major kinds of agencies. The first is composed of those agencies which were originally developed for adult educational functions, and includes agricultural extension, correspondence schools, private proprietary schools, and voluntary study groups and membership associations. The second is composed of those agencies which were originally developed for the education of children and young people but which are now taking on, not always too effectively, the additional function of adult education; this category includes public schools, colleges, and universities. The third group is made up of those agencies which were developed originally to serve the whole community, and includes libraries, museums, community centers, and social settlements. The fourth and probably the largest group includes agencies which were originally developed for noneducational purposes but which have undertaken adult education in order to serve their basic functions more effectively; in this group are included industrial and commercial establishments, churches, labor unions, cooperatives, prisons, hospitals, and government departments dealing with such functions as health, welfare, recreation, and conservation.

Adult educational activities in these agencies are typically still in a developmental stage, with much reliance on improvisation and trial and error. In every kind of agency some extraordinarily effective work is going on. Some agencies have developed a uniformly high standard of service. It must be admitted, however, by even the most zealous advocate of adult education that the present level of performance is low. The leaders in each kind of agency have developed and apply some sound principles of method, but the understanding and use of such principles is far from uniform. Furthermore, there is as yet no clear and general body of theory which applies to practice in the entire field.

All lines of evidence available indicate that the phenomenal growth of adult education will continue. Only yesterday the high school was attended by the few; now it is attended by the many. Similarly adult education even yet is for the few; it is reasonable to suppose that, as a result of broad social forces and an increasing individual realization of the values of learning, it will become the concern of the many. Even as three-fourths of all young people of high school age are now in high school, so perhaps, in another twenty-five years, three-fourths of all mature people will be engaged in conscious learning programs of some sort.

In the future it is likely that the Army and Navy off-duty programs will be considered to have been among the first of the large-scale adult educational activities. It appears important, therefore, to identify and record any principles which educators in the armed forces discovered or which they supported by additional data, even though such principles cannot be stated with any finality or exactness. This task is the function of the present study. No attempt can obviously be made to state a comprehensive theory or structure of principles, for none emerged from the Army or Navy activities. It may only be hoped that the implications here pointed out will be useful in the eventual development of such a theory. Furthermore, if the military programs used successfully a principle which is already evident to some civilian adult educators, that fact itself is an additional indication that a common body of theory can exist.

Underlying the various opinions summarized earlier in this section were several major contentions. The proper scope of the implications which will be enumerated later can perhaps best be seen by a brief examination of each of these contentions.

The military programs were generally excellent or generally bad. This is clearly an overstatement. Some were good and some were bad. In each program, there were some successful and some unsuccessful elements.

The military programs cost more than civilian agencies can afford. Frequently this was true. Sometimes, however, good programs were operated with shockingly inadequate resources. Furthermore, in some programs the chief cost was developmental. It is now possible for similar activities to be undertaken at far less expense, because materials have been made available or methods demonstrated.

The military programs dealt with more powerful motivations than exist in civilian life. This fact may have been true of the regular training activities of the Army and Navy in which survival itself was at stake. It was less true of the off-duty programs, however, where the motivations to attend were markedly parallel to those which are current in civilian life.

The principles which can be derived are already known. For the most part, this contention is true. It is doubtful whether any of the implications which will be enumerated at length below will come with any shock of surprise. And yet such principles are ordinarily known and acted upon only by the very best programs of adult education, which, for the most part, are of small scope and size. If such principles are also valid in a mass enterprise serving an enormous number of people, it would seem that new support has been found for old generalizations and that, in view of the probable growth of adult education, such support will be extremely useful.

There is not enough objective evidence on which to base generalizations. Sometimes such objective evidence does exist, but, generally speaking, the contention is correct. Objective evidence which is sufficiently careful and exact to withstand all questioning usually is not available. It must, therefore, be understood that most of the following implications rest upon the judgment of the authors of this study and those persons with whom they have consulted and for whose opinions they have respect. Under the circumstances, the implications as stated must be considered to be more hypotheses than principles.

The armed services' structure of authority made their programs unique. Any director of public-school or university adult education who has attempted to develop his program in the face of lack of understanding or even opposition will smile ruefully when he hears this contention. School superintendents, college presidents, presidents of corporations or labor unions, and directors of library systems can be just as uncomprehending of the values of adult education as any Army colonel or Navy captain. Furthermore, it is interesting to note how frequently successful military programs were developed and operated by civilian educators in uniform. If they could use civilian principles in the military service, the reverse may also be the case.

There can be no general implications applicable to all kinds of adult education. The only way to answer this contention is to present such implications.

WHAT ARE THE IMPLICATIONS?

The particular problems with which individual adult educators are beset are usually specific forms of certain general questions which all of them face. What objectives should the program have? How should it be organized and administered? What methods of instruction should it use? What instructional materials will best help it to achieve its purpose? How can it secure and maintain the best kind of staff services? What are the best ways of guiding and counseling students? How can students be best recruited? How can the program be evaluated? How can it be financed? And, finally, what kind of physical facilities are best for its purpose? These are the problems which the Army and Navy programs encountered and they are, likewise, the questions which civilian institutions face. It is in terms of these questions—and the answers which the military programs found to them—that most of the implications will be presented.

GENERAL IMPLICATIONS

Some of the implications are, however, so broad that they cannot be reduced to such categories. In a sense, these are the most important implications in terms of their far-reaching influence, although, because they are general, they are less immediately applicable to the solution of particular problems.

1. *Interest in education on the part of adults is very widespread.* Because adult education on a mass basis is still relatively a new undertaking, many persons have a real skepticism concerning its future growth. The success of many of the Army and Navy efforts, however, serves as a powerful argument that, when programs are geared to real adult needs and interests and carried out effectively, mature people will respond.

2. *A large number of service people have been introduced to education as part of their adult experience and will be motivated to continue learning if opportunities are present for them to do so.* This conclusion seems clear for two major reasons. First, adults who have become accustomed to the idea of learning will not consider it strange to go on doing so. Second, many have discovered new interests which will lead them on to further learning. Civilian adult educational institutions can expect to recruit students from returning servicemen and women if their programs are sufficiently flexible to attract them and deal with their interests, or can compete with their other interests. For example, a number of service personnel were introduced for the first time to libraries and to reading as a way of solving problems or broadening background. Civilian libraries, therefore, have a group of potential borrowers which they did not previously have.

3. *Adult educational activities should be introduced into the primary associations and institutions to which people belong.* The Army and the Navy were basic social organizations influencing and commanding the loyalty of their personnel. Because those organizations themselves conducted programs of adult education, it seemed more natural and right for their personnel to participate in them. This principle operated also in a more specific way inside the Army and Navy. Men in hospitals found that an educational program was a part of their environment,

being sponsored and carried on by the institution which, for the moment, was the major organization with which they were concerned. In civilian life, this same principle obtains, to the extent that there is a community of interest in an ongoing organization. Men and women are more likely to be interested in and to participate in activities which are part of the program of their churches, their service clubs, their unions, their community houses, or their places of business. They are less likely to undertake learning if it involves making a completely new association. It is probable that this generalization is particularly true of people who, because of their low incomes, little formal schooling, or membership in a marked minority group, are less adept socially than others.

4. *The more education mature people have, the more likely they are to want more.* In a sense, this principle is included in Implication 2 above, but, as stated here, it is far broader in its reference. Again and again, both the Army and the Navy found that there was a positive correlation between formal education and participation in their programs. In one study which questioned a large group of soldiers, 73 percent of the college men said that they were interested in taking educational courses during demobilization, while only 32 percent of the men with less than grade-school education had the same intention.[1] This fact has several meanings for civilian adult educators. As more and more of the population is made up of people who have had formal schooling, there will be a greater and greater demand for adult education. The most immediate market for adult educational activities is among those who have had formal schooling. And, finally, as those who have not had formal schooling are introduced into adult educational activities, the motivation to continue to learn will be increased.

5. *Adult educational programs are especially successful where opportunities for recreation are limited.* Numerous observers have reported that interest in Army educational programs varied inversely to proximity to organized forms of amusement. On the surface this implies that civilian adult educa-

[1] "Soldiers Want Education," *What the Soldier Thinks* (Issued by the Information and Education Division, Research Branch, U. S. War Department, and now discontinued), No. 9, p. 7.

tional agencies will be more successful when they have less competition with organized amusement. More basically it means that people, in their leisure time, will want to do things that they enjoy or from which they get some creative satisfaction. Adult educational institutions must, therefore, meet this challenge in their programs of service. One partial answer would be to correlate their activities more closely with those of public and some private recreational agencies.

6. *Participation in adult educational activities will be increased if they are located geographically close to the students.* Army and Navy libraries, for example, found that their circulation was increased if they used a number of branches scattered through a camp or base rather than if they had one single central deposit of books. It might seem that this principle is too obvious to mention were it not for the fact that many adult educational agencies now place primary emphasis on concentrating their program in a few centers of a single location. Libraries, public schools, universities, museums, and all the rest of the general agencies will increase the extent of their service if they decentralize their activities to take them where the people are.

7. *Adult educational activities may provide for marked increases in racial, religious, and social tolerance.* Two different kinds of evidence support this conclusion. Some of the programs—notably the Army I and E activities—attempted to teach tolerance directly; those responsible for such efforts concluded that they had had some measure of success. More broadly, representatives of all different racial and religious groups participated together without serious difficulty in educational programs. They, therefore, had direct experience in working together toward common objectives. In civilian life, adult educational activities may prove to be one of the best means for bringing people of diverse cultures and backgrounds together easily and naturally and thus, through joint activity directed toward a common goal, reduce the tensions which they otherwise feel.

IMPLICATIONS CONCERNING OBJECTIVES

It is a truism in education that all activities should be governed by the objective sought: its clarity, its scope, and the extent to which it may be realized with the means available. The objectives of off-duty programs were various. Some were for recreation, some to fill leisure time, and some to achieve more positive purposes related to military or peacetime life. In their experience, those concerned with the off-duty programs learned a number of things about the objectives of the men and the ways in which such objectives may be met.

8. *Programs of adult education must be directed toward the achievement of goals which the students feel to be real and significant.* Probably no principle of adult education is already so well established as this one. It is significant to know that it prevails equally as well in military as in civilian life. With monotonous regularity, programs succeeded when they were based on needs and interests and failed when they were not. In one camp, a well-meaning I and E officer, carrying on the only kind of educational program with which he had experience, developed a program of high school courses in English, history, and mathematics. Two months later, only one small and struggling class in algebra was still under way. On the other hand, the Army university at Florence, using to the fullest extent the interests of the men, sponsored a number of discussion groups of a highly successful sort, including such topics as: The Atomic Bomb, Should We Join Veterans' Organizations?, What about Conscription?, Educational Opportunities under the GI Bill of Rights, Galileo as a Mathematician, Can Opera Appeal to Americans?, Can Marriages with Italian Girls Be Successful? [2] Similarly, an evaluation of the Biarritz University analyzed its success in part as being caused by "the high motivation of the students. They attend chiefly because of a sincere desire to study, and not because of parental wishes, desire for prestige, or similar extraneous motives." [3] The implications for civilian adult education are all too clear: their programs will succeed if they are built directly on those things which mature men and women need or want to know.

[2] W. C. Eells, "How Mussolini Provided for a G.I. University," *The Educational Record,* XXVII (April 1946), 183.

[3] J. D. Russell, "Biarritz American University," *Higher Education,* II (January 15, 1946), 3.

9. *The success of an adult educational program is enhanced if it starts at the level of the student and then proceeds to more abstract or broader things.* This, too, is a commonly understood principle which has been borne out by Army and Navy experience. Men who were at first interested in relatively trivial books or classes could be led to have a much broader pattern of interests and understandings.

10. *In any large group of mature people, the demand for adult education will be highly diversified and may change greatly from year to year.* Those responsible for the Army and Navy programs quickly found that they were dealing with men and women who came from a broad range of backgrounds and therefore had a variety of needs and interests. Programs which were restricted to a few activities never drew as many people as did those which offered a varied bill of fare. Many public-school and university adult educational programs which consist of only a few offerings might well be broadened in line with this principle.

11. *The motivations for learning grow in part out of the social climate in which the students live.* Army and Navy programs built on interest inventories which explored the desires of individual men and women were frequently not as successful as those which studied the patterns of values created by immediate social groups. A group of "buddies" wanted to take courses together; the choice of the group depended on its pattern of values, frequently being most influenced by the opinions of the natural leader of the group. The implications of this principle are extremely important in civilian adult education. Community surveys and analyses will usually be more significant than "interest-finders." A greater attempt should be made to identify and analyze existing social patterns and groupings. And, finally, an attempt to discover and interest natural leaders will bring about a greater response than a direct attempt to reach all individuals alike.

12. *The attitudes of adults may be changed—at least to some extent—by the provision of factual information.* The orientation programs supported this contention fairly clearly. Furthermore, in a study of enlisted men in twelve infantry and armored

divisions, men were given a brief quiz on current affairs. The men were then divided into four groups of equal size, based on scores made. An attitude analysis revealed that the top fourth of the men had the best attitudes. To demonstrate this principle further, the men were later given varying amounts of information. Results demonstrated that those who gained the most information also displayed the most improvement in attitude.[4] It may be true that it is not so much the information given which affects the student as his increasing awareness of points of view other than his own; but, in any case, the result is the same, for his attitude is changed. Many civilian adult educators, with the impression that the attitudes of mature people are so fixed that nothing can be done about them, have restricted their objectives to skills and knowledge. They may be encouraged by these findings to attempt to achieve more significant goals.

13. *Almost all people without the basic tools of learning can achieve them if courses are well taught.* The Army literacy program succeeded in giving almost all of its students at least fifth-grade competence after several weeks of full-time training. Since 13.5 percent of all adults are functionally illiterate, a most important objective is indicated.

14. *Adults may be more interested in studying broad cultural subjects than has heretofore been thought likely by educators.* On a number of Army and Navy bases and in the Army universities overseas, the demand for art, music, dramatics, philosophy, and other kindred subjects far outran expectations. Clearly such courses must be directed toward adult interests but if this condition is met a very broad area of development appears possible. The interest of most mature people in adult education as a form of personal expression can in large measure be met in this area.

IMPLICATIONS FOR ADMINISTRATION AND ORGANIZATION

It is in the area of administration and organization that the Navy and Army programs have generally been thought to be least like civilian agencies and activities. While the armed

[4] "Influencing Attitudes with Information," *What the Soldier Thinks,* No. 11, p. 9.

services do have rigid and clearly defined systems of control, certain principles did appear in military experience which bear out or have additional values for civilian practice.

15. *Adult education cannot be successful unless those in charge of the total organization within which it works are impressed with its role.* Always, throughout the Army and Navy experience, the quality of the off-duty program was in part a reflection of the interest and cooperation of the higher authorities in the chain of command. An educational officer could sometimes surmount many of the obstacles placed in his way by his commandant, but his program was always made more difficult by them. Civilian adult educators will recognize certain similarities between their own experience and that of the Army and Navy. Often, in civilian life, there exists the problem of working with a superior—the president of the university, the corporation, or the union—who does not fully understand adult education. The solution of the difficulty appears to be the same in both cases—to try to convince the superior officer of the value of the program in question. Educational officers who tried to circumvent their commanding officers—like their civilian equivalents—were sometimes successful but more frequently came to grief.

16. *The organization and administration of a program of adult education should be kept, as far as possible, under local control, and initiative and the development of aspects of the program, uniquely suited to local conditions, encouraged.* It may appear surprising that this principle should grow out of the experience of the armed services which, in popular fancy at least, are the best examples of centralized control. One educator who had an excellent opportunity to see the Navy program in many circumstances, however, points out [5] that "the Educational Services officers who depended on the Bureau [of Naval Personnel] became frustrated and beaten individuals; those who lived off the land and developed their own programs on the basis of their own talents and the local support they could obtain were, on the other hand, extremely successful in achieving the objectives of

[5] From a letter to the authors of this study. Later quotations in this section, unless otherwise credited, were drawn from the extensive correspondence with persons who had had experience in off-duty programs.

the program." This principle seems to argue, in civilian practice, for as much localized autonomy in the particular library branch, school center, factory, union local, and extension center as the dictates of uniformity of policy will allow.

17. *An adult educational program will succeed only when there is inspired and driving leadership.* It must be remembered that educational activities are not as yet part of the normal life of all adults. In the absence of interested leadership, groups do not ordinarily grow up or, if they do, they do not persist and broaden the scope of their interests. The entire program of *G.I. Roundtables* was based on the thought that informal discussion groups would spring up unaided. In practice this hope was not borne out. It would appear that, in both military and civilian practice, adult education cannot succeed without administrators who are in part leaders and in part promoters in the best sense of that term.

18. *Supervisors should be given frequent opportunities to test the practicalities of their recommendations.* Few would doubt this principle theoretically and yet, in practice, it is frequently neglected. The Army, however, continually stressed the importance of going into the field—particularly overseas—as the best way to help Pentagon supervisors build programs of real and practical assistance. Civilian programs might well follow the Army's example.

19. *Course offerings in adult education should be organized in integrated blocks of work, each requiring a limited period of time for completion.* A large number of Army and Navy officers felt this principle, which is well known in informal adult educational agencies, to be of importance. It was particularly appropriate, of course, in a situation in which men were often transferred, but it appeared to be true as well in other locations. Most men in the services—like most civilian adults—are not as yet used to extensive learning programs and would rather pursue several short courses, each complete in itself, than one long one.

IMPLICATIONS FOR METHODS

Despite all popular reports to the contrary, the Army and Navy did not develop any basically new instructional techniques.

The value of the military experience comes rather from the fact that recognized methods were extensively used and, in that use, various criteria of success were further validated.

20. *Adults will learn to do a task better if careful explanations are given as to both the immediate steps to be taken and the larger goal.* This principle is borne out by extensive experience and by research investigation. In a study of thirty-three rifle companies the following facts emerged: Among men who rated their company's battle teamwork very good, over half felt their leaders had carefully explained the combat mission of the squad as well as told about how the company's part fitted into the campaign as a whole. Among men who rated their battle teamwork as not good, less than a quarter felt that proper explanations had been given.[6] This principle has applications for virtually every organized and sequential learning activity designed for mature people.

21. *The learning of skills is enhanced by a presentation of the basic theory involved.* This principle bears out among adults the results of a long line of psychological investigations made with children. In a study of inductees at a reception center, men were placed in two paired groups. One group was asked to participate in a class which presented basic theory and the other was not. The men who participated showed an 18 percent gain in mastery over those who did not participate.[7] Like the previous principle, this one has universal application wherever educational activities are designed to teach skills to adults.

22. *The use of a variety of methods is better than reliance on a single method.* This principle was followed again and again in the Army and Navy off-duty programs, particularly in attempts at orientation. It rather effectively negates the yearnings of some extremists to establish some one method—usually discussion, apprenticeship, or the presentation of audio-visual aids—as the chief or indeed the only valid method of adult education.

23. *At every stage of the instructional process the student should see clearly how his learning is related to the other aspects*

[6] "Keep Your Men Informed," *What the Soldier Thinks,* No. 7, pp. 6-7.
[7] "Learning Through Active Participation," *What the Soldier Thinks,* No. 16, pp. 14-16.

of his mature life. This principle had fairly diverse applications. In discussion programs, for example, interest was generally higher and participation greater when the topic discussed had relevance to current world events, immediate problems, or the geographical surroundings. In so different a situation as the Army literacy program, the same rule applied. "All teaching materials are presented in the form in which they appear or will be used in the soldier's daily life. The functional approach is designed to relate closely to life experiences and needs; by its very nature it promotes and sustains interest. Through this approach the program offers the student immediate use and application for his skills. At the time he acquires the simplest skill, such as writing his name or his army serial number, he finds an opportunity to use this skill promptly in satisfying an immediate need. Thus, he comes to realize that education pays profits. Reinforced by this knowledge, he often turns to his studies with renewed interest and effort." [8]

24. *Learning will be improved if the student is constantly made to feel responsible for his own education.* This motivation is more inherent in adult education than in the education of children; mature people simply do not undertake learning experiences unless they feel they need them. The Army and Navy found, however, that this initial motivation must be maintained or the learning program failed. The self-study courses were developed primarily because the difficulties of transportation and communication with correspondence courses made the men and women in remote locations feel that education by this method was not feasible.

25. *Informality of approach is helpful in the teaching of adults.* The Army library program, whose aim was chiefly recreational, created informal and relaxed situations in its reading-rooms. In other programs, as well, it was customary to permit smoking, to carry on discussions informally, and in other ways to avoid a rigid and formal approach to learning. Adults expect this kind of freedom and they will respond to it as well in civilian as in military life.

[8] M. A. Seidenfeld and P. A. Witty, "Adult Elementary Education in the Army of the United States," *Adult Education Bulletin,* VIII (October 1943), 4.

26. *In using the discussion method on a sequential basis, greater response will be found if the meetings are regularly scheduled without too much intervening time, if the leaders have some authority and are especially trained, and if the topics are of current or personal importance.* This rather specific set of dicta grew out of a study of the Army orientation program in which it was clearly demonstrated that men favored a once-weekly meeting, leadership by the company commander or officers specially trained, and topics pertinent to their immediate situation.[9]

27. *The use of the discussion method in educational activities has implications for the more effective performance of the basic work of an agency.* It was found in both Army and Navy that the educational program gave an opportunity for natural leaders to manifest themselves, for men to relieve personally felt tensions, and for problems which need special handling to come to light. This principle has application particularly in educational programs carried on within broad agencies such as industrial and commercial concerns, labor unions, and co-operatives. It also has a more general application for all kinds of agencies. A discussion group sponsored by a library, a church, a public school or any other agency may have important consequences for the improvement of community life.

28. *Correspondence instruction is a useful device for educating adults.* The Army and Navy programs gave great impetus to this kind of instruction and indicated its potentialities to many people. It is apparent that civilian adult educational institutions—particularly university extension divisions—have a field of service open to them if they wish to develop a broader range of activities. One person who was connected with the Army program has commented that "the Army's difficulty in finding enough really top-notch correspondence courses for military personnel suggests a need which has yet to be met in the field of civilian adult education." It is possible that smaller adult educational institutions could well plan to expand their offerings with correspondence courses.

[9] "What the Soldier Thinks about the Orientation Course," *What the Soldier Thinks,* No. 4, pp. 14-15.

IMPLICATIONS FOR INSTRUCTIONAL MATERIALS

It was in their development of new instructional materials that the Navy and Army showed most ingenuity and ability. Faced with a specific training need, they had the resources to meet it by preparing special instructional aids. Money was available for development and publication. Even more important, technical experts in film production, writing, and illustration could be secured readily. Because of these facts, civilian adult educators throughout the war gained increasing respect for the instructional materials developed.

29. *The armed services have developed a large number of materials which may be used directly or with little change by civilian programs.* Many instructional materials were developed to meet such specifically service-related needs that they have no peacetime application. A vast range of others, however, would be exceptionally useful if they could be made available. Such use requires some method of channeling the resources. A civilian adult educational association, a government agency, or some widespread service agency might well accept responsibility for canvassing the materials, securing surplus stocks where available, and setting up means for making the military instructional aids serve a peacetime purpose.

30. *Much of the instructional material used for adult education must be especially developed with that use in mind.* The Army and Navy found again and again that textbooks and other materials built for high school students were not appropriate for use with adults. Teaching was markedly improved if special materials adapted to the particular purpose of a program were developed centrally by experts, tested out in sample situations, revised, and then made generally available. The two chief sources of supply of civilian adult educational materials—commercial publishing houses and government agencies—might greatly broaden the scope of their service by developing special instructional aids designed to be used in the typical courses found in civilian life.

31. *Instructional materials for adults should be oriented toward the life situations in which mature people usually find*

themselves. The Army literacy program, for example, loaded its content heavily "with content that stresses the military tasks ahead. The individual is made to realize that he cannot be successful in the Army if he is unable to read, write, and perform simple calculations. . . . Motivation thus is intimately associated with the soldier's life pattern as are the instructional methods used." [10] It is sometimes thought by novices in adult education that the teacher can make all of the necessary adaptations of generalized material, or material prepared primarily for the use of children, to the particular situations in which adults find themselves. The experience of the Army and Navy has revealed that teaching is ordinarily much better if this additional burden is not placed on the teacher.

32. *Those who took part in military programs will have an increased respect for print as a vehicle of communication, instruction, and recreation.* Books of all types were used by men who had not used books before. Advancement in rating and increase in pay came chiefly through reading and passing examinations—though some other less respectable methods were occasionally used. Survival itself depended in part on learning information contained in books. Libraries were a chief means of recreation. The Armed Services Editions went everywhere. In one area almost half the soldiers questioned said they had read one book of this series and about half of these said they had read at least five titles. Libraries particularly, but other agencies as well, can capitalize on this newly awakened interest in purposeful reading and in reading for information and recreation.

33. *Instructional materials can be made more widely usable through the inclusion of self-teaching devices.* The idea of self-study is an attractive one to Americans, as the success of various "self-teaching" books on bridge, foreign languages, social dancing, and muscle-building clearly shows. The editorial staff of USAFI continually worked to change regular textual materials into self-teaching materials. Civilian agencies of a noncommercial sort might well explore this field of development.

34. *Phonograph records, coupled with instructional manuals,*

[10] Seidenfeld and Witty, *op. cit.*, p. 4.

provide an effective method of teaching foreign languages, music, shorthand, and radio code. The materials used by USAFI proved this rather specific contention beyond any question. It is true that a very real motivation existed, since the men concerned were ordinarily going to the country where the language was spoken, but the increased ease of communication and transportation will make this same motivation ever more prevalent in American life. Yet it is impossible in most American communities for adults to secure adequate instruction in foreign languages.

35. *The range of knowledge about and experience in the use of audio-visual aids was greatly extended.* Audio-visual education has a kind of superficial appeal to almost everyone. Motion pictures, slide films, charts, phonograph records, mock-ups, and other devices attract an immediate interest which often makes them effective. The Army and Navy used audio-visual aids very extensively and, as a consequence, learned something about them. It was found, for example, that films provide a good means for presenting basic background understandings. Men who had seen no orientation films of the *Why We Fight* series showed considerably less understanding of the reasons for fighting than those who had seen one film. Those who had seen two films had a better understanding than those who had seen only one.[11] Furthermore, the effect of such films, the same study showed, persists over a period of time. Three matched groups were surveyed. One did not see the films. Another was tested five days after seeing the films. Another was tested nine weeks after seeing the films. More than half the effect on attitudes which was noted in the five-day group persisted after nine weeks, and more than a third of the short-term increase in factual knowledge persisted after nine weeks.[12] At the same time, leaders in the armed services programs gradually came to realize that, while audio-visual aids had certain distinct advantages in creating interest and in coming closer to concreteness than can a book, they were distinctly limited in their application. One astute critic comments: "Some

[11] "Attitudes and Orientation Films," *What the Soldier Thinks,* No. 1, pp. 12-13.
[12] *Ibid.*

Army people really became visual-aid crazy, and their idea of 'improving' a course was to double the number of flash cards used. Let's hope that civilian adult education never goes to that extreme." There is a great deal of evidence to indicate that many men in the armed services became somewhat bored with the constant use of visual aids in their training. It gradually began to be realized by all but extremists in the field that audio-visual aids are valuable only when they can be fitted easily and well into a program and are directly related to the objectives sought. Civilian educators may well take this conclusion of the specialists in military training seriously in their use of audio-visual aids.

36. *The use of a variety of kinds of materials is more effective than the use of a single kind.* It has already been mentioned that foreign-language records also require the use of manuals. Similarly, it was shown on many occasions in the Army and Navy that visual devices were more effective when they were coupled with other methods of presentation. In one study, three groups were given a short test. Group A saw no films and heard no talks. Its average test score was 20. Group B saw the film only. Its average score was 29. Group C saw the film and heard a short explanatory talk. Its average score was 35.[13] In another study, *Newsmap* was found to be more helpful when used with talks on the news.[14]

IMPLICATIONS FOR LEADERS AND LEADER TRAINING

One of the chief problems military adult education had to face was that of developing leaders who, in a variety of situations, could develop educational programs which would have significance for mature people. Because civilian adult education is itself so relatively undeveloped, this problem is also one with which its agencies are vitally concerned.

37. *A large number of persons were for the first time concerned with the teaching and administration of adult educational activities.* The successful conduct of the off-duty programs re-

[13] "How the Effectiveness of Army Training Films Can Be Increased," *What the Soldier Thinks,* No. 1, p. 14.

[14] "Specific Problems of Orientation," *What the Soldier Thinks,* January, 1944, pp. 9-11.

quired a large number of persons to serve as leaders. Since such persons do not exist in large numbers in civilian life, it was necessary for the Army and Navy to impress into this kind of service a wide variety of people—school teachers and administrative officers, college teachers, librarians, and many others whose connection with formal education had been even more tenuous. Such persons had to learn about adult education the hard way, but many of them did learn. They returned to civilian life with some competence in adult education, but even more with an interest in the field. A school superintendent who was an Educational Services officer in the Navy will have some concrete experience on which to build an educational program for the mature citizens of his community, and he will be motivated to do so. Similarly librarians, college teachers, and all others who have responsibility for educational programs will have a greater interest and ability in extending the scope of service of adult education. Also significant will be the interest of many persons who are not connected with formal education in civilian life but whose experience as leaders in the off-duty programs will lead them to give support and encouragement as citizens and as possible leaders to peacetime programs.

38. *Students in the armed services programs considered the quality of the instructor to be one of the most effective factors in the success of such programs.* While this principle can hardly be considered new, it is interesting and significant to realize that civilian experience was also borne out in the military programs. In a study of attitudes toward orientation meetings among soldiers in an overseas area, of those who thought leaders "knew their stuff," 83 percent approved of such meetings. In cases where men felt leaders were not well-qualified, only 37 percent felt the meetings were worth while.[15] Studies done by the Navy also show a positive relationship between men's appraisals of the value of off-duty classes and their appraisal of the quality of instruction.

39. *Many persons who have marked competence in subject-matter skills or understandings may be used as instructors for*

[15] "Improving the Orientation Program," *What the Soldier Thinks,* No. 12, pp. 12-13.

adult educational activities. Both the Army and Navy were able to organize classes nearly anywhere and in nearly any subject-matter area. The implication has been well-stated by an eminent adult educator who had an extensive experience with the military program. "I believe that the armed services proved beyond a shadow of a doubt that in many instances teachers developed who had never thought of teaching before, and that perhaps some of the paraphernalia with which we surround our certification of teachers is not as necessary in the adult field as it might be in some other. In other words, I believe that the armed services showed us what many who had worked in civilian adult education know, but made it more impressive on a large scale. Teachers were selected from among the ranks and from people who had had very little experience in teaching but who had the knowledge of certain subject matter, or at least had an interest and desire to carry on with helpful guidance and patience. Good teachers developed in the armed services program who had never taught school in their life and never would have thought that they might be able to do so. We have in our civilian population millions of people who are potentially good teachers of something."

40. *The ability of teachers of adults may be markedly improved by training in methods of instructing mature persons.* The Army particularly stressed method and attempted to give some training in this regard to the people who took part in its program. Such training was given on both a pre-service and an in-service basis. The desire for such training was marked among those persons who were chosen as leaders because of their subject-matter knowledge and ability. Unfortunately many adult educational agencies in civilian life do little or nothing to provide such training in method for their personnel; yet where it is done, as in the agricultural extension program, the conclusion as to its value is the same as that reached by the Army and Navy.

IMPLICATIONS FOR GUIDANCE AND COUNSELING

The life of the Army and Navy was so different from that which the civilian soldiers had previously experienced that many of them were unable to cope with it without personalized help. Many distinctive counseling services had to be set up for this reason. Above and beyond this need, however, the men and women in the armed services had much the same problems of adjustment in their personal, social, and future vocational life as are encountered among those who are civilians.

41. *The need for counseling and guidance among adults is very great.* It is frequently thought that mature people have achieved a stage in life in which they are able to solve their own problems satisfactorily. The experience of the Army and Navy would uniformly tend to disprove this conclusion. The need for counseling was emphasized perhaps more than any other point by the persons who were consulted by the authors of this study. It is apparent that adults need "adjustment" counseling which helps them solve the basic personality problems which they face and which are usually emotional and social in character. They require assistance in analyzing their educational needs and selecting those learning experiences which will help them to meet them. The need for opportunities for counseling and guidance in civilian life is very strongly indicated.

42. *A truly effective adult educational program cannot be established or maintained without guidance procedures.* Both the Army and the Navy found that, where guidance was not available, men and women failed to engage in those activities which would be most helpful to them; consequently the retention rate was often extremely low. Entrance counseling appears to be essential in order that the instruction may be given most profitably to those students who clearly need it, are ready for it, and are motivated to take it. Most civilian adult educational institutions offer little or no guidance; it is likely that many of the difficulties they face, particularly the low retention of students, would be eliminated if they did.

43. *A sound program of guidance rests in part on effective testing and evaluative procedures.* The enormous size of the armed services required classification systems of great magnitude. These systems were based in part on comprehensive testing programs. It was found by both Army and Navy educational officers that guidance was greatly facilitated by the information

thus provided. In addition, specialized testing procedures were used in many programs. In the Army literacy program, for example, "there has been an effort to utilize testing and evaluative procedures to place men and to guide and direct the learning process in the most efficient manner. One of the most important initial steps involves the use of tests to facilitate accurate placement of the men so that no part of the training period will be spent in wasteful or needless drill." [16] The comprehensive testing employed in the Army and Navy does not, of course, have a parallel in civilian life but educators might well use the principle indicated so far as they can. Adults like to take tests so long as they are put on a self-evaluative basis, and this interest is a resource which many civilian adult educators have not used adequately.

IMPLICATIONS FOR STUDENT RECRUITMENT

Because mature people do not now take education as a matter of course, adult educators must give thought to methods of stimulating participation. In one sense, this problem was more easily solved in the Army and Navy than in civilian life, for the men in the armed services had a compactness and regimentation which could be more easily manipulated. On the other hand, civilian agencies have the great advantage of a much more stable population with which to deal. It has been pointed out earlier that those who have taken part in an educational program will be likely to continue and will bring their friends. On a Navy or Army base this principle does not have the same possibilities of operation as it does in civilian life.

44. *The more people know of the availability of adult educational programs, the more they will participate.* Studies in both the Army and the Navy showed that men who knew of the availability of the educational program and had a good bit of specific information about it were more apt to participate. Both services, therefore, used extensive publicity, based on modern advertising methods, to recruit students. It is likely that in the more diversified and fluid life of the civilian, this kind of promotion is even more essential.

[16] Seidenfeld and Witty, *op. cit.*, p. 6.

45. *Basically recruitment of students rests on the excellence of the program.* Despite the necessity for the use of promotional techniques as pump primers, there is a great deal of evidence to show that the most effective asset for recruitment in both the Army and Navy was a good program, and that educational officers who concentrated on sound objectives and techniques had no difficulty in securing students. One Army officer with extensive experience in the program has commented that "there was too much 'overselling' of courses, as a result of which an abnormally large percentage of the men who began a course would drop out after the second or third session." This point is corroborated by the testimony of a naval officer that "student recruitment resulted from the word getting around a station that the Educational Services officer 'knew his stuff', 'had something to offer'." It is evident that the same factors prevail to an even greater extent in civilian life as was pointed out in the introduction to this section.

IMPLICATIONS FOR EVALUATION

The use of tests and other methods of evaluation of educational achievement received a powerful impetus during the war. In particular, the USAFI General Educational Development Tests showed the way for the measurement of educational maturity. This aspect of adult education is now largely neglected in civilian life.

46. *Research in evaluation will improve the effectiveness of an adult educational program.* One of the main jobs of the Research Branch was to make studies of the Army's program in order to appraise its success and indicate how it might be improved. The research findings supported sound educational principles which would otherwise have lacked concreteness and concerning which it might have been particularly difficult to convince old-line Army and Navy officers. Individual student progress was also evaluated extensively; as a result students were given definite ideas concerning their accomplishment and the respects in which they needed further development. Usually, because of their lack of resources, many civilian adult educational agencies have not done this kind of careful research

and testing; its importance, however, is indicated by the experience of the military services.

47. *Attitude surveys are a helpful means of attuning an educational program to the needs of adults, particularly since such surveys are welcomed by participants.* The value of such studies has been amply demonstrated in the preceding pages. The interest of participants was shown in one study. In an overseas area, men questioned about attitude surveys favored them six to one.[17] Such studies are not easy to make but can be undertaken by large civilian programs; indeed, agricultural extension is already doing so.

IMPLICATIONS FOR FINANCE

The financial resources of the Army and Navy were proportionately greater than those of most civilian adult educational agencies. Nonetheless, resources were not unlimited and the Navy and Army both had to consider the question of securing additional funds.

48. *If a program can be objectively demonstrated to be useful and practical, objections to expenditures for it are less intense.* This technique was used again and again with telling effect by those responsible for both Navy and Army off-duty programs. One good illustration is the Army orientation program, which could demonstrate its effect in increased morale. Educational directors in corporations, in labor unions, and in other kinds of agencies might use this same method of securing additional funds if they believe that their programs should be extended.

49. *Evidences of student interest in an adult educational program make it more possible to secure funds.* Despite the fabled rigidity of control from the top down in the Army and Navy, officers tended to be impressed if the men in their command showed a wholehearted enthusiasm for the educational program. Such enthusiasm was used as an effective argument for more funds. Frequently adult educational agencies, particularly those provided at public expense, are timid about extending their program, pleading that they do not have adequate resources

[17] "What Soldiers Think of Attitude Surveys," *What the Soldier Thinks,* No. 8, p. 16.

to extend a new service to all the people who might use it. The military experience would indicate that, if people like a service, their enthusiasm may be used to secure greater financial support, particularly when those served are themselves taxpayers.

IMPLICATIONS FOR PHYSICAL FACILITIES

The Army and Navy had to use many kinds of physical facilities, some of them shockingly inadequate, others good. From their experience, at least two principles may be derived.

50. *Facilities used for adult education should be informal, flexible, and attractive.* This principle is, of course, true for all education but it is particularly required for adults who voluntarily attend educational activities and who expect to find the facilities available attractive and useful. Both Army and Navy found that this principle held true. It will be significant, for example, so far as libraries are concerned. The librarian of the Montclair Library, Montclair, New Jersey, solicited suggestions for a new building from local men and women in the services. In the tabulation of the first seventy-five replies, some fifty suggestions were in terms of comfort, color, and informality ranging from "reading-rooms with soft chairs and sofas" to "spots where smokers can light up."[18]

51. *Physical facilities must be designed in terms of the physical size of adults.* It would seem almost impossible for a principle to be more self-evident than this one. Yet both military services and civilian agencies were often satisfied to undertake programs in facilities which were ludicrous for mature men and women. As a result, programs were seriously hampered and the drop-out rate was large. The implications of this principle are particularly evident in schoolhouse construction where they are now, all too frequently, being ignored.

CONCLUSION

Most Americans believe that the fundamental issue of both world wars was the preservation of democracy. Many of

[18] "First Tabulation of Replies of Montclair Men and Women in the Service to a Letter from the Montclair Library Asking Their Suggestions for a Possible New Post-War Library Building" (MS on file in the Montclair Library, Montclair, New Jersey, 1945).

them fear that still another war on the same issue is inevitable.

This fear can lead only to despair if it is not balanced by a belief in the essential goodness of man and in his continuous improvement through the increase of his understanding. The institutions of the democratic state are founded upon this belief. Society can improve only as individuals grow. The method of that growth is education.

But society cannot depend merely on the education of children. There is not enough time. The interval, between the First and the Second World War, for example, was too short to permit even one generation of children to grow to full responsibility for the affairs of the world. Even if there were time, a school system in a democracy cannot go far beyond the conceptions of the citizens who control it. More basically, however, education is important not only for the facts and skills it conveys but also for its continuing effect in helping men to be broader, more flexible, and more understanding of their own and society's problems. Democracy, which requires that men jointly determine the policies which govern them, is dependent on the quality and scope of the adult education which permits that determination to continue to be sound and fruitful because men continue to learn.

In the last war, the Army and Navy did not and could not regard off-duty education as their first and most important function. When a nation is at war, destruction of enemy power becomes the encompassing end. But the educational programs, even though incidental to the main issue and therefore always subject to neglect, were so vast that they influenced millions of men. The armed services blazed a tortuous trail toward a great truth, the truth that everybody has a natural desire to learn and can profit from that learning. If civilian society is willing to accept this basic truth and begins to realize its fullest promise, a great good can be said to have come out of the war. Through the very struggle for democracy, a new implement for democracy will have been forged.

BIBLIOGRAPHY

ARIS, R. "Problems of Army Education," *Contemporary Review*, CXLVI (July 1944), 42–45.

A general article issuing a challenge to the adult educators to make preparations immediately (1944) in order to meet the tremendous demand for instruction and guidance, if they desire to use the educational opportunities that are peculiar to the situation in the armed forces.

"Army Orientation: To Make Men Think about Why They Fight," *Fortune*, XXIX (March 1944), 150–55.

A good study of Army orientation with illustrations of material and techniques used in teaching adults (soldiers) about why they were fighting in World War II.

BELTRAMO, ELVIRA. "GI Bookmobile in Austria," *Wilson Library Bulletin*, XXI, No. 1 (September 1946), 58–61.

A personal account of a bookmobile unit in operation by one of the one-hundred Army librarians sent to the European theater in 1945.

BENBOW, S. D. "Army Education Program for Inactive Theaters," *Occupations*, XXIII (March 1945), 320–23.

An excellent description of the educational program offered to Army enlisted men and officers. Its purpose was to provide an opportunity for the effective use of the waiting period following the defeat of Germany through courses of study in keeping with individual postwar plans and ambitions.

BOGOSLOVSKY, B. B. "Wartime Contributions to Post-War Education," *Harvard Educational Review*, XV (October 1945), 278–84.

The author places great importance on the forthcoming transition from textbook instruction to screen instruction. Financial resources necessary to implement such a program will tend to impede the movement.

BRADFORD, L. P. "Adult Education's Responsibility to the Veteran," *Adult Education Bulletin*, IX (December 1944), 53–54.

"It is only as adult education recognizes that the education of returning veterans must demand careful and comprehensive planning on the part of the total community and that this education cannot be remedial but must be dynamic in terms of the veteran's problem, that adult education will fully meet the responsibility and opportunity before it."

BROWN, F. J. "Adult Education Programs and Facilities for the Armed Forces," *Journal of the American Association of Collegiate Registrars*, XVII (July 1942), 444–54.

A good description of the activities of the Education Section of the Special Service Branch as it existed at the date of writing.

———. "Off-Duty Educational Services in the Armed Forces," *Annals of the American Academy of Political and Social Science*, CCXXXI (January 1944), 47–52.

This is one of the better analyses of the off-duty educational programs of the Armed services, emphasizing the United States Armed Forces Institute program and the Navy's Educational Services Program. It includes a brief treatment of the general postwar implications of these off-duty programs.

BROWN, M. W. "Adapting Adult-Education Programs to Post-War Needs," *Forty-Fourth Yearbook*, Part I, The National Society for the Study of Education. Chicago: Department of Education, University of Chicago, 1945. Pp. 57–59.
A challenge to adult education with a list of certain "musts" to be accomplished in the tremendous task of postwar "reconstruction."

BRUMBAUGH, A. J. "Cooperative Approach to Evaluation of Educational Experience Gained in the Armed Forces," *Higher Education*, I (May 15, 1945), 1–3.
A good description of the cooperative effort in the production of "A Guide to the Evaluation of Educational Experiences in the Armed Services." The article discusses the need and usefulness of the "Guide."

———. "Implications for Post-War Education of Credit for Military Experience," *North Central Association Quarterly*, XIX (January 1945), 285–88.
This is a good statement of the problem of accreditation for military experience with emphasis on its implications for all institutions of higher education. A few of these implications apply directly to civilian adult education.

CARPENTER, CLARENCE R., and GLICK, CLARENCE E. "Future Educational Plans of Soldier-Students in Europe." Unpublished Report of Research Unit, Academic Division, No. 3 (Biarritz American University, A.P.O. 268, Biarritz, France, February, 1946).
Generalization advanced that two-thirds of soldiers with capacities, interests, and educational backgrounds similar to those at Biarritz will want to continue their education.

CARTWRIGHT, MORSE A. "A Preview of Post-War Adult Education," *The Educational Forum*, X (March 1946), 273–80.
A very general statement of the problems facing adult education in the postwar period. It is illustrative of several such articles dealing in generalities with these problems. The author makes little mention of the off-duty educational programs in the services' adult education.

CASWELL, H. L. "Progressive Education Principles Used in the War Effort," *Teachers College Record*, XLV (March 1944), 386–97.
A defense of the principles of progressive education. Points out their application in the Army and Navy training programs. Discusses the differences in the objectives of the peacetime educational institutions and the training programs of the armed services.

COMMITTEE TO STUDY ARMY TRAINING METHODS AND PROCEDURES. "Training in the Armed Forces: Implications for Post-War Education," *High Points*, XXVI (December 1944), 10–29.
A good, though incomplete, report by a New York City committee established to study the methods and procedures now being used for training in the armed forces, which have implications for the establishment, organization, and operation of proposed institutes and other forms of postwar education.

ESPY, H. G. "The Correspondence-Study Program of the United States Armed Forces Institute," *Higher Education under War Conditions*. Proceedings of the Institute for Administrative Officers of Higher Institutions, Vol. XV. Chicago: Department of Education, University of Chicago, 1943. Chap. iii.
A description of the United States Armed Forces Institute program.

LANCOUR, HAROLD. "Army Library School Tries New Methods," *Library Journal*, LXXI, No. 4 (February 15, 1946), 239–43.
A description of the organization, aims and accomplishments of schools established in the European theater for training of army personnel for duties as unit librarians.

LIEBERMAN, IRVING. "Soldiers Do Read in the European Theater," *Library Journal*, LXXI, No. 5 (March 1, 1946), 307–12.
The scope of the Army library program in the European theater outlined in a report well substantiated by facts and figures.

LOMBARDI, JOHN. "Service Schools Teach Us Many Lessons," *California Journal of Secondary Education*, XIX (May 1944), 230–33.
Of great social significance will be the fact that an adult educational program was developed on a truly universal scale. Thousands of men and women have learned for the first time that purposeful education does not require formal prerequisites such as are commonly found in many of our civilian institutions.

LYNDE, S. A. "Schooling for the Under-Educated Veteran," *National Association of Secondary-School Principals Bulletin*, XXIX (March 1945), 14–17.
A stimulating challenge to the adult educators for the provision of educational opportunities for the half million men in the armed services who have not gone beyond the fourth grade and yet are interested in increasing their educational status upon returning to civilian life.

LYNDE, S. A., and SCHULER, E. A. "The Undereducated Serviceman and the G.I. Bill of Rights," *Adult Education Bulletin*, IX (December 1944), 35–40.
A statement indicating the importance of the fact that if the undereducated returning GI's are to attain the benefits of Public Law 346, existing educational agencies must conceive and establish appropriate programs.

MCGRATH, EARL J. "General Education in the Postwar Period," *Annals of American Academy of Political and Social Science*, CCXXXI (January 1944), 74–80.
This article is not specifically directed at adult education but is of interest in its treatment of the relationship between the armed services' efforts in general education through their off-duty educational programs and the problems of civilian general education after the war. Mr. McGrath was the officer-in-charge of the Navy's off-duty educational program at the time he wrote this article.

———. "Navy Off-Duty Education and Post-War Educational Readjustment," *Harvard Educational Review*, XIV (March 1944), 91–104.
This is the best published description of the Navy's Educational Services program. Mention is made of the possible postwar effects of such a program on educational institutions of all types.

NASON, J. W. "What Have We Learned?" *Journal of Higher Education*, XV (June 1944), 287–98.
Some implications of the Army and Navy programs for higher education which are offered more as "a stimulus to reflection than as results which have been adequately tested."

NATIONAL EDUCATION ASSOCIATION. *Education in the Armed Services.* Washington: NEA, Department of Supervision and Curriculum Development, 1944.
This pamphlet presents a picture of the existing (1944) training programs of the armed services. It dismisses major policies and practices which have

been widely followed. It contains a series of representative statements of members of the training staffs of the Army and the Navy.

POINTON, FREDERICK C., and HARVEY, HOLMAN. "G.I. Joe Goes to School Under Fire," *Reader's Digest* (January 1945), 61–63. (Condensed from an article in the *American Legion Magazine.*)

The United States Armed Forces Institute was amazing in the number of courses it offered and in the number of "lands" it reached—860,000 servicemen and women in every part of the world studying and every day 1,100 more asking for courses.

PONITZ, H. J. "Public Schools and Postwar Adult Education," *Adult Education Bulletin*, VIII (December 1943), 46–50.

A general statement of the needs for and the nature of an over-all program of education suited to the needs of adults in the postwar era.

POULLADA, LEON B. "Army Library Service in the Pacific," *Library Journal*, LXXI (April 1, 1946 and April 15, 1946), 439–41; 562–66.

An account of the organization, expansion and activities of the Army Library Service in the Pacific theater by a former library officer, Central Pacific Base Command.

RICHARDSON, B. "On a GI Campus in England: Ex-GI's Report on Shrivenham Army University Center," *New York Times Magazine*, October 21, 1945, 22–23.

A brief but interesting nonacademic story of the Army University Center at Shrivenham.

RUSSELL, JOHN DALE. "The Army Universities in Europe," *North Central Association Quarterly*, XX (April 1946), 291–300.

An excellent description of the university centers in European theater written by the dean and academic adviser to the Biarritz American University.

———. "G.I.'s at College," *National Parent Teacher*, XL (April 1946), 16–18.

A description of the GI reaction to the programs of study at the two Army Educational Centers at Biarritz and Shrivenham and reasons for the enthusiasm of the soldiers.

SENTMAN, R. A. "Post-War Educational Opportunities for Naval Personnel," *Journal of Educational Sociology*, XVI (May 1943), 551–56.

The title is misleading in that for the most part the article is devoted to a brief description of the Navy's Educational Services program as it existed in 1943. The article was written by the retired naval officer who was at the time officer-in-charge of the program.

SPAULDING, F. T. "Education for Men and Women in Military Service," *American School Board Journal*, CVI (March 1943), 43–44.

An excellent general presentation of the nature of the five major programs of education in the armed services. Emphasis is placed on the provisions that the Army and Navy were making for the healthy and constructive use by soldiers and sailors of their off-duty time.

"U. S. Army Education Program in the European Theater of Operations," *Adult Education Journal*, III (April 1944), 49–52.

A good description of the Army educational programs prior to VE day.

WENDT, P. R. "Postwar Implications for Education in the Audio-Visual Programs of Our Armed Services," *Virginia Journal of Education*, XXXVII (May 1944), 316–17.

An excellent article discussing the production and utilization of visual aids and the values of the wartime procedures for visual teaching in the postwar period.

WITTY, P. A., and GOLDBERG, S. "Army's Training Program for Illiterate, Non-English Speaking, and Educationally Retarded Men," *Elementary English Review*, XX (December 1943), 306–11.

YALE, JOHN R. "Army Vocational Kit," *Occupations*, XXIII (March 1943), 324–28.

A good discussion of the development, purposes, contents, uses, and implications of the self-contained library of more than four hundred pamphlets classified and filed in folders by major occupational fields.

YOUNG, KIMBALL. "An Army Venture into Adult Education; Report on the Army Orientation Courses Given at the Command and General Staff School, Fort Leavenworth, Kansas," *School and Society*, LVII (May 8, 1943), 546–48.

A brief but excellent description of the purposes, nature of the program, clientele and appraisal of the Army Orientation Course for nonmilitary persons chosen by the War Department.

THE AMERICAN COUNCIL ON EDUCATION

GEORGE F. ZOOK, *President*

A. J. BRUMBAUGH, *Vice President*

The American Council on Education is a *council* of national educational associations; organizations having related interests; approved universities, colleges, and technological schools; state departments of education; city school systems; selected private secondary schools; and selected educational departments of business and industrial companies. It is a center of cooperation and coordination whose influence has been apparent in the shaping of American educational policies as well as in the formulation of American educational practices during the past twenty-eight years. Many leaders in American education and public life serve on the commissions and committees through which the Council operates.

The Commission on Implications of Armed Services Educational Programs began its work in July 1945. It undertakes to identify features of the wartime training and educational programs worthy of adaptation and experimentation in peacetime civilian education of any and all types and levels. It also undertakes to make available to the public well-considered answers to the questions: What should education in America gain from the experience of the vast wartime training efforts? What are the implications for education and the national culture and strength, now and in the future?